PORTAL TO GENIUS

FROM VISION TO REALITY

Leslie Householder

Garrett B. Gunderson

Rare
Faith
PUBLISHING

This book presents ideas for solving medical, financial, and other various dilemmas in a fictional setting. Neither the publisher nor the authors assume responsibility for outcomes resulting from the reader's interpretation or implementation of these ideas.

Portal to Genius: From Vision to Reality

Rare Faith
PUBLISHING

www.RareFaith.org

Fourth Printing - includes grammatical improvements, additional setting and character descriptions, two additional chapter breaks, and updates on the publisher's information, additional resources, and author bios.

Printed in the U.S.A.
ISBN 978-0-9816749-2-6
Library of Congress Control Number: 2009939313

*Dedicated to the part of you
that is ready to take flight.*

"We are enjoying your wonderful book.... I think it could change the world!"

—*Cat Spalding, West Fairlee, Vermont*

"Astonishing! I absolutely LOVE it! I really can't say enough good things about what I have read. As a story, it is captivating but it also reads like a parable with so much more to offer! I am making my own notes all over it and it has given me much to think, ponder and pray about already. It is ...so real and genuine that I can't imagine anyone having to try at all to find him or herself as a character (or two or three) in this. There are so many stages of life and progression to identify with, reflect upon and move toward. It is truly an inspired work, thank you for sharing it with me. [It was] powerful...easy to read...brilliant! There is clarity within me now that I had been struggling to have, and after reading this it is simpler, and I am at peace. Page [undisclosed page number] changed my life.... I was constantly amazed that each page brought with it something new and powerful. Lessons kept appearing and were seamlessly woven into a life experience that anyone could relate to. There was no hype or attempt to sterilize or pretty them up. It is honest, truthful and refreshing."

—*Kelli King, Mesa, Arizona*

"I haven't read a book quite like this before...and I am seeing my life from a new point of view.... I have a teenage son and really want him to live a wonderful life using these principles. I feel strongly that [I must]...experience it myself and let him see the way."

—*Julie Prosser, Western Australia*

"Motivating and inspiring. ...Whether you're a business man/woman, a homemaker, or a middle-class person living from paycheck to paycheck, this book will teach you how to bring passion and purpose to your life. ...You turned a self-help book into an inspiring story that was so intriguing to read. I could hardly put it down!"

—*Leasel Highsmith, Queen Creek, Arizona*

"Portal to Genius has helped me better understand why I have usually walked a different path in life and why I had so much trouble when I tried to take the road 'most traveled.' It has helped me to celebrate being myself and thank God for the wonderful things and people who have come into my life when I needed them. Many times, when talking to people words have come out of my mouth that I can't explain where they came from. Now I know!!"

—*Heidi Adams, Mortlach, Saskatchewan, Canada*

"It was a huge breakthrough for me to see how these struggling characters went about finding their own rabbits. I have shared their same fears, dreams, concerns and roadblocks. I have been so focused on overcoming my fear, but after reading this book, I seriously can't believe how hard I was making it. This will be my guidebook for my future! I will gladly buy several copies and give them to my friends and family."

—*Krista Nebeker, Ammon, Idaho*

"Love the book. I have started to see my own Jackrabbits. It's amazing just how many there are when you start looking.... Leslie hooks you with great characters with whom anyone can identify. The conversations between Richard and Felicity are almost verbatim between my wife and myself. IT'S

SCARY!! You will learn some very powerful lessons in *Portal to Genius* that can change your life."

—*Glen Fitch, Washington Terrace, Utah*

"Engaging and thought provoking... *Portal to Genius* underscores that there is genius in being open to receiving direction and guidance in forms we may not have even thought of...."

—*Dawnalee Shields, Utah – Arizona – Oregon – Washington*

"I cried, because I know how it has felt to have great things happen in my life after all I could do. What I was not aware of, however, was that this could happen as often as I want. I, too, believe in miracles."

—*Leah Hansen, Saratoga Springs, Utah*

"What a delightful read! ...Wondrous, inspiring ...Get it! Read it! Go after what you most desire!"

—*Kristie Luane Chiles, Macon, Georgia*

"I loved your book. It is amazing. No matter where someone is on his or her path to thinking and being abundant, the book covers it. The stories show how the real-life application of the principles of success and happiness work."

—*Tim Cardon, Idaho Falls, Idaho*

"WOW! What more can I say? This book has really hit home. Again, WOW! So many questions are answered. A tearjerker; you have really brought out some great emotions. There is so much that I relate to. Excellent story and very fun to read! As I was reading I kept looking for critical analysis of what could be improved; I read and read and kept thinking, 'She nailed it; she's really nailed it'. *Portal to Genius* has provided me with greater vision, clarity, and purpose. It prompted discussion between my husband and me. I love reading non-fiction-fiction. You have taken what could have been dry and boring and turned it into a page-turner. Once I started reading I couldn't put the book down. It sent shockwaves through my life and my vision for the future. It created a fire within my soul to continue on the path even when everyone looking in only sees a 'crazy dog'. Great job with all of your long hours and hard work! Really fantastic!!! You are an inspiration!"

—*Linda Knudsen, St. George, Utah*

"*Portal to Genius* can be described in one word: *Masterpiece*. I have to admit that when I heard Leslie was working on a sequel to *The Jackrabbit Factor*, my reaction was that sequels are pretty much always disappointing and I didn't really expect to like it. The funny thing is I live my life by intuition, by gut instinct, if you will. So, in spite of intellectually feeling disdain about the idea of reading a sequel (any sequel), I was compelled to read *Portal to Genius*.... Leslie once again combines clarity and wisdom into a book that you won't be able to put down once you pick it up.... My life is full of challenges that seem at times to be insurmountable. *Portal to Genius* gave me HOPE that I am going to be okay. It shares knowledge and wisdom in an easy-to-understand way. It was FANTASTIC."

—*Valerie Dansereau, Greenville, South Carolina*

"This is well-written, engaging, and powerfully motivating! I am excited to start applying these principles in my own life. You have helped me see how I have been undermining my own success by allowing negative 'little voices' to interrupt the natural flow of resources."

—*Roger Kennard, Midvale, Utah*

"Well my head is spinning with words and ideas.... Thank you for this opportunity. It has been enlightening. You have presented me with life altering lessons to be learned through *Portal to Genius*. Thank you, both. Thank God."

—*Sheila Nagle, York, Pennsylvania*

"THANK YOU!!!! Thank you for sharing your gifts and knowledge to help others. That's what it's all about. What an amazing gift! Amazing!! Jewels of truth and wisdom taught in a clear and enjoyable journey. It brought together so many truths I have believed all my life. I was so excited to learn the lessons and even more eager to apply them that I felt as if I was devouring the book; I couldn't get through it quickly enough. What an invaluable resource! Truly life changing; thank you!"

—*Julie Brown, Cedar City, Utah*

"WOW! After reading *Portal to Genius*, I have greater clarity on how to apply the laws of the Universe into MY life. I have hope again. I have courage to shut out the fear that has been holding me back since, since I can remember. I have read so many books on this subject. THIS one really hit home. I kept saying, 'Hey, that's my life!' over and over again. I know what to do now. I have concrete examples in this book to help me. I could go on and on. I am a renewed person! My life is different from this time forward.

I finally get it. I am living on purpose, with purpose. Thank you for writing this book! Thanks a million!"

—*Leah Adair, Stansbury Park, Utah*

"I finished reading your book tonight. It went from being very profound, to mind opening and mind-bending! I read the book in parts because I'd start thinking about a thought provoking idea I'd just read, and I'd go off for the rest of the day doing a lot of soul searching, thinking about just one paragraph. That happened a few times. I have changed somewhere on the inside. I have my own personal dragons to overcome like everyone else, but thanks to this book I just got my passion back. I see now where my rabbits have been all along. I know what I need to be doing and the future is looking a whole lot brighter!"

—*Kim Snyder, Elk Grove, California*

"I want to begin by saying how richly and deeply *Portal to Genius* has impacted me. Thank you for this experience. It came in the perfect moment. There are no greater stories than those of loss and redemption and this book abounds with them for each masterfully crafted character. It's amazingly easy to identify and empathize with each one on a visceral level. What I appreciate most is the absolute humanity that permeates the book.

"As you so eloquently point out, change comes when you begin to ask the right questions. Not only is it humbling, it can be downright scary. We seem to do this only when our back is up against the wall and there is absolutely nowhere to go. If, at that point, we ask in the right way, our portal is unlocked and the genius pours into us. Or perhaps, more accurately, we finally discover what's been there all along and was simply waiting to be recognized.

"This is a good work! I encourage any and every one to read it, not just for the amazingly heartfelt story it is, but for the wonderful lessons it contains. You've managed to weave a tapestry of ideas and tools for every 'Goodman's' life. It's a parable of the highest order. It should be brilliantly obvious to everyone. But sadly, as we know, not everyone can see rabbits. Mine is just over there, scampering around and taunting me. I'm learning to be patient.

"This book has already changed me. I must admit I'm going to have to re-read because of the huge emotional impact. Yes…tears and all. Shhh… don't tell anyone…. I have a reputation to protect!!"

—*Jim Allmon, Roswell, New Mexico*

"I loved every page and have experienced several of the same things that occur in the story. It's amazing and I love sharing what I've learned from *The Jackrabbit Factor* with others; especially the young people I work with. They eat it up!"

—*Tom Stanley, West Jordan, Utah*

"If ever I am stranded on a deserted island with just one bag, I hope it contains the book *Portal to Genius*. The writers have skillfully and artistically woven the Laws of the Universe and an endearing story into a beautiful tapestry with divine impact on its viewers. *Portal to Genius* has injected me with a generous amount of insight, inspiration, and more importantly: love and gratitude for life and living it to my fullest potential."

—*Monique DiCarlo, Springfield, Virginia*

CONTENTS

PART 2: PORTAL TO GENIUS

PREFACE

While this book is the long-awaited sequel to the international best-seller, *The Jackrabbit Factor,* in truth, it is much more than a sequel.

It also supplies a *prequel element,* taking the reader back nearly a decade prior to the opening scene of *The Jackrabbit Factor: Why You Can* (which I'll call *JF*), as well as filling in the twelve-year gap between *JF* and its epilogue. Besides offering a more detailed foundation to *JF*, *Portal to Genius* answers the questions: *Who was the unknown gentleman, and what was his amazing idea? What transpired during those next twelve years, and how did Richard become the success implied in the conclusion?*

We initially planned to exclude the *JF* text in this book, until it became clear that it did not adequately stand alone without it.

While *JF* will continue to facilitate a powerful internal transformation for its readers across the globe, *Portal to Genius* is designed to help a reader more easily move into implementation and execution mode, affecting real-life victories. It's written to help the reader discover how to overcome each challenge faced on the real-life path to financial freedom and excellence in all areas of his or her life.

The principles contained in both books are universal, and the lessons addressed are applicable to all challenges. Though *JF* is included in the pages of *Portal to Genius*, the original story will continue to be available independently as a primer—a short and easy read for those who are particularly busy, for those who are skeptics, or for those who recognize its power and want to bring its life-changing introductory message into the hearts of those who look to them for leadership.

To learn from the documented mistakes and victories of others is to achieve greater success in a shorter period of time. Although this story is fictional, every encounter is based on true happenings, experienced by us (the authors), and tens (if not hundreds) of thousands of people, or more. Life has a way of bringing all people through experiences common to humanity, and we do well to learn from one another new ideas for conquering such challenges.

As you'll see through these pages, Richard becomes a giant in his own right, and it's your opportunity to *stand on his shoulders* to reach great heights of your own—even greater than perhaps you ever thought possible.

Enjoy the journey!

Leslie Householder
Garrett B. Gunderson

ACKNOWLEDGMENTS

From Leslie

A special thanks to all who have contributed to this story: through example, encouragement, and other types of support.

To my family, beginning with my husband Trevan, for his unending support and encouragement to follow my heart in all I do. To my children: Jacob, Nathan, Kayli, Jared, Nicholas, Bethany, and Sarah; you have all sacrificed so much to allow this book to become a reality. I couldn't have done this without your love, patience, and your individual contributions that held the family together throughout its creation.

I'm grateful for my parents, for their unconditional love and belief in me. For my mother's literary brilliance and my father's natural talent for taking difficult concepts and conveying them in interesting and entertaining ways. You both inspire me.

I acknowledge and am grateful for Garrett B. Gunderson, who recognized something special in the message of *The Jackrabbit Factor*, and who has been generous with his time, resources, wisdom, and encouragement to help me get its sequel completed. It has been an honor to study his perspective on success principles. His knowledge and experience have helped take my work—and many aspects of my life—to a higher level.

Thank you, Garrett, for your voice of experience, which has been an additional witness to the validity of the principles, and which has helped me illustrate in *Portal to Genius* how *The Jackrabbit Factor* concepts play out in the world of reality.

Heartfelt thanks go to Nancy Genys, the inspiration for several key elements in the story. Her determination to rise above the pain of tremendous loss, and her brilliance for transforming that pain into a powerful and meaningful contribution to society has been exemplary. I wish her and her family much success.

I'd like to thank my dear friend Carolyn Cooper, founder of *Simply Healed*, for her down-to-earth approach for helping me rapidly overcome internal blocks that were holding me back from achieving my best. Carolyn, I wish you great blessings and much success with your book. It was a pleasure to work on my manuscript while you worked on yours during that quiet week in the mountains.

I am grateful for the many teachers and mentors I've been blessed to know, and for their timely counsel and support over the years. I could never list the hundreds of inspired friends and leaders who said just the right things at the right times to help me keep going.

Additional gratitude goes to all who reviewed the manuscript to offer recommendations, and to those who played a special part in the completion of this project: Bob and Patricia Broyles, Rich Christiansen (author of *Bootstrap Business*), Sheila Nagle, Tim King, Marnie Pehrson-Kuhns, Shantel McBride, Kirk Duncan, Mark Hovda, Naji Nassereddine, Barry Markowitz, and fellow authors and friends Becky Thompson, Martina Muir, Tina Kurrels, and Carrie Newman. The powerful messages of each of your books inspire me and I wish you much success with them. I also owe a debt of gratitude to my editor, Kim Clement (kimclementediting.com), for her patient and thorough work in the book's final preparations.

Finally, I acknowledge that all credit belongs to my Creator; for all that I am and ever hope to be.

—Leslie Householder

From Garrett

I'd like to express gratitude to Leslie and Trevan Householder who allowed me to collaborate with them on the creation of this book. I am honored and humbled. It inspires me to see real life experiences (including mine) articulated through this story, as well as the principles I hold dear, and the lessons that can deeply impact people, helping them live a more joyful and prosperous life. It is always fun to engage in conversations about lessons learned and future possibilities when we spend time together.

I am grateful for those who have been so instrumental in my learning, loving, and personal prosperity. As it relates to the concepts of this book, I want to especially thank those who have given the most for this message to impact more people:

My wife Carrie, who has been such a support. She has invested more than anyone by sometimes sacrificing time together, by taking money from our savings or letting the cash flow go to business, and by supporting me emotionally in the most difficult of times. Carrie teaches me the greatest lessons of love and compassion (as well as insuring that I practice what I preach, and keeping me humble, by having me take out the garbage, do dishes etc., especially after I am recognized publicly for my accomplishments).

I am grateful for my boys, Roman and Breck, who teach me to be playful and responsible at the same time. These adorable guys rejuvenate me and always make me feel important and loved—except when they throw fits or wake me up in the middle of the night, but truly, it's those kinds of things that make the good times all the better.

My mom who helped me through some of the toughest financial times by working her magic to keep my firms financially viable with her resourcefulness, and Grandma and Grandpa who came through on a moment's notice when I had no other financial options available.

For the mental and relationship capital of some of the greatest contributors, mentors and friends in my life: Brett Harward, Rich Christiansen, Joe Polish, Woody Woodward, Kevin Thompson, Dan Sullivan, Steve D'Annunzio, Manisha Thakor, Alex Mandossian, Jon Butcher, Garrett White, Rick Sapio, Michael Drew, Roberto Monaco, Eric Lansky, Moe Abdou, Chris Miles, Dale Clarke, Ryan O'Shea, Brandon Allen, Trent Williams, all of the members of The Accredited Network, and all of my team with the Freedom FastTrack.

For those who provided financial capital to further this message, increase its reach, and deepen its impact: Dee Randall, Abby Moneyhun, Sally Eliason, Randy and Roslyn Gunderson (Mom and Dad), James and Kathleen Eaquinto (Papa and Grandma), Greg Blackbourn, Andrew Howell, Chaz Reist, Frank Sacco, Brandon Fry, Roger Gomez, and Scott Kirby.

And finally, to you, the reader, for demonstrating your commitment to overcome the obstacles that prevent *you* from living your

Soul Purpose by investing time and/or money to read this; for doing what it takes to courageously impact the world the way you were meant to impact it regardless of your circumstances; and for seeking answers on how to love life more completely. You're worth it.

—*Garrett B. Gunderson*

INTRODUCTION

John W. Sims, a highly successful businessman, spoke of a time when he was traveling with an associate. The associate said, "John, aren't you going to put on your seatbelt?"

John replied with his raspy tenor voice, "Why, are we going to get into a crash?"

"Well, no, but you know, seatbelts save lives...."

John retorted abruptly in his usual blunt way, "Seatbelts don't save lives."

"Of course, they do! I was driving down the road once with my family when something told me to make sure everyone was wearing their seatbelts. So, I turned around and had the family get all belted up. Right after we turned a corner, there was another vehicle coming straight at us in our lane; it was a head-on collision, and we all survived because of those seatbelts!"

John was firm, "No, the seatbelts didn't save your life, *whatever told you to put them on* saved your life."

More than two decades have passed since my wife, Leslie, and I heard John relate that story. Leaving a lasting impression on us, its message has deepened and taken on new meaning. The more experiences we have, the more profound the idea becomes. He is right. It wasn't the seatbelts that saved their lives. True, they played a part in the actual physics of keeping the bodies secure during impact, but the credit belongs to the voice of warning. The "life-saving" seatbelts were there during the entire trip. But the timeliness of the prompting, *and the man's response to it,* changed the would-be tragedy into a miracle.

This reminds me of a time when Leslie and a friend planned to take me and another young man on a double date in high school. They drove us to an apartment complex, abandoned us at a pay phone, told us to wait for a call, and then promptly disappeared. A few minutes later, they called to tell us where to find a hidden audio player and instructed us to turn it on.

The audio sent us walking along the winding sidewalk path throughout the complex. Each time we heard a 'beep,' we were supposed to take another step onto the next sidewalk block. But the beeps were inconsistent—sometimes they came slowly, causing us to nearly fall forward in anticipation of the next beep. Other times we were surprised by a rapid run of beeps, causing us to jolt forward to keep up with the pace. As a result, instructions to turn left or right were often missed at the junctures intended.

Meanwhile, the girls followed us, incognito. As we fell out of step, their instructions no longer suited our surroundings, and they laughed until they cried, watching from the bushes. At the end of the journey was a picnic fit for a king, but we couldn't find it by relying on their instructions alone. If we had only known *where* the girls were trying to take us, we could have improvised and found our way without needing their help to get us headed back in the right direction.

The scenario was so hilarious to them that it wasn't the last time Leslie did this to me.

On another occasion, she and her friend prepared a recording that described their every move as they traveled—by car this time—from a starting point to the planned dinner destination. "We're pulling out of the driveway," they recorded. "Now we're heading north, going twenty-five miles an hour. We're slowing to fifteen, and turning left, *right now*. Now we're speeding up to forty-five." The voice pauses for a minute or so. "Now we're turning right...."

"You forgot to tell them we slowed down first."

"Oh! Yeah, we slowed down first. Now we're back up to thirty five, and—hey! Dude! Watch where you're going!"

They continued recording their instructions (and random out-bursts), as they headed toward the dinner location for at least twenty minutes. They documented it all—not by describing landmarks, but by describing their actions alone. With the recording complete, they were ready.

When it was time for our date, the ladies put themselves in the back seat of the car, instructed us men to sit in front, handed us the recording and said, "Take us to dinner."

I knew the drill, but even still, despite how hard we tried to follow their instructions, we inevitably got off track. More than once we had to stop, back up, re-sync with the audio and correct our mistakes.

After a long and challenging journey, and only with their help (between their fits of laughter), we finally ended up at the dinner location.

While this type of activity might be good, clean fun for teenagers going to a picnic, it's an entirely different story when applied on life's journey to happiness. Yet, this kind of nonsense happens all the time.

Sometimes we look at someone who has reached an admirable destination and then imitate their actions or follow their instructions expecting to achieve the same results. While we may learn a great deal from people who have what we want, we must realize we are not always on the same sidewalk, so to speak, as they were when they began *their* journey to the picnic. We also must not be so surprised when we end up with undesirable results after duplicating someone else's instructions.

Have you ever seen the disclaimer attached to success stories, "results not typical"? Believe me; I *know* legitimate training programs *can be* fabulous, for we've had many of them help us achieve wonderful things in our life. But, why *aren't* the results typical? What about the people who followed the directions perfectly but failed to enjoy remarkable results? How can we know if a "get wealthy," "get skinny," or "get happy" program is going to deliver in *our* life?

If we want the same results as someone else, we shouldn't just *do* what they did, but rather learn how to *think* like they do. What they *did* may very well be exactly what is required to achieve the same success; but we each bring with us different life experiences, and a different variety of baggage. These elements make a difference in our results.

Therefore, we must discover the little voice inside of us that helps us get the direction *and the timing* right. If we have our eyes on the picnic table, and it is in clear view, then instinctively we will know how to get there. If we face an obstacle and cannot get past it on our own, then inspiration can lead us to the *right* instructions that will speak directly to our condition. That personalized guidance takes us from where we are, to where we want to be, at a pace that is right for us. We can enlist that divine "inner voice" to help us find our way simply by keeping a clear image in view of exactly where we're trying to go.

By learning to recognize the voice, and submitting to its advice, soon enough *we* become the latest success story and provide the next inspiring testimonial for the fabulous "get happy" program. Is the "program" responsible for our success? Not any more than the seatbelt was exclusively responsible for saving the family from death.

Success comes as a result of preparing oneself for inspiration, and then being willing to pay attention to it and do what it says. I've learned that before I make big decisions, I must first have a clear picture in mind *and on paper* of the outcome *I* am seeking. What is the lifestyle I'm after? In what kind of home do I want to live? What kind of relationships do I want with my family members? What kind of friends do I want to enjoy? (Which picnic would I like to attend?) I must answer these questions in detail and commit the answers to paper. Then, and only then, do I look for inspiration to direct me. *That* is when I'm ready to listen to and consider someone else's advice. *That* is when I am the student who is ready for the teacher to appear.

However, since every idea that comes may be either a proverbial lifesaver or the gate to a path of devastation, who can know the difference? It's therefore natural to be paralyzed with fear and remain in our familiar misery than to take a risk and hope for the best.

The message in this book will teach you how to take the risk out of taking risks. You will be able to move forward with *confidence* in pursuit of your dreams. You'll know who to listen to, and you'll be able to trust what they say. In short, you'll be able to proceed methodically toward your worthy ideal, whatever it may be.

You might be thinking: *How could anyone be so certain?* If that's *your* question, this book is for you. This story is about one man's struggle to thrive financially, but the principles apply to any objective a person might have. Having enjoyed a measure of financial success with the principles contained in this book, we've also applied them to more trivial things, such as locating a roll of lost packaging tape in our utility closet, or obtaining the perfect parking spot in a time crunch. These principles are even effective in simply finding the answer to a pressing question on my mind. Bottom line, it works. All we must know is what we really want. In other words, the first thing we must do is simply "pick our picnic."

Following is a modern-day allegory. Leslie has taken a brief analogy from another one of John W. Sims' dialogues and created a story around it so its profound message can reach a greater audience and change lives for the better. What we learned from John has certainly changed ours.

—*Trevan Householder*

CHARACTER GUIDE

The following story spans twenty-two years. You'll soon discover several important characters that will be followed throughout.

To glean the *most* benefit from this book, unimpeded by the multiple storylines, a **complimentary character guide** may be obtained at www.portaltogenius.com/guide.

The authors strongly recommend you obtain the complimentary character guide prior to beginning your experience with *Portal to Genius*.

PART 1

WHY YOU
CAN

1

THE TROUBLE

"Richard, why can't you be more like your brother?" Felicity muttered as she flung the handful of envelopes across the bed. The bills were left strewn across the old patchwork quilt with the laundry piled next to them.

Injured by her comment, Richard pressed his lips together and swallowed hard. Clearly, she was at the end of her rope. Again.

"Felicity," he sighed heavily. "Honey, I've been doing the best I know how." Richard slumped in the old recliner; his shoulders hung forward as he took a deep breath and closed his eyes. Then slowly opening them again, he glared at her from under his dark, thick eyebrows. "Besides, my brother is a crook. You really want to be married to a crook, huh? Well, sorry to break it to you, but I'm no crook. I'm just not."

"Crook or not, Richard, his kids have food on the table! And I don't believe all those stories about him anyway."

"Oh, come on. How else do you explain all that money?"

"I don't know. All I know is that I am tired of living like—like this." Felicity's throat tightened and her eyes closed. She let out an angry groan and collapsed onto the bed, sending half of the bills sliding off the blanket and striking the floor on their corners like falling daggers.

Richard reached deep down and mustered one more attempt at moving forward. "Okay then, what should I do? Insurance? I've heard there's a lot of money in insurance. They say you can retire from selling it, and the money just keeps coming. What about that?" His voice was bland and it was obvious that this insurance idea did not thrill him. Still, he was searching for some hopeful idea that might finally please Felicity.

"Sales? I thought you said you were no crook." Felicity's brief, playful smirk was her own feeble attempt at lifting the mood in the room, a mood she was responsible for ruining.

Richard was not amused. It took too much energy to respond the way he knew she wanted; this was supposed to be a serious conversation. "I've tried everything else, Felicity." He stared blankly at the floor in front of him. He felt weak and tired, but no emotion. It was killing him to face the facts of their financial condition and realize his powerlessness to do anything about it.

Just then the bedroom door that had been slightly ajar flew open and the doorknob banged on the wall next to Richard's chair. Richard didn't flinch, but Felicity shot an angry look toward little Matthew. Matthew didn't notice and scampered up onto Richard's lap. With the door wide open, the television could be heard in the kitchen as it played the whistling theme song to the *Andy Griffith Show*, which was having no positive effect on the cold feeling in the room.

Exasperated, Richard finally spoke with sudden rage. "Felicity, what the heck am I supposed to do? I've done everything I've ever been told! I finished school because they—the proverbial committee—always said I'd need a degree to get a good job. I hired on with

Wheeler because everyone said his company was growing so whoop-de-do fast that the profit sharing would blow our minds. I invested the LAST of our savings just the way Barry told me because HE'S done so well with the stock market. I bought this house because of all the HOOPLA that it was such a great deal. And now? NOW? Look at us! We're STILL eating oriental noodles once a day! Do you know how sick I am of NOODLES? Let's just UP and MOVE TO CHINA for crying out loud! Oh yeah, we couldn't even SELL this dump if we WANTED to because we OWE more than it's worth!"

Matthew sat frozen on his father's lap. Neither Matthew nor Felicity was used to this kind of sarcasm coming from Richard. Felicity looked deeply into his eyes as he continued to fume, until he finally turned his face away from hers.

Under his breath Richard continued, "And don't even mention that fiasco with my brother. All that money we spent and it just didn't work—for us, at least." He took a deep breath and shook his head, as if to shake off rising emotion and to steady his voice. More calmly, he spoke, as if to himself, "How does Victor do it? I'm respectable, aren't I? That's all I can figure: the rich guys have GOT to be crooked, because good guys like me get nowhere."

Felicity approached him and gently turned his face back to her, looking into his eyes. A new kind of fear washed over her. She realized this was the first time he had verbalized his defeat. Up until now, he had always gathered the strength to offer words of encouragement and hope. This time was different. Unconsciously tucking a loose strand of blonde hair behind her ear, she suddenly felt ashamed for the verbal beating she had given him. If only she could rewind this moment back just ten minutes, she could play the part she had expected him to play. But it was too late. What was that look on his face? What did it mean? What comes next? This was a scenario with which she was not familiar. Whatever happened to the predictable routine: wife feels discouraged, wife complains, husband comforts wife and expresses confidence and determination to make things right?

Just then, Richard gripped Matthew's arms, and in one robotic motion stood up and put his four-year-old on the bed next to his mother, forcing Felicity to slide out of the way. Matthew also seemed perplexed by the deadpan look in his father's eyes, and looked at his mother, searching her face for a little reassurance. Had he done something wrong?

Richard left the room and mechanically picked up his jacket on his way through the kitchen and left through the side door. The door shut quietly.

Felicity looked at little Matthew as if he might have the answers to the questions spinning through her own mind. He was wide-eyed and silent. If Richard had slammed the door, she would have at least known that he was letting the last of his frustrations out, after which would have come about two hours of angry silence, followed by ten minutes of quiet co-habitation, followed by an "I'm sorry," a healing conversation, and a kiss. But this? This was new.

"Mommy, where's Daddy going?"

Felicity wondered the same thing but said, "Uh, he's probably just going to visit the neighbor."

Without another word, she slowly walked to the window. She could still make out his figure through the old-fashioned, warbled pane of glass; he was walking resolutely across their neighbor's pasture, but he was not headed toward their neighbor's house. She sat back down on the edge of the bed and observed, perplexed. In the other room the television rattled on unnoticed.

"…forecast through Wednesday is partly cloudy with temperatures ranging between 76 and 80 degrees...." The disregarded noise only added more muddle to the clutter already filling her head. "Breaking news... Local authorities have confirmed that the cause of death in the Upnow case was suicide...."

Suicide. Felicity hadn't even noticed the television was still on, but the word lingered in her mind nonetheless. She didn't even realize it was the television that planted the word in the first place. Suicide? Suddenly a new thought took root and she shuddered. He wouldn't... no. Would he? Things aren't that bad, are they? Richard? Felicity stood again and gently touched the window with her fingertips. Pressing her forehead against the glass, she squinted and focused intently on the dark figure, now barely visible, as if a better look would help her know what Richard was thinking.

"Matthew, get your shoes, honey. We need to go for a walk."

2

REFLECTIONS

The Kansas winds blew softly through the cottonwoods along the Whitewater River as Richard glanced over his shoulder at the pale-green farmlands disappearing behind him. He went into the breezy woods, searching for a secluded place that would be invisible from his little century-old home. *I just need to get away for a while. Clear my head.*

He spotted a large, smooth, mossy rock about twenty-five yards into the woods and headed toward it, carefully stepping over the twigs and roots encumbering his way. Upon reaching the rock, Richard squatted down and rested on its smooth, clean side. He rubbed his face slowly and forcefully, as if he could push the financial stress right out of his life somehow.

Lord, what do I do now? Richard gradually slid down until he was sitting on the ground, leaning back on the cold, hard rock. Pulling out his pocketknife and selecting a broken stick from the ground, he let out a heavy sigh and began fervidly scraping off some bark to the emphasis of certain words which were running through his mind. *I've DONE all I know. I DO what I'm told, and LOOK where it's put me. Everyone ELSE gets what they want, and I'M the failure. It's NOT fair! When do I get to be the one to have a little bit of good luck?*

Richard dropped his knife and hurled the stick as far as he could, causing it to ricochet off the trunk of a quaking Aspen. He closed his eyes and reflected on the events of the last twelve months. He could still hear his brother just as clearly as the day it happened. "Ritchie, things are really moving. You realize I've already brought in eighty grand just this quarter? The time is right. You could make so much money with us. Buddy, your family needs this!"

"Victor, I know. It's just that I can't imagine talking to people and trying to sell anything, even if it is the greatest thing the world has ever seen."

"Look, it sells itself. How could you fail? You just do what the winners are doing, and you'll win too! It's as simple as that."

Richard hesitated, then timidly expressed his perceived inferiority, "The winners have something I don't have, Victor."

Victor raised his eyebrows lovingly and shook his head. "What are you talking about, Ritchie? You're no different from them. Okay, maybe you could use a shot of self-confidence, but that isn't anything we can't help you with. What do you say? Just think, you start bringing in the kind of money I'm talking about, and you can say 'sayonara' to your mortgage, huh?" Victor smiled and nudged Richard with his elbow. "Huh?" He repeated.

"I don't know, Vic."

"Tell you what, you come with me to the training and after you see what kinds of people are making it, then you can decide."

There on the woodland floor, Richard shifted his weight to relieve the pressure the rock was inflicting to one side of his back. He smiled sardonically as he settled down again and recalled the meeting:

"Victor," Richard whispered discreetly. "Who are these people? They're goofy, for crying out loud."

Victor chuckled, "Ritchie, this is what I'm talking about. You see that guy over by the punch table?"

"You mean the one with the real nice suit and white sneakers?"

Victor laughed, "Yeah, that's the one." He leaned in closer and whispered, "He's a millionaire." He chuckled again, as if noticing the fashion faux pas for the first time.

"NO."

"Honest, Ritchie. I know you can do it. You have a whole lot more going for you than most of these people, wouldn't you say?"

Richard was cautious to temper the excitement he felt growing inside. "A millionaire, huh?" Richard back-pedaled prudently, "I don't need a million, Victor. I just need enough to pay my bills. And maybe enough to send Matthew to college someday." His voice was reluctant but the glimmer in his eye was unbridled.

"Well, shoot, Ritchie. If they can make a million, then surely you could make enough to do that, don't you think?"

"Yeah, I think I could." There was a hint of courage and hope emanating through Richard's entire countenance now. "How much is it going to cost me to get started?"

A squirrel rustled some leaves above his head, but Richard didn't flinch. He cocked his jaw to one side, and shook his head slowly feeling the anger and cynicism building up inside.

Picking up a dirty stone, he rubbed it clean with his thumb. It worked for Victor and the others, but not for me. Settling, he concluded, *I didn't want to be like him anyway: all obsessed with riches. Money, money, money. Who needs it, anyway? I hate the stuff. I HATE it!*

He chucked the stone and rubbed his eyes with the backs of his knuckles. Emotional exhaustion settled over him, and shifting his weight again he rolled to one side and eventually fell asleep. He heard the faint call coming from the neighbor's field, "Richard? Richard where are you?"

Unconsciously he rolled slowly again to his back. But his answer, "Honey, I'm just over here," stayed inside his own sleepy mind.

3

THE PATH

"There you are," his wife said, but only in his dream. She approached him gracefully, the dappled sunlight dancing on her skin as it descended through the cottonwood trees, while she smiled and floated closer with her arms outstretched. In slow motion, she glided over the ground and then embraced him gently. He beamed as she kissed his cheek, and with an expression of adoration in her eyes she gently whispered, "Now go and seek our fortune. I know you can do it."

Richard stroked her hair lovingly and then touched her arm, smiling. "I'll do my best. Don't worry. Everything's going to be okay."

Felicity smiled back, her warm brown eyes glistening with admiration for her man.

Proud to be the invincible hero, Richard confidently marched off in no particular direction, but did it with vigor nonetheless. In only a few short steps, the trees were behind him and a worn-out road appeared before his feet. The pavement, which must have at one time been a dark, shiny black color, was now pale and spotted with potholes. Surprised at its sudden appearance, Richard rubbed one of his temples and looked into the distance where the road seemed to be going. "Hmm. This has gotta go somewhere important—looks like a bazillion people have gone this way before. It's all worn out; that many people can't all be wrong. I bet I'll find just what I'm looking for." With that, he stepped onto the old road and began his journey.

After walking for only a few minutes, Richard noticed something interesting. Up ahead on the road was a little brown paper bag. Filled with curiosity, he pressed forward and picked it up. It wasn't heavy, and upon opening it he discovered a time card just like the ones he always used at Wheeler's company before getting laid off a few years before.

The top of the card read, "Employment Incorporated," and underneath it was a blank line after the words, "Employee name." The paper sack also contained a little plastic bag with half of a peanut butter sandwich. He closed the sack, glanced around, and saw no one. Should he consider this to be the good fortune he was seeking? It was somewhat sustaining, but not enough to meet the family's needs. Nevertheless, he opened the sack again, pulled out the sandwich, and continued walking. He downed the sandwich in only three bites and felt some degree of gratitude for the negligible success.

"Wish it had been bigger," he sighed, and stuffed the plastic bag back into the paper sack. The timecard caught his eye again, but this time the blank line had his signature, "Richard Goodman." He frowned at the oddity of what had just occurred. But trying to find answers was futile as he was alone on the path. The strangeness of the experience filled his head, and he strolled down the path with his mind full of questions.

It wasn't long before he was hungry again, so the sight of another small brown paper sack along the road was encouraging. With renewed enthusiasm, he ran ahead and scooped it up, only to find that it was empty, aside from a folded "pink slip" with "Employment Incorporated" on the letterhead, and one small baggie with crumbs from an already consumed sandwich. He stopped and squinted at the road that lay ahead and he thought he saw yet another sack.

Speeding forward with anticipation, he reached the third paper sack. It was bulkier than the first. He opened it, and found another timecard with his name on it; but this time there was an entire peanut butter sandwich.

Then something else grabbed his attention. Curious, he peered into the distance along the ill-repaired road. Without shifting his gaze, he reached into the sack and slowly pulled out the sandwich as he continued to stare at the newfound images. A few men had appeared up the road, walking away from him. He hadn't seen them before, and wondered how he could have missed them. Almost magically more people began to materialize until there was quite a busy crowd, all traveling in the same direction. There must have been hundreds of people, robotically plodding along and picking up brown paper sacks.

Someone bumped him from behind, causing him to drop the sandwich. Richard turned as he heard the person apologize, "Oh, pardon me." He was taller than Richard and kept a quick and clumsy pace. In each hand were two paper sacks and a third was tucked under his arm. Before Richard could say a word, the man was gone. He had slipped ahead into the crowd and disappeared.

Richard reached down, retrieved the sandwich from the pavement, and then blew on it. He examined it briefly for any serious contaminants and glanced back up at the crowd where the awkward man had disappeared.

"What am I doing?" Suddenly he was conscious of the absurdity of the scene. The road that had seemed so promising, so full of hope that it would lead to a small fortune for his family, was clearly only going to provide just enough to keep him from ever changing his course. He dropped the sack, plopped down, defeated, right in the middle of the crumbling asphalt and put his head in his hands. Hoards of men now passed on either side of him. Each one was searching for another sack, hoping to find at least half of a sandwich. Some carried one sack, many carried two. Occasionally someone would pass by carrying three. The most frantic of the men were those who didn't have a sack yet, or those who carried a crumpled, empty one with a "pink slip" peeking out of the top.

Suddenly, Richard was kicked in the hip by a slicked-haired man with wing tipped shoes and a crisply pressed, pinstriped, button-down dress shirt. Without an apology, the man stumbled over Richard but regained his footing and continued to race ahead, darting around people and glancing repeatedly at an athletic, blonde man in sweat pants and a tank top, sprinting nervously next to him.

"Oh, come on, LOOK OUT, people!" The first man growled at everyone crowding his way. He shot an angry glance at the blonde man speeding along at his side and accidentally ran right into a curly headed stranger in a tweed blazer who had been unaware of the approaching fray. Refusing to go down, the slick-haired offender grabbed hold of the curly-head's shoulders, and thrust him, flabber-gasted, into the path of his competitor.

"Ooof!" The blonde man was hit by the poor curly-headed stranger broadside and they both tumbled to the ground.

"Aaaargh!" The blonde man punched the dusty path with the side of his clenched fist.

"I *told you*, it's *mine!*" The first man in wing tipped shoes pounced on the coveted brown paper sack, which had apparently been the object of their obsession.

Richard was already standing again, having jumped up to avoid any other reckless pedestrians. Approaching the blonde, Richard extended his hand to help him up, as well as the curly-head. The two men dusted themselves off and both slouched down the path, dejected: the stranger for the undeserved abuse he had just received, and the blonde for losing his chance to win the sack.

"Hey, mister! There're other sacks, you know," Richard called ahead to comfort the man.

The blonde stopped dead in his tracks turned around and looked sadly into Richard's eyes. "Call me Joe. Joe Bless. And no, there really aren't. I've looked for so long; I don't know when I'll ever see another sack. It's been so long since I've had one. Don't you see? That sack was the opportunity of a lifetime." The man turned away and scarcely lifted his feet as he disappeared into the crowd.

Richard squinted and looked up and down the path, eyeing at least thirty sacks placed sporadically along the road, just waiting to be retrieved. A lot of people seemed to pass them by without even a glance. Why did Richard see them, but Joe did not? Why was there such rudeness over obtaining the one bag for which the men fought?

Just then, a well-dressed woman walked by. She seemed to be about thirty years old. She carried a diaper bag which hung from one elbow, a bulging laundry bag slung over one shoulder, a spray bottle of disinfectant clipped to her hip, a purse over her other shoulder, a toddler girl in a backpack, a puppy under her arm, and a paper sack clutched in one fist.

Richard's mouth dropped open at the sight of the woman who lumbered by. He saw her twist an ankle in one of the dusty potholes. She winced but trudged on. She looked tired, and her little girl made brief eye contact with Richard. The babe's eyes held a look of weary longing. Her head was turned to one side with her cheek pressed gently against her mother's back. Blinking slowly, she closed her eyes and snuggled into her mother's warmth to take a nap.

He looked around at each of the men and women (now he saw many women) who flowed along the road where he still stood. He also noticed that regardless of how many sacks they carried, they never turned around. They were continually pressing forward. He also saw some women trying to carry several children: one on their back, one on each hip, and a sack or two tightly in their hands.

But, the most heartbreaking of the images he saw were the women who had to put their children down. The mothers were doing all they could but found it impossible to do it all. He heard one mother tell her little boy, "I'll find you a sandwich and bring it right back. Just wait here for a little bit. I promise I won't be long." The child frowned and reached up to be held again by his mother, but she could only take one hand and kiss it, then turn away to find another paper sack.

Richard ached at the heartbreak of the little boy, as he thought of his own little Matthew. The boy slumped down on the rough asphalt and looked back just in time to see another young woman approach him, smiling. She was pulling a wagon full of toys, books, and musical instruments. Over her shoulder hung a duffle bag with the zipper completely pulled open, and he could see that the bag was full of nearly eight or nine little brown paper sacks.

The next thing Richard saw sent a shudder down his spine. The woman reached down for the boy, and as if in slow motion, his color changed and he began to morph as if straight out of a sci-fi movie. *What the devil is happening?* As Richard leaned closer to get a better look, he blinked forcefully to clear anything from his eyes

THE PATH   35

that might be causing the distorted image. The boy's soft, baby skin became rigid and then wrinkled and rough. The distinguishing characteristics of a child melted away and before Richard could grasp what was happening, the child shrank and became a paper sack the very moment the woman's hands took hold of him. With a look of gratitude in her own tired eyes, she gently placed the sack in her duffle bag with the others, and walked on.

Richard was stunned. *These children—their own mother leaves, and they become someone else's paper sack? This has got to be a dream. O-kaaaay, I'd really like to wake up now!* He slapped his cheeks to no avail. He slapped them harder and was instantly sorry. Rubbing his cheeks, he thought the morphing child was bizarre, but all he deeply cared about was returning to Felicity, and waking himself up wasn't working.

His stomach turned as he thought about having to get back to finding another sack. What good would it do? He could see that nobody ever seemed to turn back. How could they? They never found enough in those sacks to ever quit the insanity. And when a man came upon a weighty sack, loaded with more than the normal portion of peanut butter, jelly, and bread inside, it only whetted his appetite for more and he would run quickly in search of another bonanza of sandwiches.

This is insane! If I continue like them, I'll never get home. He shook his head and fought back tears of frustration that welled up in his eyes. Something deep inside told him he was meant for something greater than this. *There has to be a better way!* He wanted to turn around and reunite with his wife, but he had nothing to bring her. *I need to find something enduring,* he thought.

Richard closed his eyes and tried to imagine, tried to create a solution in his mind. It was about the toughest thing he had ever done: directing his thoughts toward some unknown, unidentified, answer.

Instinctively he felt he had some kind of genius idea hidden somewhere within. But his mind was inclined to wander, to think about the images of the people that thronged him on either side, or to think about what his wife could be doing at that moment, or reflect on the paper sacks and their meager contents. But, with each temptation to let his thoughts drift, he consciously forced himself to search hard and deep for a brand-*new* idea.

But nothing came to mind.

Richard let out a frustrated sigh and opened his eyes. Strangely, he was alone. Did just the mere effort of trying to think differently from the crowd set him apart from the others, in a very literal sense? Everyone was gone! Richard was confused, until he remembered something his father had said on more than one occasion: "There is no labor from which most people shrink as they do from that of sustained and consecutive thought. It is the hardest work in the world."

Now who said that? Oh yeah, there's a name I could never forget. Wallace Wattles. Richard laughed to himself. *Who was that guy anyway?* Richard's mind meandered. Then he thought again about his father's words. *Thinking **is** hard work, isn't it Dad? I know there's got to be a solution here; I just don't know what I'm looking for.*

Richard's father had been well off. He was a quiet man, but had built a beautiful life for his family. He seemed to be such an ordinary fellow, but lived the life of a closet millionaire. Not a showy life, but an abundant one, nonetheless. He drove modest but quality cars and had a small home that was elegantly furnished and beautifully kept. He traveled to exotic destinations and returned with interesting gifts from Asia and Europe. If he hadn't passed away so early, Richard might have been more conscious of what his father was really all about. Victor was five years older than Richard and had spent long hours talking with their father, gleaning the wisdom and insight that accompanies a millionaire mentality. Unaware that such a thing existed, Richard was beginning to realize that until now he hadn't known there was more to know.

Richard answered his father out loud, "Dad, I don't even know what I am looking for!"

His father's voice spoke in Richard's mind, "What do you want?"

What do I want?

4

THE FEAR

As Richard slept by the rock, Felicity and Matthew searched on, over the rocks and roots of the ground beneath them. They still called for him, but he could no longer hear their voices. The thickness of the trees hid him from their sight, even though he slept only a stone's throw away.

"Richard?"

"Daddy!" Matthew called. Then turning to his mother, he asked, "Where's Daddy? Why are we in the woods?"

Felicity didn't know how to answer so she changed the subject. "Matthew, how are you, honey? You doin' okay?"

"I'm okay, Mommy. But my feet hurt." He raised a foot as if to show her the evidence.

"I'm sorry, sweetheart." She squatted down and briskly rubbed his pant leg. Slowly she turned around, shaking her head. She quietly muttered, "Which way do we go? How on earth do I find him in here?"

"Can I sit down, Mom?"

"Sure, honey. Let's rest a minute." They sat together on a fallen log and she closed her eyes to say a silent prayer that everything would be okay.

Felicity felt a little better, more assured that they would find Richard all right, but she quickly began second guessing her sense of peace. *What if I'm wrong, what if he's already given up, what if Matthew sees him first, and he's—?* Her imagination began to run wild. *What if we're too late?* Her body tensed with fear and she jumped up, startling her little boy, and yelled, "Richard!" She didn't mean to frighten Matthew so she quickly adjusted her demeanor. She also decided she needed to go back for help.

"Hey, I have a good idea, let's go take your shoes off at home and give your little feet a break, okay?" Felicity's voice was shaky and falsely cheerful. It even cracked a bit, but Matthew didn't notice. Scooping her four-year-old into her arms, she hurried as best as she could back toward the farmland. Her small, five foot three frame struggled under his weight as she tried not to stumble on the uneven ground beneath her feet. Soon they were back in her old kitchen.

Taking off his shoes she said, "Oh, sweetie, look at the clock. We're late for your nap." Matthew was tired anyway, and Felicity needed to think. She let him have a drink and tucked him into his toddler bed.

Felicity kissed him and then closed his door. With no little eyes watching her, she surrendered to her anxieties and became frantic. She scrambled for the phone and it fumbled out of her hands and landed under the table. Reaching down to pick it up, and having to crawl partially under the table, she pushed against the chair, which became stuck against the table leg and finally fell over. She growled, and her tightly frowning eyebrows raised a little as she tried to see the numbers through the tears pooling in her eyes.

Leaving the tipped chair on the yellowed linoleum where it lay between the table and faded avocado green couch, Felicity put the phone to her ear and paced the floor in front of the little table. "Hello, police? Um, my husband is gone; we really need to find him!"

"How long has he been missing, ma'am?"

"Uh, I don't know," Felicity looked in vain for a clock on the wall, or a watch on the counter, or anything to help her have some kind of reference.

"I don't know, maybe an hour."

"Can I have your name, please?"

"Felicity Goodman."

"Mrs. Goodman, is there a reason why you are concerned after only an hour?"

"Well, he was upset. He left without saying anything. He never does that! I just don't know what he's going to—where he's—what I—" Felicity stammered, realizing that the operator did not feel the panic that she was trying to convey.

"Please calm down, Mrs. Goodman. Do you have any idea where he might have gone?" Her inquiry was obviously a routine statement rather than a question motivated by genuine concern.

"He went into the woods behind my house."

"I've started a statement here, but to be honest with you we cannot file it as an official missing person report until he has been gone at least twenty-four hours."

"Twenty-four hours?! What if that's too late? What about—I don't know, isn't there anything you can do?"

"If he were a minor, it would be different. But the policemen on staff can't place a high priority on a case like this because, frankly, most of the time the person has left of his own free will and will also return on his own before the twenty-four hours is up."

Felicity was speechless.

"Mrs. Goodman?"

"Uh, yeah. Um…" Felicity didn't know what to say but didn't want to hang up yet either. Surely, she could say something to change the outcome of the phone call. "Uh, well, what do you suggest I do? I'm afraid he might—try something." She couldn't seem to say the word suicide because she didn't want to believe it could really be true. Speaking it out loud to the operator would have taken this nightmare out of her head and straight into reality somehow. It would have seemed so serious. She sort of hoped this whole day was just a bad dream.

"Ma'am, do you have reason to believe he is in danger?" Again, her question came out like a statement.

"Well, yes, and no—he's never threatened—" Felicity hesitated and finally got it out, "*suicide*—or anything, but he was so depressed looking, and he left without an explanation."

"Would you like me to send out an officer to talk with you and get the paperwork started, at least?" The operator seemed to be demonstrating a little more compassion.

Felicity was relieved. Albeit not the kind of help she hoped for, she thought it might be comforting to have the officer come, anyway. Even a little bit of attention from the authorities would be better than nothing. The emptiness she felt inside gnawed at her nerves. It must have been her tendency toward comfort food as well as the thought of a police officer coming over in a black and white car with lights on top that instilled a sudden craving for a nice, white, jelly-filled doughnut.

After giving the operator the needed information, Felicity hung up the phone and stepped over to the window again. She gazed across the farmer's field and into the woods. They seemed so impenetrable from that far away. They looked shadowy and harsh. *Where are you, Richard? Where are you?*

It took the officer about forty-five minutes to arrive at her home. As she waited, she searched her nearly empty cupboards for something edible to help her feel better. She wasn't the least bit hungry, but eating would calm those nerves. She finally found some graham crackers and prepared to whip up some icing sugar and milk to spread across the top.

After clearing a place at the table, she began to put it all together. Her hands shook as she thought in detail about the horrible things that Richard was probably experiencing. The depression, the anger, the loneliness, the hopelessness—and the suicide! She envisioned the funeral and how Matthew was going to have to deal with the loss of his father!

Felicity absent-mindedly stirred the icing mixture. Her mind wasn't on crackers or icing or even the chair still lying on its side by the couch. After pouring a glass of milk, she dunked a corner of the cracker, swishing it back and forth until the edge of the two sandwiched crackers became heavy and soft. Briefly allowing the excess milk to drip off, she lifted the crackers to her lips, and consumed most of the soggy clump. A small section rolled down her chin and onto her blouse. Leaving it there, she only looked down on it; then, seeing it as further evidence that her life was falling apart, her brows furrowed and the tears returned full force. Leaving the rest of the crackers on the table, she picked up the small bowl of icing. Dipping her finger in, she walked to the couch and then buried the glob of icing in her mouth. Before she knew it, she had eaten the whole batch.

Disgusted, exhausted, and scared, she set the bowl down on the floor and reclined on the couch. She was just curling into a fetal position when the doorbell rang. She jumped to her feet and shouted, "Come in!" Losing her balance, she fell off the couch, banging her knee on the fallen chair. Struggling to her feet, she kicked the chair, just as the concerned officer and his partner were swinging the door wide open. Felicity's other foot was caught in one of the rungs and she began to lose her balance.

"Ma'am?"

Felicity's hands flew out in front of her, preparing to catch herself in case she toppled all the way down to the floor. Then waving them full circle like windmills, she finally stabilized herself. Standing erect, she prudently brushed the wrinkles from her blouse, unknowingly leaving the soggy graham cracker stuck to her chest. "I was, uh, just..." Felicity drew a blank and finally just sighed, resigned to an idiotic first impression.

"May we come in?"

Recovering, she said, "Yes, yes, please come in."

Relieved by their long-awaited arrival, Felicity fought back a new release of tears which she valiantly kept at bay, for a few moments. Then failing, she rubbed them away, smearing her cheap mascara as it ran in black streams down her cheeks.

The officers watched her, uncertain about what they were getting themselves into. The thin layer of crusty icing around her mouth looked like the remains of a dreadful froth that had dried up. The senior officer glanced down at the chair, then back to her.

Embarrassed, Felicity stepped her foot out from between the chair rungs, kicked it behind her and motioned for the officers to come in.

Senior Officer Cross chose not to call further attention to the disarray. The poor woman was obviously distraught, and he just wanted to get down to business. His junior partner glanced at him, and in response, the senior officer dismissed the look with a discrete shake of his head and a slow blink.

But before the senior officer proceeded with his duties, he glanced once more at the chair. Why hadn't she merely picked it up?

"Ma'am, can I get some more information about your, um, husband?"

Felicity nodded and motioned for him to sit at the small kitchen table. She pushed the radio and crackers to one edge so he would have more room to spread out the paperwork. Junior Officer Doolittle remained standing behind Cross, and Felicity sat back on the couch not far from her visitors.

Cross, the senior officer, looked intently and directly at her, and squinting, cocked his head to one side. He found it hard to overlook the raccoon eyes, the streaks of tears turned black with mascara, and the dried froth. The dispatcher had briefed him that this was not an urgent case, so why was this poor woman such a wreck? Finally, he spoke, "Ma'am, how long has he been missing?"

"Um," she sniffed, "about two hours." She noticed he wasn't looking her in the eyes. Was he looking at her mouth? Self-consciously, Felicity tried to wipe her mouth with the back of her wrist. She glanced at the younger officer with him, who was a little uninterested, eyeing the rest of the milk and iced crackers.

Cross leaned back in the chair and his shoulders relaxed. "Ma'am, don't you suppose that he might just be out for a walk?"

How could she answer that? She was choking back sobs. Trying to speak would have only sounded like the emotional high-pitched words of a little girl. The patronizing tone of the policeman's words made her feel small. Felicity shook her head slowly, but she didn't say a word.

5

THE INSTRUCTION

Against the cool, mossy rock, Richard continued to doze. In the tree above him slithered a snake that had just caught view of the solitary man below. Slowly and quietly it crept toward a lower branch, and then paused.

The breeze was cool, but the sun shone through a gap in the trees and kept his body warm. In the meantime, his mind was far away, taking in the strange scenes of the potted road and amber fields. He once again heard his father's voice speak. "What do you want? Richard, our minds are powerful tools. Your thoughts are alive and do more than you realize. Don't be careless with your thoughts." Richard suddenly felt like he wasn't alone. He turned, and there stood his father, smiling.

"Dad?" The last time Richard laid eyes on his father was when he was twelve. Unfortunately, those final memories were tainted with the dismal images that accompanied his father's final battle with cancer. He almost didn't recognize him standing there so alive and robust; he appeared to have the strength and health of a young man in his prime.

In his younger days, Richard's father had been a brilliant businessman. So Richard had been told, anyway. What does that mean to a kid? But because cancer had cut his father's life too short, Richard, with his mother and seventeen-year-old brother, was left behind.

"Son," his father smiled and opened his arms.

"Oh, Dad." Richard melted into his father's arms just as he had dreamed over and over. When he felt alone or depressed, he often closed his eyes and visualized this very event. "Dad, I've missed you so much—you're here! How—?" Richard exclaimed through breathy sobs.

"Ritchie. Oh, my little Ritchie. I've been with you, on occasion, but you couldn't see me. At times, your thoughts drew me close to you. Just as the things you desire. That is what I am here to tell you now: You want money? Use your thoughts. You need food? Use your thoughts. Think on the worthy desires of your heart, and they are drawn to you spiritually."

"What do you mean, Dad?" Richard pulled away from his father's embrace, but continued to hold his arms.

"All physical things have a spiritual counterpart. By thinking, we draw the spiritual counterpart to ourselves. By persisting in right thought, unseen help arranges the affairs of men to cause our worthy desires to pass from the spiritual to the physical world."

Richard's brows furrowed and he shook his head slightly. "That seems too simple, and kind of weird, Dad. I've thought lots of things that never came true."

"As long as you believed it was coming, the dream was actually on its way. All things in the universe that were required to see the dream come true were gathering for your benefit. However—and this is where most men fail—the moment you entertain doubt or fear, all those forces reverse and the things, the ideas, the situations, the people you need, immediately draw away from you."

His father paused, and then continued, "Our negative thoughts actually and literally cause the blessings to be repelled. If you can picture what you want, and believe that it is on its way, by God's law it must come. Hold on to the belief, and in time you will realize it." Richard's father panned the area surrounding them and held up his hand as if to display the scenery to his son. "The earth is abundant with all that any man could need. But by his own misuse of thought he cannot see it." He dropped his hand and then tapped Richard's forehead, "Change your thinking, and you will see the opportunities all around you. You've been blind to them, but they are all around you right now."

Blind to them? Richard thought about the blonde man who couldn't see the sacks. *What am I missing? What's all around me now that I can't see?* Richard looked around. He wasn't sure what he was looking for but nothing really stood out. He saw the dilapidated road, the vast fields on each side, the tree line, and thick woods in the distance. He looked back at his father, puzzled.

"Son, you have to know what you want. If someone else has what you want, learn from them, but you must trust your own instincts to make the right decisions. The voice of inspiration will come only after you have a clear picture in your mind of what you are seeking, and after you allow yourself to feel truly grateful, as though you already enjoy the success."

This philosophical stuff wasn't making much sense to Richard. It seemed terribly vague and hardly useful. Along the path, many things had seemed bizarre. This odd conversation was no different, so he didn't take it too seriously and simply nodded graciously to his father. "Thanks, Dad."

"Now go. Know what you want, and when you find it, chase it. You'll know what to do."

Richard blinked and lifted his eyes, nodding as though he was committing the advice to memory. But before he could thank his father again, the kind, wise gentleman disappeared.

Richard spun around to see where his father had gone, but he was alone. With a sentimental sigh, he paused and then looked again at the road. "What do I want? I want to wake up already!" Then with a groan, he lamented, "I want food for my family. I want to go home to my wife and Matthew." He looked down the road in each direction, a little confused because he could not remember from which direction he had come. He saw a few footprints in the dirt where the asphalt had completely worn through. They all were pointed in one direction, so he chose to go the same way.

Somewhere off the path, something rustled the tall grass. Richard jumped, startled by the sudden noise. The tall, golden, wheat-like grass swayed in the light breeze, and all was quiet. In one spot, maybe fifty feet away, he saw a gap in the grass where something hid. In an instant he heard another rustle, and the gap was gone.

6

THE INSANITY

Coming from the hole in the grassy field, he heard the warning growl of an agitated wild dog. *Oh, no.* Sickened by the sudden rush of adrenaline, Richard froze. The dog snarled and leapt out of the grass and landed again, out of sight. After a tense moment of silence, it appeared again, barked, growled, and then darted crazily one way and then the other. Richard relaxed just a bit as he realized the dog hadn't seen him after all, but decided to move cautiously down the road away from the rabid-looking beast. The wolf-like dog's mouth dripped with saliva and his glowing yellow eyes had Richard entirely unnerved.

But before he knew it, the dog was already headed straight for him, so Richard took off like a rocket. Panting, he ran as fast as he could, and escaped into the field on the opposite side of the path. He hurdled dirt mounds and whipped through the tall, brown grass. Stealing a brief glance behind him, he saw the dog approach within ten feet—and immediately dart away just as quickly.

Richard pounded the dusty ground with his loafers as he slowed to a stop and tried to catch his breath. Leaning over with his hands on his knees, and between gasps, he raised one eyebrow and squeaked out a breathy, "Huh?"

Why did the dog turn around? Richard wondered, *Is there something worse lurking nearby?* Nervously, Richard looked about and searched for other hidden dangers. He saw nothing that would have frightened the dog. Richard was stumped. The growling and the barking continued and the dog hopped from place to place in a frenzy. *That's it. The dog's insane.* Returning to the road, Richard tiptoed along with a quicker pace and kept one eye on the dog for safety. In and out of the grass, the dog continued growling, foaming, and snarling back and forth, up and down. *Poor dog. I wish someone would put it out of my misery.* He chuckled at his witty thought, then proceeded cautiously down the path, feeling safer after determining that though the dog was crazy it seemed harmless enough.

As he turned from the dog, he thought about the visit from his father. He smiled and relived the warmth of his father's love.

His moment of peace, however, was abruptly interrupted by the appearance of the same wacky dog, which had now stumbled out into the road immediately in front of him. The dog re-established its footing, and with a rabbit in its mouth, glanced placidly at Richard and walked peacefully away into the grass on the other side of the road.

Richard paused and tipped his head to one side. *A rabbit? It was chasing a rabbit?* He chuckled out loud. *The dog was chasing a rabbit.* Suddenly it all made sense. The dog wasn't crazy, and it wasn't rabid. Richard recalled all the jumping and growling, the darting to and fro. He shook his head and laughed at himself for feeling so anxious before.

"Ooh, I'd like to have a rabbit, too." Someone spoke from behind. Richard turned around, taken aback by the unexpected company.

"Yeah, a rabbit would be nice. Much better than all those peanut butter sandwiches, eh? Name's Richard. What's yours?" Richard extended his hand to the small, round man now standing next to him with a five o'clock shadow and somewhat disheveled comb-over.

The man didn't break the stare he had fixed on the dog as it sauntered away, but politely replied, "Harold. Harold Ashway." He exhaled slowly and sighed, "I've always wanted one of those rabbits." Harold's face lacked expression, mesmerized by the lingering memory of the dog's prize.

Without another word, the man stepped off the road into the sheaves of grass and jogged clumsily ahead about forty feet. Then with a wave of his hand and a smile in Richard's direction, he turned and began to leap around as if he was chasing an elusive rabbit. Except, there was no rabbit.

Richard squinted. *What is he doing?*

The man paused, scratched his head and then got down on his hands and knees. Then he started darting around like an animal on all fours; and to top it off, he started barking. And growling! Barking and snarling and jolting all over the place, the man carried on and Richard's mouth dropped open. *You've got to be kidding me.* Richard tried his best to make sense out of the man's odd behavior. Was he imitating the dog's actions without seeing something to chase? Did he think he would gain a rabbit by doing so?

What was he barking at, anyway? Does the fool think that mimicking a dog on the hunt is gonna somehow PRODUCE a rabbit? There's no rabbit! Even if there was one out there somewhere, all that craziness would scare it away!!! "Harold Ashway!" He shouted, "If you carry on like that…!"

Richard paused when he caught sight of three or four jackrabbits behind the man, frightened by the commotion. The man was oblivious to them; he never even heard them scamper away, nor did he pay attention to Richard's exclamations. Richard attempted to hold back the laughter he felt rising in his chest but failed to suppress one massive snort that escaped through his nose. Rubbing the back of his neck, he turned away to leave the man to his business.

Just then his father's voice returned to his mind, "Know what you want, and when you find it, chase it. You'll know what to do."

Richard began slowly walking down the path again, rehearsing his father's words and contemplating the ludicrous scene he had just witnessed.

Then he thought about his brother, Victor. He remembered all the things people had said about him, how crazy he was, how he'd burn the candle at both ends, and how doing the same things had never produced the same results for Richard.

Richard stopped dead in his tracks. That last thought sunk into the deepest recesses of his soul, and he clapped his hand to his mouth. *I always tried to do what Victor did to get what he got. I always tried to do what someone else did to get what they got, but it doesn't work that way, does it, Dad? I was scaring away any success that might have been nearby! Doing what someone else has done is like imitating a crazy dog, isn't it?*

Richard thought deeply about this new perspective. He thought about the way he should behave instead to get better results. It seemed so simple, philosophically, at least. He realized that, first, he needed to be calm and confident. *But how* could he *be confident when he had doubts about so many things?* Well, he wasn't sure about that; he just knew that he needed to find a way. He knew that to catch a rabbit, he had to be calm, or they would detect him and disappear. He needed a way to attract the thing he wanted, because it was clear that busy-ness without focus can be a waste of time.

What did he want? *A rabbit would be nice*, he thought. It would be something he could take home to his family and they could make stew. That would be much better than all the sandwiches he had found. He stepped off the path and sat down on an old, dried-up stump, scoping the area for rabbits.

Nothing.

Opportunities all around me, huh? He began to feel cynical again. Shaking his head, he looked over his shoulder and studied the old road again. With a heavy sigh, he stood up and decided to speculate some more after gathering another sandwich. He needed the energy. After all, this thinking business was tough, exhausting stuff.

He plodded along, and before he knew it he was shoulder to shoulder with hundreds of men and women in search of brown paper sacks once again. But this time all the crowds annoyed him more than ever. He knew better. He knew there was a way to leave the hordes in the mindless quest for mediocrity. *Oliver Wendell Holmes. Didn't he say, "A mind once stretched by a new idea never regains its original dimensions?"* Now he understood why the sack race suddenly felt so intolerable to him. Never did that saying mean as much as it did now. He could not stand this way of life, knowing that something better was waiting for him.

In fact, he was sure he hadn't noticed them before, but occasionally he spotted individuals out in the field, well off the beaten path, who strode along in the opposite direction. Each of them had an aura of confidence and hurried anticipation as they rushed alongside of, but against, the crowd.

Where were *they* going? It didn't take long for Richard to deduce that they were on their way home to their families, because they each carried a captured rabbit. On top of that, gathering behind them was a small but growing drove of rabbits, appearing from nowhere and following these people like rats in the story of the Pied Piper.

Richard nudged a man who was walking next to him. The man glanced over with a questioning look.

"Did you see that?" Richard threw a thumb in the direction of the latest rabbit captor.

"See what?"

"The people with the rabbits."

"Oh, them. Yeah, I notice those kinds of people every once in a while, and I swear they are so irritating."

"Irritating?"

"Yeah, now and then they stop to get on the path right in front of me."

"Serious? Why would they do that?"

"I think they get a kick out of being annoying. They get in my face with all this talk about how I could have my own rabbit," the man chuckled. "I mean really, when would I ever have time to catch myself a rabbit with so much to do here on the path? I wish they'd just leave me alone."

"So, what do you tell them?"

"I tell them they're full of baloney and to get out of my way. I've always known that if something sounds too good to be true, it probably is."

Richard didn't say anything. He kept pace with the man and remained silent for a while. Finally, he had to know, "What if they really could show you how to get a rabbit? Wouldn't you want one? Don't you have a family you could go back to if you had one?"

"Oh, sure I have a family. But it's my job to collect sandwiches until I retire. I've only got about twenty years left of this."

Richard winced. "Wouldn't you want a rabbit?"

"Oh, see, that's just too good to be true. I could never get a rabbit. In fact, I don't think I'm supposed to have one, anyway."

"Why is that?"

"God said I can't go to heaven if I get a rabbit."

"What? What are you talking about?"

"He said that rabbits are the root of all evil."

"No, he didn't."

"Yes, he did. Now if you'll excuse me…" The man tensed up and nervously hurried away from Richard.

"The root of all evil?" Richard whispered to himself.

Richard attempted to run the man's logic through his own head. Here was a man planning to spend the next twenty years away from his family, with most of that time in pursuit of little brown paper sacks because it was taboo to find a rabbit. So, *was* it wrong? Was he on some forbidden quest that would alienate him from the Source of all Good? He didn't want a rabbit for the sake of having a rabbit; he wanted one because it would allow him to return with complete focus to his family.

Looking at the panorama of individuals in perpetual search for sandwich after sandwich, Richard couldn't help but wonder what was going on in the lives of *their* families back home. Did they have any idea what they were missing? *Do I have any idea what I am missing? What would it be like to be a room parent at school in Matthew's class next year? I wonder what a room parent does, anyway. And then there's Felicity. Wouldn't my marriage thrive and grow like never before if I had the time, means, and freedom to continue developing that relationship the way I really want? If my family is the most important thing to me, am I spending most of my time developing those relationships? NO! I'm spending all my time looking for stupid sandwiches in dad-blasted paper sacks!* Richard suddenly yelled out loud, "The root of all evil? I just want to go home. I just want a rabbit so I can finally be home."

Was that so wrong? Maybe so. Maybe he was supposed to engage in the sack race his whole life if for no other reason than to build his character. After all, that's what everybody else does. Stick with the program. Don't deviate. Do what you're told, and you'll succeed. A little bit of fear spread over him as he spotted a sack and numbly picked it up.

He decided to put the whole rabbit idea away for a while. It was too conflicting and frankly, a nagging nuisance. He knew it was what he wanted, but there was just too much of a mental wrestle to try to do anything about it.

The crowds of people around him became thicker. Soon he couldn't move without bumping someone. He was in a veritable foot-path traffic jam. Richard groaned inside as he came to terms with the fact that unless he chose to think differently from the crowd, he would only drown in the floods of mediocrity, and probably perish from the conscious awareness of his own failure to achieve his dream. Would he miss the chance to enjoy watching Matthew grow up? How long would his wife keep holding on to the hope that he'd one day accomplish what he set out to do?

The thought of disappointing Felicity yet again was more than he could bear. He stopped abruptly and realized that it was too late for him to ever be satisfied with keeping up with the crowds. He closed his eyes and held still. For a short time, he was bumped over and over from the masses that pressed on. Occasionally the blow was so abrupt and forceful that it almost knocked him over, but he didn't flinch.

He envisioned his wife smiling at him, and his little Matthew running and jumping into his arms. These were the images that brought him joy. He could hear Felicity say, "Oh, honey, you did it. I knew we could count on you." With his eyes still closed, he relished her adoration and could feel the joy that swelled up inside from reuniting with his loved ones.

When he opened his eyes, the crowds were gone.

7

THE IRONY

Silently, Felicity felt her mind slip into a fog. This wasn't going right. She had very real concerns, and who could she turn to if the police weren't going to take her seriously? They just glared at her; what could she do? She couldn't even speak to them without feeling like a fool.

Whether or not my fears are justified, I deserve at the very least an empathetic ear! Who's going to help me? Who'll listen to me, and convince me that everything will be okay? Who'll change the way I feel?! Who'll save me from this nightmare?!

Officer Cross exhaled a forceful, frustrated sigh. "Ma'am, if you're not going to talk to me, there isn't a whole lot I can do for you."

If you're not going to treat me with some respect, then I'm not going to talk to you.

"So, what's it going to be?" Cross glowered at Felicity with his eyes half closed and his eyebrows raised high. He glanced at his junior partner who stood apprehensively near the wall. The younger Officer Doolittle seemed to want to say something to break the tension, but showing Felicity any compassion at that point would have undermined the arrogant superior, and undoubtedly be met later with a reprimand.

Still refusing to respond, Felicity looked at the floor defiantly and prayed for some kind of advocate to save her from the humiliation she felt growing inside.

Cross knew what would change the stalemate. "Perhaps you know exactly where your husband is, and you just don't want to tell us what happened, is that it?"

Felicity finally looked up, incredulous. Cross stared her down, searching for any hint of guilt in her response. She crumpled her eyebrows, closed her eyes and shook her head, whispering, "This can't be happening to me."

8

THE DIFFERENCE

Richard opened his eyes and realized the group had vanished. He turned around, looking to see where they had gone but they were nowhere to be seen. *Whoa*, Richard thought. *That was easy.* He took mental note that if he ever felt crowded among the masses of mediocre minds, he needed first to close his eyes and imagine what he wanted, and most importantly, imagine the feelings that would go with it. He guessed that most people never take the time to really do that.

That's when he noticed a sack at his feet. With a new attitude toward it, realizing it wasn't his ultimate goal, he nevertheless felt a degree of reverent gratitude that it was there. He looked heavenward and thought, *Thank you for this. It gives me the energy I need to pursue my goal.* He reached down, picked it up and carefully pulled it open. Smiling, he pushed aside the timecard and pulled out a triple-decker sandwich.

A voice inside his head spoke to him, "Ah, you keep on this path and the sandwiches will just get bigger and bigger! See? All you need is patience and persistence and you'll get all you need right here on this path."

In the woods where Richard slept, the serpent lifted its head and quietly loomed over him. Suddenly a thin twig cracked and fell, dropping the baleful creature next to his arm. It crept up his sleeve and then settled onto his chest. It remained poised, hovering over his shirt pocket, gazing at Richard's face.

In his dream, Richard paused to think. He looked down the path, as if to somehow determine whether the voice was telling the truth. Would he really find all he needed along this road? But instead of seeing sacks, he began to see people again. *No, that's just what everyone else thinks. I need to think differently than the others. I must think differently.*

It bothered him a little that he wasn't alone on the path anymore. He felt like he must be slipping into popular mentality for them to show up again like they did. He closed his eyes and imagined his family. He thought about standing near his back porch in the thick, cool, green turf, and picking up Matthew and twirling him in the air. He saw the trees zoom past behind his son as Matthew giggled and thrust his head back in sheer delight. Even with his eyes closed, Richard's thoughts put a real smile on his face and upon opening his eyes once again, he found himself completely alone.

There. Now, where was I?

He stepped off the path, and sat on an outcropping of rocks about ten feet from the road. He was consciously aware that thinking and feeling the happy images set him apart from the crowds. Now, he began to wonder what it might be that he should do next to get a rabbit. *Use my thoughts, huh, Dad? I wonder what he meant by that.*

He closed his eyes and imagined a rabbit in front of him. Richard found this difficult, as he wasn't good at keeping his thoughts from darting all over the place. But he managed to see in his mind an outline of a small, gray animal with tall ears. The shape of the creature was sort of abstract for the moment that it won as the dominant image. It seemed dark all around and almost like a watermark, nothing more.

But he did hear a rustle. Richard opened his eyes and looked into the distant field. He was certain he saw the tall grass move in one spot. All the grass was swaying in the mild breeze, but in one place the grass remained fixed. Something seemed to be hiding there.

He stood up cautiously, and saw it: a small animal with two long ears, far away and somewhat vague. But he saw it!

He fixed his eyes on the animal and slowly, vigilantly approached it.

It was impossible to move through grass without making noise, so it wasn't long before the rabbit looked his way and darted toward the woods at the edge of the field.

"Aargh! There's no way I'm going to be fast enough to catch a rabbit like that!" Richard threw his hands up and let them fall to his side.

He moaned and returned to his perch on the rocks. He looked back to the path, feeling lonely. *There's nobody out here. At least the path never lacked company when you wanted some.* He shouted out loud, "At least I wasn't alone in my misery!"

Richard moped for a while. Finally, he muttered, "What am I doing? Who do I think I am, anyway? I'm no Victor. I don't know how to do this."

He looked up just in time to see a smiling man holding a rabbit by its ears. Lifting it up, he greeted Richard as he passed by, about thirty feet away, well off the worn-out path.

The voice in his head spoke up, *"Oh, would you look at the showoff. He's just rubbing it in your face that you don't have a rabbit."*

But Richard reserved judgment. He acknowledged the impish voice, but he wasn't choosing to believe it, not yet.

Richard waved his hand to return the greeting and forced a smile. With a friendly jerk of his head, the man invited Richard to come along. Richard glanced around to determine if the invitation was truly for him, or intended for someone else. When he saw no one else around, he shrugged and stood up to join the rabbit man.

Something about the man was magnetic. He seemed so self-assured. So at peace with himself. So directed. Richard wanted to be like that. He wanted to know what the man knew. He wanted to know how to catch a rabbit.

"Good day," the rabbit man greeted.

"Good day." Richard responded.

"I saw you sitting in the field, and thought you might be interested in having a little chat."

"How did you know?" Richard was puzzled by the man's intuition.

"Because I was just like you only a little while ago. It's my guess you stepped off the path in search of a rabbit. Am I right?"

Richard nodded, and his eyes lit up in anticipation that the man might reveal a profound secret. "You know what, you're right! I've been on a heck of a journey, and so far, I've figured out that I must visualize what I want, and feel what it would be like to have it. The strangest things keep happening. I know I want to be with my family, and each time I think about it, and feel the feelings that go with it, all the people around me just vanish."

"That's because you've set yourself apart from the masses. Most people wish for a rabbit, or say how nice it would be to get off the path, but only a rare few ever take the time to visualize doing it."

"How does visualizing help? Does it just sort of act as a mental rehearsal, so I'm not as afraid to take the necessary steps?"

The man shook his head and grinned, as though he was about to share the most priceless secret of all. "Oh, no. It's so much more than that." The man paused, and Richard leaned in, baited and waiting for more. The man looked intently at Richard, and then changed the subject.

"What's your name?"

"Richard. Richard Goodman."

"Good to meet you. I'm Andrew, but you can call me Andy. Andy Zauff. You got anything to eat?"

"What? Um, yeah, I have part of a sandwich," Richard became guarded. "Why?" he asked with suspicion.

"Hmm. Oh, never mind. Excuse me while I go get some lunch. Maybe I'll see you around." The man politely tipped his head and turned away with a look in his eyes that said he was torturing poor Richard on purpose.

"Now wait a minute!" Richard was not about to let the man get away precisely at the moment he was to discover the secret.

The man turned around, "Yes?"

"Weren't you going to tell me how visualizing helps?"

"Well, yeah, perhaps. But it's lunchtime, and I intend to eat now." The man was frank, but kind.

"Okay, fine, if I give you the rest of my sandwich, will you stay and teach me what you know? Please?" Richard felt an urgency to seize the opportunity for knowledge even if doing so meant he had to abandon all pride. And his sandwich. He didn't know if anyone else with this man's experience would ever come along and give him the priceless knowledge that he so desperately sought.

Andy smiled and accepted the sandwich as Richard eagerly offered it in his outstretched hand. Granted, it was all Richard had. Would he ever be able to replace it? He thought of the men who fiercely competed for the one measly sack on the path, when so many others lay around unnoticed. He knew there were other sacks, more so than some people realized. Trusting the wisdom would be worth the price, he put away his concerns about being able to get another sandwich. He decided he'd simply go find one, expecting one to be there when he needed it.

The man ate Richard's food and motioned for him to sit down with him to continue their conversation.

"Contrary to what you may think, visualizing isn't just for generating courage." The man spoke very deliberately. "Picturing a favorable circumstance in your head literally causes unseen things to happen in mysterious ways." He paused and searched Richard's face for signs of belief or skepticism. Seeing only wide-eyed curiosity, he proceeded. "Actually, some terribly misleading rumors are circulating among the paper sack collectors: they say to leave the path one must have a big enough dream to do so. The problem is that the people think that means they need to have a big enough dream to give them the motivation to do nearly super-human things." Richard was nodding, for that was a perspective he had encountered himself. "But it is the dream itself, the passionate thoughts of what they want, that emanate from their minds like radio waves and which go out into the universe, causing astonishing things to happen on their behalf."

The man's voice showed excitement, as if every time he thought about it, he was just as amazed as when he himself learned it for the first time. "In other words, if you get excited about holding a rabbit by the ears in your hands, rabbits will literally begin to approach you, merely by your thoughts. By thought they are drawn to you, by action you receive them."

"You're telling me that my thoughts make things happen that I can't see. I don't mean to be thick-headed here, but what are you talking about? What kind of thoughts?"

The man answered, "It's so simple. You've got to have gratitude for your present conditions, no matter what they are, because it is the lessons of the present that prepare you for the blessings of the future. Have grateful thoughts for your current situation, no matter what. Also, you've got to have thoughts of how you'll feel when you reach your goal."

He added, "Thoughts of trust are vital, too; trust that there's a divine power guiding you to find and catch your rabbit. And, most importantly, you must have thoughts of belief that there is a way, no matter what kind of obstacles may appear. These thoughts are all invisible, but powerful little soldiers that go out and do for you many things that you can't do for yourself."

"So, I must be grateful even though I don't have a rabbit," Richard reiterated.

"Yes. Be genuinely grateful for the way things are, and then be truly grateful for how things will be. You see, to be grateful for something before it has been accomplished, is faith. And faith can move mountains."

"So, all those people who have rabbits just think differently than the rest of us? I thought they were faster, stronger, or smarter."

"No, for the most part they're just like anyone else."

Richard wasn't quite convinced. Pointing toward a few of the folks holding rabbits in the distance he said, "But it comes so naturally to them. Every successful person I've ever known was self-confident. I've never seen them show any doubt. It's like they were born or raised that way. As for me, I would really struggle to think that way consistently. It'd be so unnatural."

The rabbit man grinned and nodded his head understandingly. "Yes, it could take some practice. But truthfully, many of the people with rabbits had to develop the thought-discipline, too. Just like you." He chuckled, "You know, you're not the only one who has mistakenly deduced by observation that the winners are somehow more gifted than the rest. Isn't it ironic that so many people without rabbits think they've figured out what it takes to get one?"

Richard agreed, "Like the guy I saw who thought he'd catch a rabbit by jumping around like a dog."

"You're kidding, right?"

"No, I'm not."

Andy rolled his eyes. "People just need to learn how to think differently. If they'd learn how to think like a winner, they'd win! For one thing, I'd like to tell them to 'see the rabbit vividly before launching a full-blown attack,' for crying out loud. I mean, that's just common sense. And I'd tell them: 'Don't make excuses. Winners don't make excuses, period!' Richard, in case you haven't noticed, excuses are epidemic out there on the path. For every person who has an excuse, there's someone else who is determined to succeed despite the same, or worse, circumstances. Nobody has an obstacle so great that there isn't also a way prepared for that person to succeed. That's a promise."

He paused as he searched Richard's face for understanding.

Richard spoke up, cautious not to sound like he was trying to make excuses, "Certainly there are times when a task is truly impossible, I mean, you'll never see a really old man place first in a triathlon, will you?"

With a slight grin, the man raised his eyebrows, blinked slowly, and shrugged his shoulders. "I've learned to never say never. I've also learned that if I believe I can't do something under certain conditions, somewhere in the billions of people on this planet someone exists who would do it anyway. So, I figure, why not me? And, if that was my dream, to win a triathlon as an old man, and if I could believe it, then it would be possible. But I might need an altruistic reason to do such a thing, and the desire would have to be intensely passionate. I'm sure that in the history of mankind, many old men have done physically impossible tasks, equivalent to a triathlon, perhaps because their life depended on it. Miracles do happen."

"I just don't understand how a person can do something remarkable if they don't already have what it takes."

"I'll be honest; most people can't achieve their dreams—as they are. But people can change. Success comes when a person submits to change, but it isn't the kind of change you'd suspect. See, although a person might not have all he needs to make something happen immediately, he certainly has all he needs to get started, and that's all that matters. If they picture themselves successful, and feel the victory as though it were real, and believe that somehow there will be a way, then they can expect it. They *must* expect it. Then, when they go as far as they can go, and reach what appears to be a roadblock, that is where they can expect to find the way around it."

Finally, Richard got it. He nodded, but now he wanted some specific advice about his own situation. "Okay, with that said, all I want is to provide for my family and spend my days enjoying their company. I don't want to spend my whole life in the sack-race."

"Do you know how you're going to do that?"

"I have no idea. But I believe that catching a rabbit will help."

"Okay, then. It's simple. You need to write it down, and know that the mere act of doing so causes unseen things to happen for your benefit."

"I need to write it down? What good does that do?"

"Well, it's funny. Visualization alone accomplishes a great many things. But it's a beautiful experience to commit a goal to paper and know that writing it down is like submitting a request to a Master Chef. There's no waitress here, so you must put in your own order. When the dream comes just as you ordered, you can know for certain that the Master provided it. And he loves the recognition! When you only imagine it, and it comes true, there's the question of whether it was just a strange coincidence."

"You're kidding, right? You mean, you write down what you want, and it comes?"

"Basically, yes. But there's more to it than that."

"Like what?" Richard's curiosity was piqued.

"Well, let me ask you something. If I were to go back to the path and tell everyone that all they needed to do was take the time to write down exactly what they wanted and it would come true, what do you think they would say?"

Richard chuckled. "I know what one of them would say, at least. He'd tell you how annoying you are."

Andy laughed. "Yeah, I've heard that one. What do you think they would do if you told them to write down what they want?"

"Well, I doubt they'd do anything. And even if they did write it down, I doubt they'd believe it would work."

"You're right. In fact, only about three percent of the population take it seriously. And, it's no surprise that only about three percent are able to get rabbits to come to them."

"No kidding."

"No, I'm not. See, the whole key is *belief*. People are used to believing in only what they can see, or detect with their senses. The three percent consciously choose to believe in something they create in their own mind. You're not presently with your family. But each time you close your eyes to imagine and feel that happy reunion, circumstances are literally changing, rabbits are approaching. Do that often enough, believing with no reservations that it is already true, and it will happen. By law."

"Law?"

"Laws of thought."

"There are *laws of thought*? What in the world does that mean?" Richard's brows were furrowed and his brown eyes were wide.

"Well, just like gravity is a law of nature, so are there laws related to how our thoughts affect our circumstances. And, like gravity, we don't have to understand them or believe in them to be affected by them one hundred percent."

"You mean I've been governed by 'laws of thought' my whole life and never even knew it?"

"Exactly. Not very many people have discovered that their thoughts significantly affect their circumstances. But those who have discovered it have found that the knowledge can be a great advantage to them. As they believe on purpose, the things they need are drawn to them. But when they let themselves doubt, the things they need are drawn away from them. This is how it works with absolutely everybody, but what do you think the problem is? Why do you think it's not *obvious* to everyone?" Andy wanted Richard to draw the conclusion himself.

"Well," Richard responded, "We think hundreds of things every day and never see evidence of them having any effect on anything."

"But they do. They really, really do."

Richard thought silently for a time. Finally he said, "I suppose our circumstances seem random because we don't hold on to one thought long enough to see it happen. We talk ourselves out of ideas. We believe, then we doubt, we believe, then we doubt, right?"

Andy replied, "You've got it. It's like a cosmic dance. All we could ever need is all around us. There is plenty for everyone, and if it ever ran out, more would be created. As we believe it's coming to us, it does. When we believe that we lack, it is drawn back. The dance: one step forward, it's on its way. One step back and it steps back as well."

"So, disbelief is the norm because all of this is happening in an invisible way. We never see the dance, so we have no idea that we're having any effect on it." Richard was energized. This knowledge felt like an infusion of confidence he had never experienced before.

Andy could see the lights going on in Richard's eyes and he smiled. "Think of it this way: a tree seed that gets planted in the earth does not have to scramble around searching for bark particles, or leaf molecules, does it? Does it worry that it might not find what it needs?"

Richard chuckled, "Of course not."

"You're right. We can learn a lot from God through his creations in nature. No, the seed doesn't even have to look very far. It just remains still, and all that it needs is naturally drawn to it. As God instructs, 'Be still, and know that I am.'"

Remembering something he had been taught as a child, Richard added, "Consider the lilies of the field, how they grow—they toil not—but never was a king arrayed—quite as well as one of these?"

Andy simply smiled.

"I butchered that one, I think. I don't remember exactly how it goes."

"You get the idea, though." He continued, "If we think of our idea like a seed, and plant it in our minds, and nourish it with belief and gratitude, then all we need to accomplish the idea is drawn to us, just as naturally as elements to the lilies."

"Pshh. That makes so much sense."

"I love to see people finally get it. I used to try to tell everyone on the path how simple it was to have all their needs met. But they were suspicious and talked illogically."

"How do you mean?" Richard was curious.

"Oh, I'd tell them they could go home to their family if they caught a rabbit, and they'd say they *would* if they had one, but since they didn't, they were trapped on the path. I'd tell them they could catch a rabbit if they learned how, and they'd say that they knew someone who had tried it before and failed. I'd tell them there's a better way, and they'd say they'd heard it all before. So I just got weary of trying to explain it. Ironic, isn't it?"

"Wow. I guess someone has to really want it before the answer will do them any good, huh?"

"That's what I've learned. Usually I just stop trying if they give me an excuse two or three times in a row. No reason to waste the answers on someone who isn't asking the questions. It's like being a store clerk and handing a bathroom key to every customer who comes along and saying, 'Here, the restroom is down the second aisle, and then turn left. It will be at the end of the hall. Here, take the key. Take it! What do you mean you don't need it? Who wouldn't want to use the bathroom?!'" Andy held an imaginary key in one hand and shook it in front of Richard's face while Richard recoiled and waved it away.

Andy continued, "I've learned it's a timing thing. The information just isn't useful to everyone who comes along. Some come in for a soda or a newspaper, with no intention of using a restroom. And when someone comes along who wants the restroom key, you certainly don't have to talk them into taking it. After all, only a relatively small number of people are looking for what you have. And you know what? That's okay."

Thinking about the hordes of people crowding the path, Richard suggested, "It's my guess there are a lot more than just three percent who want a rabbit though, wouldn't you agree?"

"Yeah, I do. But not that many understand they need to change the way they think before they'll ever get one. Too many of them wish for a rabbit, hoping one might come their way out of sheer luck." Andy grinned. Suddenly he had an idea. "Follow me. I want to show you something."

Richard and Andy hurried to catch up with a few people who were walking along with rabbits in their hands. The man conferred with a few of them secretly for a moment, and one of them threw his head back in laughter. Each of them smiled in turn, and then they all nodded their heads. Andy turned again to Richard and said, "I'd like you to meet some of my friends: Colin O'Hare, Evan Yukon, and Cary Moore. Guys, this is Richard Goodman. Now, let's take a little trip back to the path. You've gotta see this."

Returning to the old road, Richard glanced over his shoulder and politely nodded his head to the three strangers, extremely curious about what was going to happen next.

The dream itself,
the passionate thoughts of what I want,
will emanate from my mind
like radio waves and will go out
into the universe,
causing astonishing things
to happen on my behalf.

There is no obstacle so great
that there is not also a way prepared
for me to succeed.

I have all I need to get started,
and that's all that matters.

I will write it down.
I will "submit" my goal
to the Master Chef.

9

THE GIVEAWAY

Andy Zauff turned to Richard and said, "Do you want to see why our thinking has everything to do with the degree of success we enjoy?"

Intrigued, Richard glanced at the three others who stood near him, smiling. They obviously couldn't wait to witness his reaction.

Without another word, Andy gathered up all the rabbits from the group and held them securely in both hands. He had five rabbits. The other participants in this scheme made themselves comfortable on the ground next to each other, facing the path. If there had been bleachers, Richard was sure by the eager look on their faces they would have been on the front row, with hot dogs and soda in hand. With uncertainty, Richard chose to sit beside them.

Andy asked Richard, "Which one of those people on the path do you think would like some rabbits today?"

Richard's eyes grew wide, "What? What are you going to do?!"

"Just pick someone."

"Um, okay. How about that guy?" Richard pointed to an average looking fellow, wearing khaki pants and a polo shirt with a "too cool for you" strut.

"Fine. Now watch this." Andy took the rabbits, and walking away from his friends, he stepped onto the path directly in front of the khaki pants man. "Excuse me, a minute; I have something to give you."

"Out of my way, punk." The khaki pants man pushed Andy aside and walked on.

Turning to Richard, Andy hollered, "Pick someone else!"

Richard pointed to a thin man in a suit and glasses.

Andy stepped in front of the thin man. "Excuse me, sir; I have something to give you."

The thin man stopped, eying Andy suspiciously and said, "What." There was no modulation in his voice whatsoever.

"You are the lucky recipient today of five, fine rabbits."

"What's it going to cost me?" The thin man's voice remained monotone and somewhat irritated.

"Nothing, whatsoever. No strings attached; I'm just conducting an experiment."

"No thanks," the thin man put up his hand and hurried away.

Looking back at the crew who sat at the side of the path, Andy raised his shoulders as if seeking further input.

Richard held out his hands, palms up, as if to say, "You choose."

So, Andy stood in the path and called out, "Free rabbits, five fine free rabbits!" But people just ignored him or looked at him oddly and walked past.

Finally, he hollered, "Today's jackpot is FIVE FINE RABBITS! Who's got a lottery ticket!?"

With that, quite a few people frantically searched their pockets and approached him, shaking their tickets and chattering excitedly.

Looking back at his comrades, Andy saw they were doubled over in laughter. Richard was stunned.

Andy arbitrarily snatched someone's ticket and said, "You're the lucky one!" Then he put all ten rabbit ears into one hand, and offered them to the jumping, screaming winner.

The winner awkwardly took hold of the ten rabbit ears and panted excitedly. The others on the path had mixed reactions. Some cheered him and stayed close, offering to help and declaring their lifelong friendship, while others cussed, grumbled, and stormed away.

Returning to his friends empty handed, Andy parked himself on the ground, obviously not finished with his investigation. Richard was amazed that these rabbit people would sacrifice such a valuable commodity for the sake of an experiment on his behalf.

Somewhere in the cloud of dust, the winner was surrounded by crowds of people who had gathered to see what all the excitement was about. Quite a commotion ensued, as cameras flashed from reporters who had been drawn to the scene and couldn't wait to get their story on the front page of the morning paper.

Out from under the throngs of people scampered a rabbit that had escaped the madness. Hopping off the path and into the grass, it approached Colin and stopped directly in front of him. Colin reached out and took hold of the rabbit while the others patted him on the back.

One by one, the rabbits returned, and Richard was speechless. Once all the rabbits were back, Richard looked toward the path and saw that the crowd had dispersed. The only one left was the "winner," moping empty handed and searching for a paper sack.

It was a depressing sight. Richard didn't like the way this scene made him feel. Sensing Richard's concern, Andy nodded, "I know how you're feeling. Believe me, this is the most frustrating part about owning a heightened awareness of the laws. It's painful to see how blind others can be, especially when it doesn't have to be that way.

That man can have all the rabbits he wants, but he must change the way he thinks. Some people have to hit rock bottom before they're humble enough to start asking the right questions."

"Couldn't we just teach him how to think? Help him succeed?"

"Believe me, I've tried with many a sack collector and even a few rabbit owners who got their rabbits in cut-throat ways. But most people aren't interested in what I have to say, and those who *are* interested tend not to believe me. Only people who want the knowledge desperately enough seem to listen to me *and* apply what I teach. They have to want the knowledge at least as much as they want food."

It all came together for Richard now. "The sandwich. You had to find out how badly I wanted this knowledge, didn't you? You probably weren't even hungry, were you?"

"Well, actually I was. But you're right. I had to know if you were going to waste my time or not, and if you were going to waste your own time or not. Without considerable sacrifice, people don't typically follow through. That's why I started asking for sandwiches. Some people see it as greedy, but in reality, I'm doing them a favor." The three comrades stood, and Andy shook their hands from his sitting position and said, "Thanks for your help."

They each smiled and said, "My pleasure," or, "No problem," before strolling away. Andy put a hand up to say goodbye and then positioned himself closer to Richard. He casually crossed his ankles, rested his arms on his bent knees and began fiddling with a stalk of dried grass he had pulled from the ground beside him.

Richard spoke slowly to himself, "Greedy? Greedy to ask for a sandwich so he can change someone's life?" Richard wasn't sure what he thought about that.

Having overheard Richard's mumbling, Andy said, "It's like I have plenty of water, fertilizer, and sunshine that I'll gladly pour out on anyone's ground. But if they're so tight-fisted that they won't put their seed in the soil, all I have to offer will be wasted."

"Okay, I've heard something like that before: What you send out comes back to you—or that which ye sow, so shall ye reap—is that what this is all about?"

"Yep, but you have to be careful with that cliché. Too many people try to apply the principle improperly, and the money never comes back to them. Then they wonder why it didn't work, and lose faith that it's a valid promise. There's a fine line between a sacrifice or investment, and gambling. Make sure you know the difference."

"So, I suppose an investment in knowledge that empowers me somehow is a true investment, while a lottery ticket is gambling?"

"Yes, that's the one of the more obvious distinctions. Still, there are less obvious forms of gambling, too."

Richard leaned back on his elbows and waited for the explanation.

Andy continued, "Have you ever made a huge sacrifice for some kind of venture based solely on someone's recommendation; maybe an advertisement, or a well-meaning friend or relative?"

"More times than I'd like to admit." Richard shook his head and grimaced.

"What were you sacrificing for?"

"What do you mean?"

"I mean, specifically, *why* did you make the sacrifice? What did you expect to get out of it? What specific things were you going to *do* with the profits? How was it going to *feel* to enjoy those profits? About how *long* did you think you'd have to wait before you'd be able to harvest the profits?" Andy was leaning forward, throwing the questions at Richard in rapid-fire, with an obvious tone of accusation. He knew full well that Richard had not taken the time to think through these details before making the so-called investment.

Richard was feeling somewhat cornered. Sheepishly, he responded, "Oh, heck. I didn't think too much about any of that. I just trusted the people knew what they were talking about and that each of the ventures promised to make me a bunch of money. Their ideas honestly made a lot of sense to me."

"That, my friend, was gambling. I don't doubt the people probably knew what they were doing. I suspect they had those questions nailed down solid for themselves, and they probably did make a ton of money. But you're the one who didn't see your own rabbit, and you're the fool who jumped, barked, and chased nothing but air."

Richard sighed. This awareness was depressing. Trying to divert such uncomfortable focus on his past foolishness, he changed the subject back to his most recent smart investment. "Well, in case you were concerned about the sandwich thing, I'm really not put out by that. I'd do it again if I had to. You've taught me how to fish, and you can't put a price tag on that. Half of a sandwich? Pshh! What a bargain."

Andy kindly consented to the diversion. "That's right; you've come a long way. Forgive my attack on your past decisions; I just wanted to emphasize the importance of having your own dreams and goals vividly defined before taking action in any investment or business venture. With your dream securely in place, you'll be steered by a divine power toward the right decisions for you."

"I'm okay with that. I've just experienced some growing pains to face the fact that I haven't been all that wise about those kinds of things."

"But you're on your way now, and that's what matters."

"I'm on my way now. That's right." Richard stood up and extended his hand. "Well I'm awfully grateful, and can hardly wait to get started."

"Remember: for whatever you decide to accomplish, your needs will be drawn to you once you have planted the seed in your mind. Plant it, get emotional about it, be grateful for it, and KNOW that all things you will need are literally approaching. Just like the elements to the tree seed." He smiled, "Now, my fine friend, I am really happy to know you, and I wish you the best. I'm going now to have my own dream fulfilled: my family is waiting for my arrival as we speak." With a smile, he saluted Richard and held up the rabbit in a goodbye gesture.

Richard smiled and saluted him back. "Thank you, and God bless!"

Whatever I need
to accomplish my goal
will be drawn to me
once I have planted
the seed in my mind.

Whatever I need
to accomplish my goal
will be drawn to me
once I have planted
the seed in my mind.

10

THE CATCH

Richard couldn't seem to wipe the grin off his face. He knew, *he knew*, that it was in his own control to achieve his goal. No longer did his success depend upon whether a rabbit happened to come along. He didn't need to hope the circumstances would be in his favor. He didn't need to worry if he would be fast enough or smart enough or better than the next guy. Success was completely within his control! Competition was unnecessary because enough rabbits abounded for everyone! And if the rabbits ever ran out, more would be created. God had provided and would continue to provide plenty to all who believed in abundance.

In fact, he was getting hungry, so he returned briefly to the path to get himself another sack with a sandwich and realized with gratitude that God even provides an abundance of sacks on the path. He deduced if every person without a sack truly believed they would find one, and if there literally was not enough to go around, more would be created, by God's law.

Believing in plenty made it possible for Richard to always see more. He remembered the blonde competitor and wished he could have given him a shot of belief, because the act of willful belief would have opened his eyes to what had been all around him the whole time.

Richard laughed joyfully out loud, "I think I believe in abundance! There's no such thing as *lack*! There is *only* abundance!" He was energized. He had felt so hopeless for so long, having this new awareness caused him to drop to his knees, arms spread with his face to the sky, overcome with gratitude because he finally knew how to provide for his family, no matter what the circumstances. *No matter what the circumstances are, I can always choose my own thoughts.* These new ideas astonished him. He sat back on his heels and took a moment to enjoy the entire sandwich one grateful bite at a time.

While still on his knees, his heart swelled with the feeling of gratitude as he envisioned with his eyes closed the rabbit he hoped to capture. *Dear God, will you please grant me a rabbit?* This time, he put in the extra effort to add detail in his mind. He made the rabbit well-defined, and it was beautiful, with long, graceful ears and suede-like fur. He could see every detail of the creature, right down to the tiny white fuzz on the edges of its ears, and the strong, sloping back and puffy white tail. Finally, he expressed gratitude for it as though it were already his. "Thank you for this wonderful rabbit I now have!"

He opened his eyes slowly, but nothing was there. *It didn't work. I did what he said, and there's no rabbit.* Richard felt a twinge of disappointment but consciously applied the proper laws of thought he had just learned. He closed his eyes again and thought, *It's already mine, and I know that as I choose to believe, it is approaching. God, help me know what to do and where to go, so I can do my part.*

Richard opened his eyes and still did not see a rabbit, but he smiled anyway, because he knew it was only a matter of time, as long as he continued to believe.

Okay, God, tell me what to do. I'm ready to follow your instructions. Richard truly expected to hear something, perhaps a booming voice from the clouds, or an angelic, musical whisper in his ear. But he heard nothing. Maybe the inspiration would come as words to his mind. But since he perceived no communication from Deity, he decided to just get up and start walking. After all, he knew for a fact you can't steer a parked car.

As he walked, a thought did come to him that his idea to simply start walking could very well have been the inspiration he was looking for. It was a strange thought, because he had expected something more dramatic to get his attention. Rather, he chose to trust in the imperceptible guidance. He gave God the credit for getting him up off the stump. It just felt right to do so. And now that he had shifted himself into first gear, he trusted that God had the steering wheel. His job was to roll, God's job was to steer.

The grass was especially tall now where he walked, and he pushed it out of his way with each step. Before long, he pushed aside another thick wave of grass and there in front of him sat the most beautiful rabbit he had ever seen. Just as he had imagined, the long ears were graceful and looked like the finest grey brown suede. He noticed the color inside of the ears was soft and white. Tiny white fuzz lined the rims and even glowed in the lowering sun. The rabbit breathed slowly. There was no hint that it was wary. Richard's eyes followed the hunch of the rabbit's back as it sloped to a beautiful white tail. He looked into its eyes and it held Richard's gaze as though it was challenging him to succeed. How uncanny it seemed that it had just barely come out of the hole where it hid, only inches away.

Amazed, Richard did not restrain his excitement and lurched forward, startling the rabbit. Did he see disappointment in the hare's eyes? It seemed to say, "You want it to be harder than it has to be? All right, I'll make it harder."

It darted away and Richard ran after it. Diving for it, he caught hold of its foot but it was trying to scamper so fiercely that he lost his grip, and rolling over he leapt again to try to grab it. It was quick, and he missed. The rabbit didn't seem frantic, but like it was goading him. Richard had a fleeting thought that he didn't deserve this fine rabbit, but giving up at this point was not an option. He jumped and darted, chasing it hard, and finally he had it by its ears.

Panting, he stood up and turned to hear a faint chattering. He saw a woman near the path, standing with one foot on the path and one foot on the edge of the field, whispering to the child on her back that the man looked insane and they'd better hurry on.

Richard grinned, realizing she couldn't see the object of his pursuit, and held up the rabbit to explain the madness.

Shaking her head, she rolled her eyes, patted her babe's hand, and resolutely returned to the path. "Showoff," he heard her say.

Richard felt sad, and out of breath. *That was a serious workout! I couldn't take too much more of that. But at least I got him! I got him! Felicity, I'm coming home!*

In the woods, the snake spotted a squirrel. It turned, then quietly slithered off Richard's chest and wrapped itself around the trunk of the tree, creeping upward in pursuit.

Whatever my circumstances are,
I can always choose my own thoughts.

11

THE CHOICE

The officer questioning Felicity was not about to waste any more time. If she had something to say, she evidently wasn't going to say it in the next ten minutes, and he was becoming bored. Finally, he stated calmly, "Ma'am, I'm leaving. You think about what I told you, and let's hope he turns up, for his sake as well as your own."

Just at that moment his radio bleeped on with a coded message and a chirp. "Oh—see, I've got to go, but you let us know if you decide to start talking again, alright?" And with that, he quickly gathered his things in a haphazard bundle, stuffed them into his briefcase and closed the latches.

He could have said, "Lady, you're a freak," and it wouldn't have been any clearer than his condescending body language.

The worry in Felicity's eyes deepened, and a feeling of hopelessness filled her up. The officer stood, causing the aluminum-legged chair to squeak as he pushed it backwards on the aged linoleum. Without intent, he automatically tipped his hat, motioned for his partner to come along, pushed the screen door open wide so it banged hard behind them, and they were gone.

Felicity was stunned. "They aren't going to do anything. They think *I've* done something." Her anxiety suddenly mounted and she cried angrily, "He could be dead RIGHT NOW and they aren't doing ANYTHING about it!" She kicked the chair that was still tipped over and it hit the wall with a bang.

Matthew came out of his room rubbing his sleepy eyes. "Mommy? What was that?" He stopped and looked at his mother. He withdrew back into the bedroom when he saw she had black around her eyes, white in the corners of her mouth, curled tendrils plastered to her forehead, and streaks on her cheeks.

Not knowing what to think, his lower lip pouted out and his eyes turned glassy. Felicity could see he was about to cry. She opened her arms and he reluctantly approached her. She hugged the little boy and broke down. "Oh, honey, I'm sorry. I sort of kicked the chair; I didn't mean to wake you up." Felicity forced the words because she had so convinced herself that something was wrong that she struggled to provide him any comfort. What she needed was someone to hold *her* close and offer *her* some reassuring words.

But nobody would. Nobody could. Nobody knew.

"I wanna see Daddy," Matthew whined.

"But he's not home yet, sweetie."

"How come?"

Felicity opened her mouth to answer, but couldn't think of what to say.

"What's wrong, Mom? I'm scared."

Looking into Matthew's concerned face, she surrendered inside. She knew deep down that all she imagined had been without real evidence, and it wasn't fair to take her little four-year-old on this imaginary panic trip. Part of her still worried, but she forced herself to hope. It wasn't the natural way to think. It wasn't the easy way to think. But she had to imagine that Richard was well and that they would see him again. She glanced down at her palms and realized that her own thoughts, her own imaginations, had caused them to become very moist. She looked through the door into her bedroom mirror and noticed her smeared makeup and tear-stained cheeks. Finally, she saw the dried icing in the corners of her mouth, and the cracker glob on her shirt. She looked deranged. No wonder the officers had treated her the way they did.

She looked again at Matthew and with new resolve she knelt in front of him and held his arms. Gazing directly into his reddened eyes, she said tenderly, "Matthew, everything is fine. Daddy is *just fine*," Felicity's voice cracked, "and we're going to go see him now. You understand?"

Matthew's face softened and he said, "Okay." He placed his arms around his mother and sniffled.

"Let's go. We'll find him before it gets dark."

Felicity took a deep breath and stepped into the bathroom to spot clean her shirt and wash her face, patting it dry with the terrycloth hand towel and then hanging it neatly on the rack. Finally, it was also time to pick up the fallen chair and place it neatly next to the others at the table. She gently pushed it in and then touched it once more affectionately, feeling new resolve.

Hearing her own voice speak words of faith, Felicity felt her worry ease away. *What if you're wrong?* A little voice inside her head taunted her. She spoke aloud, "When I have a choice, I choose to believe." Merely believing couldn't be any more harmful than the damage she may have already done, worrying Matthew so.

What if she *was* wrong? Then she'd cross that bridge when she came to it. All she had was now, and all she would allow herself to do was believe.

When I have a choice,
I choose to believe.

12

VIOLATIONS

Richard was also on his way. He had left the path, and he had a rabbit. Looking toward the others on the path, he felt a compelling urge to teach them what he had learned. He had a rabbit! Anyone *could* have a rabbit, truly! He couldn't contain himself; he wanted to show them what could be theirs. He held up his rabbit and waved, just to see if anyone would stop and talk to him. Wouldn't anyone come ask *him* how to do it? He showed them he knew how, why didn't they want to know for themselves?

But deep down he knew what they were saying to each other. "Look at that guy, thinking he's so much better than us." Or, "What an unfortunate man; destined to lose his soul over a lust for rabbits."

He could also detect their thoughts: "Yeah, a rabbit would be nice. Maybe someday a rabbit will fall into the path right in front of me, too." Or, "I knew I should gotten my degree in Canine Muscle Coordination so I could catch rabbits just like him."

Additionally, there were the folks who were very close to stepping off the path, but were paralyzed by the same fears he had experienced himself: fearing risk, fearing answers, fearing abundance, fearing success. "What if I lose my way without a path? What if I don't know how to handle a rabbit? What if I catch one and it gets away, and then I can't ever find another paper sack? What if I catch one that snatches the only sandwich I have and then it runs away? What if people laugh at me? What if I fail?"

Taking one more look at the crowd, Richard had to simply carry on. He was breaking new ground, charting his own course. He looked ahead at the meadow that lay between the path and the woods, and pressed forward.

He seemed to travel for hours, but this time he walked in the less traveled area off the road. Along the way, he came to meet several men and women with a rabbit in their clutches. In fact, he had never realized how many people had discovered the secret, but now that he knew it, he saw them everywhere. With a heightened awareness, he realized they must have been there all along.

He gazed admiringly at the people who appeared to be strolling home, so happy and accomplished. But his feel-good warm and fuzzy emotions were interrupted by two men who arrived out of nowhere and were whispering emphatically at one another. Richard turned to see who they were and saw the men clawing each other's shirt sleeves, teeth gritted, whispering angry words that Richard couldn't quite decipher.

Finally, one of the men thrust his hands off the other man's shirt, and clamored to get ahead as they both seemed to be pursuing a rabbit.

Splitting up, they attempted to surround the creature, and the faster one leapt ahead with a full-body attack, trying to pin it down once and for all. The other man wearing a camouflage jacket pounced on top of the first, and the yelling began. Richard could not determine the fate of the rabbit, but he heard the scuffle and watched them fighting each other viciously to win the prize.

Eventually he heard a loud thud and a groan, and the second man in the camouflage jacket stood, triumphantly gripping the hare in his fist. After a forceful nudge with his foot to the fallen man, he walked away, limping and gloating gracelessly in his victory.

Richard rushed over to help the fallen man get back on his feet. The man lay there groaning, but when he slapped the ground angrily with one of his hands, Richard could see that his pain was that of wounded pride, more than any physical injury.

"I'm fine, I'm fine."

"You sure? Who was that guy?" Richard was genuinely concerned.

"Oh, he's just my best friend, or should I say, my ex- best friend. First class creep." The man brushed off his pant legs and struggled to his feet. "He and I decided to go rabbit hunting together. We were sick of the sack-race and decided to do it big by getting ourselves a rabbit. We finally found one, and when he got irritable, I realized he wasn't planning on sharing the spoils. You saw the rest."

Richard brushed some loose grass off the back of the man's flannel shirt. Bowing his head, the man held up his hand casually and said, "Thanks for the hand, uh..."

"Richard. The name's Richard Goodman."

"Gavin. Gavin Upnow. Thanks again," he replied then limped away.

Gavin Upnow? You've got to be kidding. Richard mused at the collection of characters he had met along this journey. At every turn, he seemed to be presented with intriguing, perplexing, confusing, enlightening, and even mind-bending encounters.

Richard looked over at a few of the rabbit people and the evidence of their "success" as they walked. He wondered how many of them had captured their rabbits by living in harmony with God's natural laws of thought, and how many had fought contentiously for it. *I think I'd rather do it God's way. It's hard enough catching one of the little thumpers without having some other guy pounding you into the ground at the same time.*

As Richard continued to reflect, one more question kept gnawing at him. How is it possible that some of the people held in their hands two, three, and up to six rabbits by the ears? He knew how hard it had been to catch one, even without competing for it; how did some of these people have so many in their fists? Dozens of people of all kinds held multiple rabbits: short, tall, heavy, thin, men, women, even an occasional adolescent. It seemed all kinds of people had managed to catch several rabbits. He would have expected only the most athletic and agile people to have been able to chase and wrestle a rabbit down with one or more already in their fist, but what he saw indicated otherwise.

He made eye contact with one of the shorter, heavier ones. He was a pleasant looking, clean-shaven young man in his forties, with a large round belly and twinkle in his eye. He wore a snugly fitted hunter-green polo shirt with a shiny black belt that disappeared under his gut and baggy, off white trousers. His shoes were glossy slip-ons with leather tassels. The man looked at Richard's rabbit and grinned. With a knowing twitch of his head, the man beckoned Richard to walk alongside him for a while.

Richard of course didn't need further encouragement. "The student was ready" and he was eager to learn what this man knew. The man obviously had not wrangled the four rabbits he held. That would have been physically impossible. Besides, his clothes showed no sign of dirt or grass stains like Richard had on his own clothing.

"I know what you're thinking, because I was just like you only a short while ago," the man said when Richard caught up to him.

Richard looked again at the abundance of rabbits in this man's grasp. "Oh really?" He enjoyed the mysterious air about these people who knew so much, and he thought it interesting that the more he learned, the less mysterious all of it really was.

A bird sailed by overhead and he looked up. It made him consider the laws of aerodynamics, and how scary it would have been for people to see humans put them to use centuries before they had been discovered. Imagine the alarm that his forebears might have felt, had they seen a 747 airliner soar over their heads. Oh, how mysterious that would have seemed!

Just like the laws of aerodynamics, he realized now that these laws of thought had always existed, too. But he didn't understand them before now, or know how to use them to his advantage. He remembered being taught all his life to "doubt not, fear not," and now he was finally beginning to understand why. *It just simply isn't good for me! The things I want and need are repelled, literally, when I allow myself to entertain the negative emotions of doubt and fear.*

He recalled several times when he had allowed himself to think about things he didn't want. *What if that tornado on the horizon is going to come rip my house apart?* He was eight years old and he remembered visualizing the destruction, feeling the horror as though it was already happening. It then began to come his way, and out of sheer terror he rushed down into the cellar and closed his eyes and ears, and then forced himself to picture the house standing strong and unaffected in sunny, peaceful weather. After all, it was the only thought that brought him peace, to pretend things were just the way he wanted them to be. He wanted to escape the storm's wrath, and the only way he could was in his own mind. He tuned it all out to live completely in his fantasy.

And the house remained.

Richard thought back on the experience in awe. Had he actually had influence on the elements? He wasn't sure. He remembered other experiences when he had imagined something that didn't come true, and he deduced it was probably because he didn't want it badly enough, or for long enough, or believe innocently enough. Or maybe it just wasn't an appropriate desire, and he expressed gratitude for a God who still knew what was best for him.

But as for providing for his family, and being with them, nothing but peace came as he thought about that. To him, that meant that it was a commendable aspiration, and that God would help him achieve it, as long as he did not violate the laws of thought.

Finally, the short, heavy man in the green polo shirt derailed Richard's train of thought. "Really," he said. "I know what you're thinking because I was just like you only a short while ago. I myself only had one rabbit, and I had worked up quite a sweat to obtain it. So now, you want to know how to catch more than one rabbit because that first one was quite a doozy, right?"

"Oh, yeah." Richard could sense this man was living in harmony with God's laws. Maybe it was a glow, or energy he was subconsciously picking up. He couldn't understand how he sensed it, but he did nonetheless. The feeling was just as identifiable as the times when he would walk into a room and know instantly that Felicity was in a cheerful mood, even if he couldn't see her face.

The man's eyes twinkled, for here was someone whose mind was open and was eager to hear more. "What's your name?"

Richard responded with his full name, "Richard A. Goodman."

The man remarked, "Well, Richard, I'm guessing you discovered that to visualize the rabbit in detail brought it to you."

"Right," Richard replied.

"Would you believe me if I told you that the rest of my rabbits basically tipped their head to my hands and let me take their ears?"

"No. You can't be serious." Then Richard remembered the comrades and how the rabbits had returned to them effortlessly as well.

"I'm serious. The first one is always the hardest. Let me guess, how you pictured it in your mind was kind of vague, wasn't it? And the rabbit was somewhat hard to see once you found it, am I right?"

Richard thought for a moment, and said, "You're right. You're absolutely right. I had a hard time seeing it in my mind, and when it appeared, it also was hard to see, and far away. In fact, that first one I couldn't catch at all. The next time, I visualized every detail I could imagine, and it appeared, just like I had seen it in my mind. But when I lunged at it, it ran away and I nearly wore myself out capturing it. Still, I caught it, and here it is." Richard held up his furry loot. "I was just on my way home to share it with my family."

The man grinned. "Obtaining more rabbits is a piece of cake if you know what to do."

Richard still felt the urgency to get home, but he chose to sacrifice a little more time for what promised to be the education of a lifetime. A smirk crept over Richard's face and he had to know, "Is your name something like Ina Everett Thynn?"

"Huh?" The man looked confused.

"Oh, never mind. Okay then, what do I do?"

"The name's Randy Mollup." He looked questioningly at Richard again and then continued, "So, how badly do you want to know what I know?" The man was blunt and unapologetic.

Richard sighed, knowing full well what must inevitably happen next if he was serious about gaining this higher level of understanding. He thought for a moment, and then a latent streak of rebellion emerged. He responded challengingly, "I have no more sandwiches, Mr. Mollup."

The man shrugged and gave Richard a look of pity. "I'm sorry for you then. If you can't find a way to make the necessary sacrifice, our conversation will end here."

Richard wised up. Attempting to meet the man on his own level, he said, "Now hang on just a minute." Richard held up his hand as if to say, "Wait here," and he closed his eyes. As quickly as he could, he created an image of the two men conversing, and tried to feel the wonder he expected to feel when he learned the secret.

He knew he had done just that when the corners of his mouth automatically turned up. Upon opening his eyes, he confidently told the man, "I'm going to learn what you know."

"Oh, are you?" The man was amused at Richard's under-developed comprehension and insolent remark. "And what makes you think I'm going to share what I know?"

"Because I visualized it happening, and I felt it happen, so now I know it will."

"You provide me some compensation, and I will explain to you precisely why the conversation you visualized won't happen." With that, Mr. Mollup winked and strolled away.

Doubt not, fear not!
It simply isn't good for me.

How badly do I want wisdom?

13

THE SACRIFICE

Richard stood with his jaw hanging open. *What did I do wrong?* His mind spun and he felt stupid for being so presumptuous, and unknowingly revealing his ignorance.

He could not let Mr. Mollup get too far away. *Quick! Think, Richard, think. How can I get him to talk to me?*

Just then the rabbit twitched in his hand. He looked down and his eyes widened. "Oh, no. He wouldn't expect me to—there's no way."

Richard looked up at the man who was getting farther away with each passing moment. At the same time, the man turned his head and continuing to stroll along, he met Richard's gaze. The look in his eyes said, "C'mon, haven't you figured it out by now?"

Richard could scarcely believe what he was about to do. He closed his eyes once more, bracing himself for the painful decision he was about to make. Taking a deep breath, he held up the rabbit briefly and then began to trot ahead to catch up with Mr. Mollup.

Charitably, the man stopped and waited for him. As Richard approached, he was shaking his head repeatedly, venting his disbelief that he was going to give away the biggest bounty he had ever achieved for nothing but knowledge.

Closing his eyes again, he held out the rabbit for the man to take, and winced with anticipation for the torturous exchange.

"You sure you want to do this?" Mr. Mollup asked.

"Take it already. Take it!" Richard's eyes remained closed.

Mr. Mollup carefully opened his last two fingers on his left hand, which already held his two other rabbits, and closed them again around the new rabbit's ears.

Richard finally opened his eyes and looked longingly at the rabbit. He felt queasy in the pit of his stomach, but pressed his lips together firmly, inhaled through his nose and said, "Okay?"

Nodding, the man complimented Richard. "That took some guts, my friend. I applaud your foresight. You'll be glad you did that, and with that kind of courage, you'll quickly recoup your investment. *Plus* you'll have the knowledge you seek."

"I know I will. I fully expect to." Richard straightened up, as he felt a growing confidence in his decision.

"How quickly do you expect to get your rabbit back?"

"My rabbit?"

Mr. Mollup didn't say anything; he simply waited for Richard to respond.

Richard sensed he was being tested again, and he tried to interpret Mr. Mollup's body language and verbal clues. He was gun shy for having made a fool of himself only a few minutes before. But he had nothing more to lose except his pride, and he was realizing that the last wound to his pride hadn't been exactly fatal.

The good man raised his eyebrows and Richard, throwing up his hands, let out all the stops, "I expect to get *my* rabbit back before we're done talking today." Immediately he raised his cheeks and eyebrows, squinting, bracing himself for another embarrassing correction.

There was a twinkle in Mr. Mollup's eye, and Richard felt a wave of relief. Perhaps he had said the right thing this time.

"What do you do when you want a raise at work, Richard?"

"I never got a raise at work."

"Why is that?"

"They just didn't give them out, except for the annual cost of living increase."

"How do you know they didn't give any out?"

"I don't know, I guess 'cause I never got one."

"Did you ever go into your boss' office and come right out and *ask* for one?"

"No...."

"What about your bank account? Have you ever asked your bank to reverse a service charge, or overdraft fee?"

"No, I haven't. I didn't know you could."

Mr. Mollup stared Richard down and waited for the lights to go on in his head.

Finally, they did. Richard's eyes grew large, and the man smiled. Richard held his gaze and turned his head slightly, "You mean...?"

The man responded with raised eyebrows, as if he expected Richard to make the next move.

Finally, Richard spoke. "Will—you—give me my rabbit back?"

Mr. Mollup relaxed, and it was suddenly clear that he had been waiting for Richard to finally "get it" this whole time. Handing the rabbit back to Richard, he said, "You'll get what you ask for out of life, Richard. Have the courage to ask. Have the guts to go after what you want. The worst that can happen is you'll hear 'no.' The best that can happen is you'll get what you want."

Richard was never as full of gratitude for that rabbit as he was then. He stroked it affectionately and then looking back up at Mr. Mollup, asked, "Are you still going to teach me?"

The man didn't respond.

Richard pursed his lips together and then, as if a light came on in his head, he articulated, "Mr. Mollup, will you please teach me?"

"Yes, I will. But please call me Randy." Randy smiled and motioned for Richard to sit down on the grassy mound nearby.

It seemed so long ago, but Richard had not forgotten, "You said you would explain to me why, initially, you were not going to engage in a conversation with me, even though I visualized it and felt it."

Randy Mollup grinned and nodded. Leaning closer, he gazed intently into Richard's eyes. "Tell me this: why did you want to have that conversation so badly?"

"Because I knew it would help me get a ton of rabbits."

"Then why didn't you just go ahead and visualize a ton of rabbits, instead of visualizing the two of us having a conversation?"

"What difference would that have made?"

"Two things. Number one, you have no right to manipulate my free agency by the thoughts you choose. Never try to visualize people doing things for you. You visualize the outcome, and the right people will do the right things to help it happen. But you do not know who the right people are, so you cannot decide that part. That isn't your place.

"Number two: if you had visualized the ultimate *reason* for wanting my knowledge, then you would have instinctively known what your next move should be. In this case, your move would have been to provide me with compensation, no matter what the cost."

Richard bit his lip and nodded, as the realization of his mistake sunk in. "Okay, I see what you mean."

Randy continued, "Even better, think: what are the rabbits *for*?"

"I need rabbits so I can return to my family."

"Then consider taking your thoughts a step further and imagine those happy times you desire to experience with your family. Visualize the *reason* for the rabbits, and sometimes you'll be guided instead to faster ways to achieve it without them. *If* you indeed need rabbits to achieve your goal, you'll get them. But sometimes they're not as necessary as you think."

Shifting gears, Randy continued. "Let's move on. So, you wanted to know how to catch *multiple* rabbits, right?"

"That's right. That's why I'm here."

"Then let's go back to when you spotted your first rabbit. You said it was vague in your mind, and then it was far away and hard to see when it appeared."

"Yes, that's right. And it ran away before I could do anything about it."

"And what about the first one you *caught*? It's my guess you saw it vividly in your mind, but it still wasn't easy to catch."

"Yeah, you're right. I saw it vividly, and when it appeared, it was right there, in front of me, just as I had pictured it. But I had to chase it, and it almost got away from me."

"Well, if you want a rabbit to *come to you*, then you've got to take the time to visualize the rabbit already in your hands. Feel the fur in your mind. Sense its warmth as you hold it in your fingers. Make it vivid. And even better still, visualize a look in its eyes that it is entirely pleased to serve you, and be with you, because you treat it with respect."

"But aren't you going to end up eating it?"

"Not necessarily, we may care for it and let it breed, so we can have an unlimited supply. Some will be eaten, but even those are happy to serve because they're God's creation, created to provide the needs of other creatures."

"So that's why my first rabbit was tough, because I had in mind an expectation that it didn't want to be with me? That it would be hard to get, and so it was?"

"You got it."

"So, if I want a rabbit, do I imagine one coming to me, and then picture myself grasping it? Is that how I make it happen?"

"No. You aren't going to *make* anything happen. Too many people mess it all up with that mentality. Instead, imagine it already with you. See, don't be like the people who spend all kinds of wasted time visualizing circumstances moving in their favor, trying to 'make things happen.' Instead, experience the feelings of success as though it's already been accomplished. Allowing yourself to *experience* it puts you in a state of being that is in harmony, so to speak, with the thing you want. Then the right people and things are naturally attracted to you, and do what needs to be done, because it gets them what they want as well. The fact is that using our minds to try to force things or people to do stuff is in violation of basic universal law."

"Like I tried to do with you."

"Right." Randy was pleased to see Richard absorbing the ideas so well.

"What about two guys I saw who were after one rabbit; what were *they* doing wrong? They both believed they could find one, but only one rabbit showed up."

"I've seen it all before. This is how it usually goes: the men successfully imagined a rabbit, and they undoubtedly were excited about it. But when only one appeared, all application of proper thought went out the window. Competition ensued, and the one who finally caught it probably attributed it to his wit and never discovered true rabbit wealth. As long as he thought he had done it by his own clever strategy, he never found the power of working with God to provide all his needs." Just then the wind picked up and Randy turned to watch the leaves fluttering in the row of trees behind them. Once it was quiet again, he added, "In fact, he probably lost his friend over the illusion that there was only so much to go around, and that one must be faster, quicker, and smarter than the next guy to win the prize."

"That pretty much sums it up." Richard shook his head and chuckled, *Is there anything this man doesn't know?* Gathering his thoughts, Richard asked, "So does this mean we don't have to compete with anyone else to get what we want out of life?"

"That's the reality. There is more than enough for everybody, and to compete like that is in violation of another one of the laws of thought. That's the beautiful thing about it, Richard. God has provided enough for everyone who obeys these natural laws. If everyone believed and could visualize and truly expect to receive whatever they are asking of him, then everyone would receive. The laws of nature do not play favorites."

"I saw a couple of men competing for sacks on the path."

"Unnecessary. So, long as they think there isn't enough to go around, they entertain a lie that prevents them from ever seeing what they're searching for."

"I was surprised to see the other men competing for a rabbit. I thought that to leave the path meant you were somehow on a higher plane or something, and that you wouldn't operate that way."

Randy Mollup shook his head. "Oh, no. There are marvelously honorable men who never choose to leave the path, which is entirely their prerogative. And then there are those who leave the path and do it all wrong. You'll find all kinds of people in both arenas. No, you don't have to leave the path to be happy. But isn't it nice to know you have options?"

"Yeah, it really is. Isn't that what freedom is all about? Having choices?"

"Having choices. Unfortunately, sometimes we learn too late that the choices we make limit our ability to keep making choices. Eventually poor choices lead to smothering bondage. That's how I felt right before I went on my very first rabbit hunt."

"What did you do? What was your first step away from the sack-race?"

"I imagined how it would feel to be free of it. Then I decided to find a way, somehow. Then I changed how I felt about the sacks. Instead of grumbling about them, I started to appreciate them. Gratitude is a powerful thing. I think it put me in the right frame of mind to see things I had never seen before. I started to see bigger and better sacks, and eventually I started seeing rabbits. When I felt like they were already with me, the real magic began."

"Oh, wow." Randy's words distilled upon Richard's mind and he mused out loud, "I think I finally understand the gratitude part. I can go ahead and feel grateful that a rabbit is mine, because in my own mind, it is."

Grinning, Randy nodded. "You got it. So, do you think you're ready to get your next rabbit?"

Richard panicked. Was Randy weaning him already? With his mind still in a spin, he suddenly had a hard time believing that any wild jackrabbit would be interested in going home with him, just because he felt grateful it was already his. "I'm not sure. What if a jackrabbit doesn't want to go home with me?"

"Look, I'm going to tell you something profound, and I want you to remember this, and trust me: that which you want, is looking for you." Randy looked him in the eye, and lifting a finger he slowly repeated, "That which you want, is looking for you." He put his finger down and added, "In other words, you don't have to struggle to obtain it. Change your mental picture and expect that you'll naturally attract all you need."

"In other words?" Richard thought he was grasping it, but he wanted as much clarification as he could get. He didn't want this new way to become obscure. He wanted to own this information. He wanted to understand it well enough for it to become a part of him.

"Well, changing your thinking literally changes you. You've been like a lantern with no flame, trying to—oh, I don't know—" Randy grasped for a meaningful analogy. Finally, he continued excitedly, "trying to gather an insect collection! Turn on your light, and they just come. A lot of people on the path are like lanterns that have burned out. It's a *dream* that can turn their light on, and then the bugs (or whatever they need to fulfill their dream), will be drawn to them, in a very natural way. Quite often, it isn't circumstances that need to change; it is the *person* who must change."

Change, Richard thought to himself. *Haven't I already changed? How much more do I have to change?* Changing oneself sounded harder than just chasing a rabbit. He thought back to Felicity's hurtful words, "Why can't you be more like your brother?" It was that cutting remark on top of everything else that had moved him out of their door and into the woods. Couldn't he succeed just the way he was? Hadn't he already changed significantly? He had caught a rabbit, didn't that count for something?

It must have been the fallen look in Richard's face that led the good man to encouragingly clap his hand briefly on Richard's shoulder. "Hey, it's not as hard as it might sound. Don't you see, when you allow the feelings I'm talking about to grow within you, that's what facilitates the necessary change. That's it."

Richard felt encouraged so he didn't interrupt his teacher.

"Let's test it. How would you like to try it with something small, before going off to capture your next rabbit?"

"Yeah! Let's do that! If I could see this work in a small way, then I know it would help my confidence with the big dreams."

Randy spotted a monarch butterfly flitting about, not very far from them. Richard watched him close his eyes for a moment, and smile. He opened his eyes and stood up slowly, then approached the patch of blossoming clover where ten to fifteen more butterflies danced. But before getting too close to them, he sat down again and held out his finger near a cluster of dainty white clover blossoms. In a minute or two, he slowly lifted his arm to show a butterfly comfortably perched on his finger.

Richard was amazed; Randy made it look so easy. Standing and then approaching the man, Richard said, "I don't think I could do that!"

"Then you can't, Richard. Pay attention to your thoughts. To accomplish this, you must choose to allow yourself to believe in the impossible!"

Richard raised one eyebrow and bit his lip.

"I have an idea. How do you feel about ants?"

"Ants? Now there's one thing I can believe will come to me. I'm a magnet to the little creatures, they love to bite me and I happen to be allergic."

"Perfect. Let's go find some ants."

"But that's not requiring I believe in the impossible; It's asking that I simply believe in the inevitable!"

"Oh, no, Richard. This is all about getting whatever it is you want. Do you know what you want?"

"I don't want to get bit!"

"Then let's go find a massive colony of ants!"

I'll get what I ask for out of life.
I'll have the courage to ask.

I'll visualize the outcome,
and the right people will do the
right things to help it happen.

There is more than enough for everybody.

14

THE REGRESSION

Richard puffed his cheeks and exhaled forcefully. "I thought this mental stuff was all about attracting what you want, not repelling what you don't want." Richard's trepidation about subjecting himself to a swarm of ants was terrifying.

"You're right. It's completely, one hundred percent about attraction. In your case, you will be attracting a healthy state of being, a condition of peace and contentment amid a colony of little red insects."

Randy grabbed Richard's shirt sleeve and pulled him over to a small clearing. Richard's heart began to race and his palms became sticky.

"Here are some. Now Richard, just do exactly what I say. I know you can do this."

Rubbing his hands on his pants, Richard took a deep breath and said, "Okay, I hope you're right."

Observing his moist hands, Randy asked, "What's wrong?"

"All I can see in my head is my poor hand all swollen and pocked with little red ant bites."

"Oh boy. This will be a challenge. Richard, do you think you could try to imagine your hand completely well and safe instead?"

"That's what I must do, isn't it?"

"Yeah, it is."

"Okay...." With that, Richard closed his eyes, feeling silly, but not wanting to disappoint his mentor. He visualized his hand, just as it truly was, and breathed deeply until he had convinced himself that his hand was completely well and fine. Without opening his eyes, he told Randy, "I think I'm ready."

"Then come sit down and gently place your hand on the ground over here. If you start to panic, close your eyes again, and *picture it* again. Believe in the reality of the images your mind creates. The truth is: your hand *is* well. If you believe that truth, it will continue to be reflected in your circumstances, for that is the circumstance with which you are in harmony. Remember the proverb, '*As a man thinketh in his heart, so is he.*'"

Richard sat down and placed his hand on the ground near the ants. It was a continual act of will to keep discarding the fearful thoughts that nagged him. He had never exerted so much energy to discipline his thoughts before. But he held firm to the image in his mind.

Finally, Randy spoke. "Richard, they aren't bothering you. Do you see that? You did it."

Richard wasn't all that impressed, even though he was plenty grateful he suffered no bites. He wasn't entirely sure it wasn't just a coincidence.

Randy detected his thoughts, and said, "It's okay to believe. It'll only strengthen your ability to have faith, and that's not a bad thing."

Richard nodded, "Okay. I'll try to believe."

"Would you like to try it with something bigger before venturing back to the quest for rabbits? We could try for birds."

"No thanks. I'd have to visualize my shirt remaining clean and fresh to avoid what the birds usually do to me. I'd like to just get on with the rabbit hunt, if you don't mind."

"That's fine, so long as you understand that if you put mental energy into images of things you don't want, you will be counter-productive. You'll attract things you don't want."

Richard couldn't quite put his finger on exactly why he was feeling this way, but he sensed he was going into overload. Maybe it was just too much information too soon. His eyes scanned Randy's face, so animated, and so enthused to share.

What was that on his nose? A hair? Richard was stunned. It was a long hair. It must've been almost an inch long, coming out of the crease on the side of his nostril and curling slightly toward his cheek. How in the world had he missed it before? Distracted, Richard found it much easier to think of that hair than to think of what the man was saying.

Randy Mollup was still talking, and yet there was that hair. Richard couldn't stand it. He imagined plucking it out so he could finally concentrate again. *No, I couldn't do that. It would be bad to reach out and grab hold of that hideous hair. I can't let myself lift my hand, grip the hair and pull hard. I'd guess it would be tough to yank. Huh, he chuckled to himself, I can nearly feel the brief resistance, and the almost audible 'doink' I'd feel in my fingers if I were to pull it out. No, I could never do such a thing.*

Without purposely replacing the thoughts in his mind, Richard eventually could even see Randy's face as though there was no hair. The thought was relieving and he felt like he just might be able to pay full attention again. With the distraction gone in his mind, he no longer felt irritated!

The smile spread across his face and Richard heard Randy continue, "…you'll find that your actions and your circumstances are nothing more than a reflection of the images in your subconscious mind."

Richard nodded. But before he knew it, his hand went up, and he reached out and snatched the hair right off Randy's nose.

"What th–?" Surprised and shocked, Randy rubbed the side of his nose.

Richard's eyes were wide and he was mortified at what he had just done.

Gratefully, Randy only snickered. His snicker turned into a chortle and finally into an infectious belly laugh. He knew exactly what Richard had done: he had allowed a distraction to steer his thoughts. "A hair on my nose? You are distracted by a hair?! My friend, resolved thought takes practice." Randy pointed to Richard's rabbit, "And with a hare in your grasp and one less hair on my nose, you're on your way!" His eyes sparkled with humor.

Embarrassed, Richard laughed; then apologizing, he urged his mentor to continue. After all, the hair was gone, so it would be easier to pay attention, anyway. "I'm sorry. I'm afraid I allowed my thoughts to wander too long."

"That's okay. I think you have what you need to take it from here." He chuckled again and said, "Richard, it's no secret that the laws of thought played a predictable part in your behavior. You used the principles unknowingly to annihilate my nose hair. I suggest you pay close attention to your thoughts, for they *will* bear fruit. No action ever occurs without first a thought of the same kind. So always choose those thoughts of yours carefully." Randy warmly whacked Richard in the leg with the back of his hand.

Richard was grateful that Randy was self-assured enough to gracefully handle the awkward moments they had experienced together.

Neither man spoke for a few minutes, yet the silence was comfortable. The mentor leaned back and watched the clouds travel by, and Richard remained thoughtful. He analyzed what had just happened with the hair incident. He realized he truly had applied the laws of thought, as he had unconsciously moved into action to remove the hair. He had done something completely out of character, without hesitation, and as a result, his immediate environment perfectly mirrored his thoughts. In his mind, he had seen his instructor with a bald nose, and he had entertained some pretty strong feelings about it. As a result, he had moved automatically, almost unconsciously, into action to make it happen.

Undisciplined or improper thoughts could certainly get a man into trouble, Richard concluded.

The wind picked up some speed and the clouds rushed by. Richard wasn't sure how much time he had left with the good, round-bellied man, so he finally asked, "Let's say I do precisely what you're teaching me. How long could it take for my next rabbit to appear?"

"That depends on how long it takes for you to allow the changes inside of you to take place."

"So, thinking and feeling will change me, eventually, huh." Richard still wanted to have a time frame on which he could rely.

"I know this part can be frustrating, the waiting part. But you have to understand, your lantern must burn bright with the dream, and you must believe strongly. Or even just believe a little bit, but without any doubt. Sometimes it only takes a moment to truly believe something you can't see; but sometimes it takes months or years to develop that kind of expectation."

Months? Years? Richard fought the doubt that was creeping in. Richard wasn't a lazy man. He could work as many hours as anyone, but this was asking something else. The rabbit wriggled in his grasp and Richard snapped his attention back to their conversation.

Randy sensed Richard may not be ready for all he wanted to say. But when Richard suddenly became alert, he continued. "Richard, for everyone who is committed to believing, no matter how long it takes, his or her dream eventually comes true. Isn't that a better guarantee than none at all? People who keep at it, trying to live in harmony with the laws of thought, will grow in skill and self-belief until their confidence in getting everything they will ever need is virtually unshakable."

Forcing a smile, Richard reluctantly accepted that he would just have to take Randy's word for it. Patience was something he would have to work on and he knew it. "So, you believe until it happens, and it doesn't matter how long it takes? Isn't it harder to believe, the longer you have to wait?"

"Now, remember, these principles can be used in small things that don't take a long time, all along the way. Such an exercise strengthens your will and deepens your faith. Shoot, you could even use the principles to get better sandwiches in nicer bags if that was your dream. If you do, nature will create a need in one of the rabbit chasers who provide the sacks; and they will feel compelled to leave just the right one for you to discover. As for the tougher dreams, you're right. It can be harder the longer you have to wait. But on the other hand, the longer you must wait, the more detail you can be putting into the image and the more certain you can become of precisely what you want."

"That sounds like a scapegoat to me, to be completely honest. Like, if it never happens, are we just supposed to say, 'Oh well, I guess it's still on its way, forever'?"

"No, Richard. You can trust that each idea has a finite 'gestation period,' if you will. That period of time is specific and certain. Your job is to hang on to the belief throughout the required period of time. Pass the test, or should I say, the trial of your faith, and the reward is yours. Trust me, it's easier to do, just knowing the time required is certain and finite. And one day, you'll be the one to provide a few bags for the good people on the path."

"Wouldn't it be nice if we had some sort of chart, listing all of the kinds of ideas in the world with all of the corresponding gestation periods?"

"Man, that would be something, wouldn't it?"

Quietly the men contemplated the philosophies they had been discussing. Finally, Randy broke the silence, "Richard, you can choose to be skeptical about dreams that don't show up on time. You can choose to think that what I'm telling you is a hoax and that somehow my advice about unfulfilled dreams is a scapegoat. It's your choice, Richard. But remember, while you're wasting energy doubting, someone else out there is spending the same amount of energy believing and achieving, and it might as well be you."

Not completely satisfied, Richard nevertheless recognized he needed to try to do away with his analysis paralysis if he wanted to be a dream achiever.

"If you choose to believe, then you can always chase doubts with this one idea: The times when we don't get what we want exactly when we want it, we simply express gratitude to God for his wisdom and get excited because it either means something better is on its way, or it wasn't what we would have wanted after all, or that it wasn't yet the right time. It's all good, and just thinking so will attract as much good to yourself and your family as you are capable of enjoying."

Richard conjectured, "So what if I get stuck just living my whole life with unfulfilled expectations?"

Sighing patiently, Randy thought for a moment, then shared an analogy that he thought might be helpful now. "A woman expecting a baby knows the baby will come. She doesn't have to know exactly *when* it will arrive, but she has a general idea, and she does not have to worry that she will live out her entire life with the unfulfilled expectation." Randy paused and raised his eyebrows for emphasis. "Like I said, each of our dreams has a finite gestation period, Richard. Do not entertain doubts or fears, and you can be certain your dream will happen at the right time. Just as the woman doesn't want her baby to come too soon, neither should you want *your* dream to be realized too soon, either. When it doesn't seem to come on schedule, we must feel gratitude that it will come at the *right* time."

"Okay. Okay. I can see it in that light. If a woman is going to have a baby, she can predict its arrival give or take a few weeks. She'll calculate a specific due date, which she usually marks on her calendar. But you're right, it could come a little early; and she isn't going to get doubtful if she goes overdue. In fact she'll get more and more certain all the time, won't she? She won't give up and quit preparing; she'll just keep getting herself more prepared with each passing day. After all, she's *expecting*!"

"Well said, Richard. Imagine feeling that way about your dreams and goals. Expect them. And imagine becoming *more* sure the longer you have to wait."

"Now there's a new way of thinking. I like that."

Finding examples in nature always seemed to help. Once each idea 'clicked,' Richard felt amazed at how familiar it all seemed, like the laws of thought had always been a part of him, but he had not been aware. Perhaps the ideas resonated deep within him because he, himself, was a part of God's natural world, too. "Thank you, my four-rabbit friend. Thanks a million. I can't wait to use what you've taught me to get my next rabbit."

"My pleasure, really. I wish there were more like you, because there's so much joy in sharing what I've learned."

With that, the small, heavy man smiled and nodded his head to say goodbye.

I'm expecting!

I want my objective to happen
at the right time.

15

THE SUCCESS

Richard looked down at the rabbit in his hand that had long since relaxed and accepted its capture. The rabbit belonged to Richard, and it seemed to be okay with that.

Richard closed his eyes and tried to visualize a rabbit in his other hand. It wasn't hard; all he had to do was duplicate how it felt from one hand that really had one, into the other. He realized it was so much easier to imagine holding rabbits after having been successful in catching one. And he finally understood why people like his brother Victor never seemed to worry about having what they needed, even when appearances indicated otherwise. Victor had always seemed to attract more opportunities and money so easily, according to his needs and desires. Additionally, he realized Victor was not all-consumed with riches like he had once thought. The process of accumulating wealth had happened naturally as he simply continued in right thinking.

He pulled his mind back from wandering to thoughts about Victor, and again focused on the second rabbit. He pictured it white, with brownish gray fur down its back and large feet, and he felt the muscles in the ears twitching in his fist. Did it want to get away? No. It was twitching with excitement, because it wanted to be just where it was. A smile spread over Richard's face and he felt a swelling sensation of gratitude fill his chest.

His throat tightened and his eyes became misty. Oh, how wonderful it was to have such an abundance! How amazed he was that God had blessed him with so much, and so quickly! *Thank you! Thank you for such a wonderful blessing as a second rabbit to take home to my family! We are so happy and grateful to be together again, and to feel peace and joy, and for the time I have to play with my son! To dance with my wife! To enjoy the wonderful things that were created for showing mankind how much God loves his children!*

Richard didn't want to open his eyes, but when he did, there was the rabbit.

It didn't surprise him, for he was already grateful for it, and he already knew what it would feel like to hold it in his other hand. It was as predictable as an image in a mirror, only the reflection of his thoughts had not appeared immediately, but with a slight delay. He realized: *that's okay.* He was learning that he could expect his circumstances to mirror his thoughts, and he would be able to hold on and believe until they all came true.

The rabbit in front of him, this situation, was in perfect harmony with Richard's mind, and so it came together effortlessly. This time he didn't lunge at the hare, all he needed to do was open his fingers, and place them gently around the beautiful creature's ears.

16

THE RESOLVE

Felicity and Matthew walked into the woods; it was nearly dark. Each time she felt herself fear, or slip into a brief panic, she closed her eyes and whispered to herself, "When I have a choice, I choose to believe." She imagined hugging Richard again, then holding his face and telling him how sorry she was for not believing in him. She imagined saying how grateful she was for all his attempts to provide. She pictured herself letting him know that it didn't matter if nothing changed, she could be happy just the way things were. After all, they had a roof over their head and they had each other. That's all they really needed, anyway! If they ran out of food (something she had worried about but never really expected could happen), then they'd starve together. But at least they'd do it as a couple.

Felicity and Matthew walked hand in hand, talking about how good it was going to feel to find him. This lifted Matthew's spirits considerably as well as Felicity's, and they began to quicken their pace and leap the logs and rocks playfully together. He was out to find his Daddy, as in a game of hide and seek! "Dad-dy! I'm gonna find you! You can't hide from me!" Matthew jumped off a rock and let out a giggle.

Felicity smiled and followed Matthew through the trees.

17

THE TASK

Richard kept on. He had two rabbits in hand, and a heart full of gratitude. These should last us a while, he thought. Then, looking down, he spoke out loud, "Oh my! A boy and a girl rabbit! God sure knows how to give good gifts!"

A woman and a man passed by holding hands. "Isn't that the truth?" They smiled and Richard saw that they each held a rabbit, and at least twenty more were following behind, freely!

"What—how—?" Richard was speechless.

"Oh, this is what happens when you get good at writing your goals down and when the goals are unselfish. All these rabbits are for others who are in need and are unable to provide for themselves. God has proved that he can trust us with abundance, because we keep giving a portion away! The more we give, the more we get!"

Richard smiled. Once again, he had that warm, familiar feeling of being right at home with a new idea.

The woman continued, "We gave even when we didn't have much to share. But we just decided early on that we would commit to giving away a percentage of all we were blessed with."

"I've known people who give and give and give, but I have never seen this kind of *getting* in my life!"

"That's because giving is only one part of it. The other part is knowing exactly what *you* want and *writing it down as though it is already yours.* If you don't make the formal request, sometimes it can seem like God operates as though you want things to stay just the way they are."

"I have to write it down?"

"Well, it certainly can't hurt. What it really requires is clarity and focus. Writing it down tests your clarity. If you can't put it in writing, then you probably aren't clear enough. Sometimes you'll find that until you *try* to put it in writing, you don't realize how vague your thoughts really are. Anyway, after it's in writing, you know the rest. I see you've been successful in your own right." The woman gestured to the two rabbits in Richard's hands.

"You mean, visualizing and feeling?"

"Yes, that's it."

Richard was no longer so amazed because now he was surrounded with people who had discovered the same principles. It just seemed normal to think this way. It would take some time to completely understand the gestation period thing in practical application, but he was willing to figure that out along the way.

He had some uncertainties, but at least he knew his part. He had control of, or at least growing control, of his own thoughts. After all, that's all he could control, anyway. The timing didn't really matter; he would leave that in God's hands.

So, he planned to write down a detailed description of his life as he wanted it, as though it had already happened, with a future date at the top like a journal entry. He would allow himself to feel gratitude as though it was already his. Then he would let go and let

God do the rest. And when a doubtful thought would come into his mind, he'd discard it. When he sensed that he should do this or that, he would do it, because he would trust that it was the voice of inspiration, leading him to accomplish his goal.

Then what about reuniting with his wife and son? He had what he needed. When would he get to be with them? How long would the rest of this journey have to take?

He realized there was something he hadn't done. He looked around because he didn't *have* a pen and paper to commit his desire in writing; and out there in the wilderness there was no hope of finding them. In fact, even if he did have a pen and a paper, his hands were busy holding jackrabbits. *I can't write it down; I don't even have a pen and paper. Surely, I wouldn't be expected to chop a tree down and manufacture a pencil and paper just to write my goal! Besides, I don't have the foggiest idea where to get graphite for the lead. Now, if there was a store anywhere in sight I might be able to do something, but there's nothing around. Now what?*

Richard was frustrated and somewhat discouraged. *This isn't going to work for me. I don't have what I need, and couldn't do it even if I did, because my hands are full. Besides, there's nowhere to put the rabbits down without them wandering off. I don't believe they'd just stay by my side, at least not yet.*

Then he remembered what to do. He closed his eyes and imagined a pen and paper in his hands, generating a feeling of gratitude. With not a clue about how it would help, he did it anyway.

Someone tapped him on the shoulder, interrupting his meditation and said, "Excuse me, mind if I hold your rabbits for just a moment? I've really needed to know what it feels like to hold rabbits; see, I'm trying to catch a few myself."

Richard smiled and said, "Of course."

But the man's hands were full. He was holding tight to a notepad and a pen, for he had just written down a goal of his own.

Richard offered, "May I hold your things for a moment so your hands are free to hold the rabbits?"

"Oh, sure!"

"Would you mind if I took one of your papers for myself and borrowed your pen?"

"I'd be pleased."

The men traded rabbits for paper and Richard remembered: *That which you desire, is looking for you.*

Richard wrote a future date at the top of the paper. Then under the date he wrote: "I'm so happy and grateful now that Felicity and I are together. Matthew is here and we are joyful and full of amazement at God's goodness to us. We have two rabbits and know how to get more as needed! We feel peace and happiness as we play. Matthew and I enjoy throwing the ball and learning how to play catch together. Felicity and I enjoy dancing together and Matthew feels happy and secure in knowing that his parents love each other. We enjoy sharing the laws of thought with friends and family, and anyone else who is seeking the wisdom of the ages."

The man saw that Richard was done with the pen, so he held out the rabbits and said, "Thank you very much, Mister. This is really going to help me imagine what it will be like for me to catch my first rabbit."

"My pleasure, young man. Thank you for the paper."

With that, Richard tucked the paper into his back pocket, took the rabbits from the young man, and walked on with an assurance and expectation that he would very soon be reunited with his family. After all, he had finally done all that he had been taught to do. Expecting it, now, was easier than he ever thought it would be.

I will write a detailed description of my life as I want it, as though it has already happened, with some future date at the top like a journal entry. I will allow myself to feel gratitude as though it is already mine.

That which I desire is looking for me.

18

THE BEGINNING

"Richard!" Felicity followed Matthew and continued to call for her husband.

"Dad-dy! Daddy, daddy, daddy!" Matthew sang, "I'm gonna find you!" Matthew climbed up on a large boulder and turned his head. "There he is, Mommy! I did it! I found him!"

Felicity ran to catch up with Matthew and sure enough, she saw Richard resting under the tree against the rock.

"Is he asleep, Mom? Is that why he couldn't hear us?"

"Yes, Matthew." Felicity was confident. They approached him and Felicity gently shook his shoulder. "Richard, honey, it's time to wake up."

Richard mumbled in his sleep, "Oh, thanks, but I already found a paper...."

"Richard, it's Felicity." Her eyes were moist.

Richard opened his eyes and blinked a few times. Out of the corner of his eye he thought he saw a wild rabbit thump on a snake, leaving it almost, but not completely lifeless, and then dash away. He looked at Felicity and then at Matthew and tears of joy came to his own eyes. "Honey, it's so good to see you."

Felicity held his face and spoke softly, "Richard, I'm so sorry about what happened and how I acted. I'm grateful for you, Richard, and if nothing were to ever change, I'll be happy enough to just be with you."

"Felicity," he beamed. "Everything is going to be okay. I know for a fact that everything is going to be just fine. Do you realize we have all we need to live abundantly and share a lot!? We're gonna be wealthy!"

Felicity pulled back with a perplexed look in her eyes. "How on earth is that going to happen?"

"I have no idea, but I know where to start. Felicity, what we want, wants us!"

"You know, Rich, it's gonna take a miracle."

"Yeah? Well, Felicity, I happen to believe in miracles."

Only a moment later, an unknown gentleman on the other side of Richard's town paused mid-sentence and told his dinner companion:

"*I just had an amazing idea.*"

PART 2

PORTAL TO GENIUS

1

PREMONITIONS

Ten Years Earlier and
30 miles northwest of Great Bend, Kansas

Morgan's heart pounded in his head as he frantically placed his suffering boy in the back seat of his car and threw the .22 caliber rifle in the trunk. As he raced to the main highway, he knew he might still be forty minutes away from anyone who could help, and his mind flooded with echoes of his last conversation over the phone with Rita:

"Hunting Jackrabbits? Honey, he's only six! Can't you wait until I get back from Mother's so I can keep him out of the line of fire? I know how focused you can get and I know how spontaneous he can be. I just can't help thinking he might race ahead of you, and you might not notice."

"Rita, don't worry, I'll be careful. *Nothing will happen to him.*"

"*Morgan Stillwater,* you *promise* me he'll be safe." Her blue eyes widened in a plea. "This is our only child. Please don't make me worry about life without him." There had been a long pause until she softly asked, "Are you going to let him shoot?"

"Been thinking about it. I was six when Dad let me try the rifle."

"Please don't do it, at least—will you just—wait until I get back? Mother's doing better, and if she remains stable, and if Dad's feeling like he can handle everything without me, I think I may be able to catch a flight to get me home by dinnertime Thursday. What if you save it for next weekend? Maybe we could all go hunting together."

"Honey, let me have this time with him. Ever since the day you told me you were finally pregnant, I've been dreaming of doing this sort of father-and-son thing with him. No offense, but I just don't think it would be the same with 'Mom' coming along to make sure we're okay."

Rita's voice turned grave. "*Promise me, Morgan*. Promise me you'll have your eyes on Isaac the whole time. I don't care if you don't come home with a single rabbit. All I care is that this family stays intact. Got that?"

"*Everything's gonna be okay, Rita. It's just a rabbit hunt.*"

Morgan glanced in the rear-view mirror. Isaac was breathing faintly and his lips were darker than the last time he checked. Cursing the day he had to drop out before getting into medical school, Morgan hit the steering wheel hard with both hands. "I could have helped him! I might have known what to do!"

He picked up his cell phone, hoping that somehow it might have magically charged itself, even though it had died more than an hour previously. No luck, and no charger.

Suddenly the anguish overcame him and he began to sob uncontrollably. A weak, but restless movement from the back seat and the boy's pallor caused Morgan's foot to press harder on the accelerator.

"*Oh, Rita,*" Morgan moaned through clenched teeth as his speed reached 95 miles an hour. The grasslands whooshed by in a blur under glowing clouds against an electric blue sky. *"I was careful, I was so careful!"*

Finally, the barren landscape gave way to an occasional silo and farmhouse. *Do I stop and call for an ambulance, or do I just look for a hospital on my own?* He didn't know how serious Isaac's condition was, or how much time he had to work with. He decided to press on.

After another five long minutes, as he entered a small country town, Morgan heaved a sigh of relief to see a blue sign on the side of the road with the large capital "H" and an arrow, Pulling in under the portico labeled "Emergency," Morgan screeched to a halt and labored to carry his son through the automatic glass doors. The receptionist stood, responding to Morgan's alarmed expression and she signaled a nurse from triage to come quickly.

Miraculously, there were no other patients waiting to be seen in this sleepy little town hospital. The nurse quickly provided a bed, called for a doctor, and began asking questions.

"Is this your son?"

"Yes, he is." Morgan was in a daze.

The nurse checked Isaac's vitals while asking, "What happened?"

"Uh—," his voice cracked with a spontaneous whimper, but he quickly continued between anxious breaths, "we were hunting jack-rabbits, and I spotted one, and I shot, and then I don't know why, but Isaac collapsed, because he wasn't even in my way, and I can't find a wound *anywhere*. I don't *know* what happened."

"Has he been ill?"

"Uh, I don't know, I mean, he's been extra tired lately, but he's been in a growth spurt, and today I thought it was because I woke him up so early."

Just then the doctor arrived and Morgan watched intently as the two professionals quietly searched for an explanation. At length, the doctor spoke. Addressing the nurse, he instructed, "Darla, arrange transport. Mister, uh—"

"Stillwater. Morgan Stillwater."

"Mister Stillwater, we're a small facility; and we don't specialize in pediatric cardiology. I'd like to have him transported to Wichita right away."

"Cardiology?" Morgan fell back in his chair. Shaking his head, he explained, "Doctor, I had a valve replaced five years ago. You think he might have the same condition?"

"These things *can* be hereditary. We'll only know for sure after he's seen in Wichita."

Speaking to himself, Morgan scoffed sadly, "So a bullet *didn't* hit him." Blindsided, he rubbed his face. Weakly, numbly he asked, "Could you contact Dr. Ray Golward at the Cypress Heart facility? He's an old friend from high school who is also my cardiologist now. I'd trust his recommendations."

"Certainly." The doctor nodded and left the room.

With one horrific fear put to rest, Morgan realized the real one had only just begun. *"Oh, Rita. How am I going to tell you?"*

2

NACHOS AT HALFTIME

Cypress Heart facility, Wichita

The air was stale and heavy in the waiting room when the doctor found Morgan lingering with eager anticipation for a positive report of Isaac's condition. Morgan's face fell when he saw grave concern in the doctor's eyes, and his own eyes turned glassy and red with raw emotion.

"Dr.—" Morgan stammered. He had never grown accustomed to calling him by such a formal title. Because they had been close friends long before he received his license to practice, the doctor didn't look bothered when Morgan continued more informally. "*Ray*, I don't know what to do."

"Morgan, he needs the procedure. Remember, your valve replacement was hard because of the additional stress: college, a new baby. But *you* made it through, even with all that; and I'm sure he will too."

Morgan shook his head despairingly. "Sure, I made it through, but I had to drop out of school. There's got to be an alternative."

Dr. Golward pursed his lips together, "When did you say Rita would be back from her mother's?"

"Tomorrow."

Knowing Morgan's wife would help him recognize what was medically necessary, he suggested, "Why don't you talk to her about it then and give me a call."

"I already have. She can't understand why I'm holding back. I know. I know; there's really no question. We've just got to do it." After a halting pause, he nodded, "It's okay." Morgan sat quietly with the doctor for a moment, gathering his thoughts. His brows furrowed slightly before asking directly, "But what if it doesn't work?"

"Morgan, you've experienced this as a patient. I don't need to explain the risks; you know them as well as anyone. But you've also seen it *work*, and Isaac really has no other choice."

"I know. You're right."

"Just let me do my best, and pray for God's hand in his full recovery."

Morgan nodded and took a deep breath. "You know, if I'd been able to stay in medical school, you realize I might be the one performing this surgery?"

"No, Morgan. Everything happens for a reason. It's not your job to do this for your son. And somehow, all that's transpired will ultimately reveal a grander purpose for your life and greater meaning to your challenges."

Morgan lamented, "I never aspired to work for a medical devices company; I always thought I'd be in the trenches saving lives like you."

"Well, we all play our part. I couldn't do what I do without the tools your industry provides. And look at you now, succeeding magnificently right where you are. Honestly, it was your interest in medicine that made you uniquely equipped to bring passion and purpose to an industry often driven by profit alone." Dr. Golward smiled. "No wonder you've done so well. In your wildest dreams, did you ever think you'd end up as the company *president*?"

Morgan was too numb to respond.

After a reflective moment, Dr. Golward put his hands on Morgan's shoulders and reiterated, "Now. Let's help your son. That's *my* passion and purpose; I want to see him grow up to play football for our old high school. Deal?"

"Alright," Morgan nodded, "I trust you."

"No, don't trust *me*. Trust *God*, Morgan. I'm just an instrument; and like I said, all I can promise is to do my very best. You know, my own heart is in this one. I want him well."

Eight months later

"I'm so sorry, Morgan." Dr. Golward looked at his hands, wringing them as he prepared to deliver the devastating news. Then, bravely making eye contact he stated, "He's dealing with infective endocarditis."

Morgan closed his eyes and Rita put her arms around him, hiding her face in his shoulder. Morgan looked up, shaking his head: "Why *Isaac*? How can thousands of people come through without a hitch, and Isaac's little body goes septic? Can you *explain* that to me?" Morgan was angry and Dr. Golward just listened. "This was supposed to *work*, Ray!"

It's not that Morgan didn't understand the medical terminology or anticipate the potential setbacks of his son's condition. He had spent hours at the hospital library learning everything he could about the aspects of cardiology that had impacted his family twice now, but Isaac's situation wasn't a story in a medical textbook. This wasn't just O positive on a chart. This was real blood, and not just any, but his own, coursing through the veins of his very sick, but cherished offspring.

This was his own flesh, under conditions beyond his control. Thoughts of helplessness pulsed through Morgan's throbbing head. If only he had been able to finish medical school, he might have had more power and knowledge to avert the tragedy in the first place.

Finally, the doctor responded. "The valve is compromised; the leaflets seeded bacteria. We hope to get the infection under control with antibiotics, Morgan, but I'm afraid the valve is only temporary. The leaflets are damaged."

Morgan's anger melted away as he mustered some weak but hopeful determination. "So now what?"

"He'll need another surgery. How soon? Not sure. We'll wait as long as we can, managing his condition with medication to delay the second procedure."

"So, what's to keep this from happening again?"

The doctor silently pressed his lips together and then replied, "There are no guarantees. There are inherent disadvantages to both the mechanical prosthetic valves and the ones made from animal tissue. We do the best we can with what we have."

Unsatisfied with the doctor's response, Morgan replied resolutely, "I believe in miracles, doctor. I still envision Isaac leading a normal life."

The doctor cautiously assured, "I believe in miracles, too, Morgan." After a sympathetic pause, Dr. Golward smiled faintly,

"I'm looking forward to the football game we'll watch him play in about ten years. Mark your calendar; we'll eat nachos at halftime."

The doctor would never express such confidence to just any of his patients' families, but he knew Morgan needed his buoyancy more than he needed a report of the apparent truth. Their enduring friendship transcended the typical professional protocol, and he knew the friendship would endure, even if his words proved to be a lie.

3

A BOLD REQUEST

Two months later

"Ray, look at this." Morgan held up a pale, yellow gadget, about the size of a quarter.

"What *is* that?"

"This," Morgan paused for emphasis, "is a valve. I haven't slept since we brought Isaac home." Morgan continued more quickly and energetically, "My mind's been racing, knowing there has to be a better solution, and after researching everything I could find on his condition, expecting there had to be an alternative, one night I woke with a start—and could see with perfect clarity exactly what he needed. In full color, three dimensions, I saw the very thing that would solve the problem, and I've spent the last four weeks 'round the clock developing it. This is it."

The doctor took the device and examined it from all sides. His mouth hung open slightly, as he considered the challenges that artificial valves had always been known to have, and with every turn of the object and every twist and bend of his fingers, the realization washed over him that *this* inspired design avoided both the coagulation problems of the more durable mechanical devices, as well as the durability problems of their bio-prosthetic counterparts.

The features were so advanced it seemed like science fiction. Dr. Golward turned the valve over in his hands many times as he continued to examine the device. He muttered thoughtfully, "*This porous element might actually promote a strong matrix bond between the heart tissue and valve, maximizing implant stability....*"

Morgan interrupted his thoughts. "The valves are made of a synthetic polymer that possesses the physical qualities of natural valves: elasticity for preventing deformation and adhesions, efficient opening and closing of valves, and compatibility with the natural healing process. So, no deformity, flow, clot or infection problems, essentially eliminating the need for multiple surgeries, heart failure, blood thinners...."

"Unbelievable, Morgan." Dr. Golward examined it pensively one more time, then began to question, "But—"

Reading his thoughts, Morgan interrupted. "Ray, get this." Morgan brought out a notepad with his midnight scribbles on it. Enthusiastically he pulled his chair closer to Dr. Golward and spun the pad around on the desk to face them both. "Look at this—with thousands of medical devices and a lab full of building blocks for everything my company makes, when I saw the vision for *this*, every solitary thing that needed to go into it was apparent as well." Morgan chuckled, "I jotted it all down, wondering if it would still make sense in the morning."

Dr. Golward pored over the notepad and eventually whispered, "This is a dream." Looking up at Morgan, eyes wide, he continued, "Can this be for real?"

Morgan rattled on, "Thrombosis: not a problem. We take the DXio45 melding component, combine it with ROJ-62, overlay it onto the methyl methacrylate fiberflex and you have an ideal replication of the endothelium of the connecting heart chambers."

Dr. Golward remained in a daze, and Morgan kept going. "With the new technology for fusion in cranioplasty, it seems the same process could bond *this* compound to the outer surface of the prosthesis, and *voila*! You've got built-in endocardium—the body won't even know the valve is there." After a moment, he burst out a chuckle and excitedly pointed to one part of his diagram, "Do you see how this combination could even lay the foundation for potential self-repair?"

Dr. Golward sat back and closed his eyes, looking for a hole in Morgan's theory. Finding none, he began with a sigh, "If this is truly what it seems to be, it's revolutionary. The world will know about this, Morgan! It needs testing and mass development!" Leaning in he continued, "You've got to submit this to the medical journals—it'll save thousands of lives every year! You always said you'd be saving lives in the trenches!"

Shaking his head and smiling, Morgan countered, "Oh sure, who would listen to me? I'm no medical doctor; I'm just a parent who is obsessed with seeing my *son*, the only child I *have*, grow up. No, Ray, the world isn't ready for this. It's for Isaac, and we don't have time to wait for the medical community to accept it."

Dr. Golward cautiously tempered his excitement. With his thoughts racing faster than he could speak, he blurted, "What are you saying? Wait—no. This can't be for real. It's—you—what about..." With his thoughts in a blur, he eventually formulated a question. "Morgan, how in the world did *you* think of it?"

Morgan replied, "I couldn't have designed it on my own if I tried, Ray. I'm not that smart. It's bigger than me, and so I've got to go with it, follow where it's leading."

Thoughtfully Dr. Golward tried to process this incomprehensible event. He was witnessing the birth of a groundbreaking innovation and had trouble digesting the significance of the moment. Slowly muttering out loud, he finally concluded, "You're right, you're *not* smart enough to come up with this on your own; somehow this *passion* of yours has become your portal to *genius*!"

"That's about all I've got, Ray. I feel the passion in my veins. It keeps me awake at night. There's nothing more I want than to know Isaac will give me *grandchildren* to carry on the family name. I want people—family—a hundred years from now to know and *care that I lived*." By now, Morgan's eyes were misty. One tear eventually fell, and embarrassed, he quickly wiped his face dry. "I need my son to live a full life, without the constant threat of another operation, and I believe this will do it." Morgan took a deep breath, and mustered the courage to say, "That's why I need you to perform the surgery."

Dr. Golward's face fell. "You want me to do *what*?"

"I need you to give him this device. Put it in there. I can't do it myself, or *you know I would*."

"It's too experimental—too infantile! Where's the lab testing? Years of experimentation? This is your *son*, for crying out loud, not a laboratory rat! Have you gone mad?"

"You said it yourself, doc: *this is genius*; I didn't come up with it on my own. I've been given a solution to save my son. Who am I to reject it?"

"How will you pay for this? The hospital, equipment, medications, physicians? No insurance company would ever touch this."

"I've already cashed in my entire portfolio. Much of the equipment can come from my own company, and—since on paper it can be considered product development and testing—I can utilize company funds, to an extent. I'm prepared to cover the facility, medications, and most of what your team would require, but I'm hoping you'll do your part—as a favor." Morgan searched the doctor's face, which showed no sign of cooperation. "Let me try to simplify the idea. This proposition is not really that difficult, Ray. The procedure is the same routine, only with a different device—same contact points, same procedure. Only this time, no complications."

"Do you have any idea how much red tape there is to go through? This sort of thing takes paperwork, releases, legalities. I'm not sure Isaac has that kind of time, Morgan."

"You can push it through, can't you? I'm on my knees, Ray. I don't know what else to do. He won't always be a candidate. I'm afraid we'll lose Isaac if we don't do this."

"*You could lose Isaac if we do*, Morgan."

"Just tell me this. Is it possible? Can you use a device that has only been tested in the research and development lab at the plant? Can you get a team to do it?"

"It's complicated. I can get the facility and a team, but this is a Class III device, so without approval from the FDA, we need an investigational device exemption—an IDE—and even with that we can't do anything for at least 30 days, probably more."

"But if you recommend it, and I consent—I'll sign anything you need me to sign—then what does it matter to the FDA?"

Even though Dr. Golward could see the feasibility and genius of the invention, there was a part of him that had a hard time *not* seeing the gadget as homemade, and the thought of being responsible for its performance to any degree terrified him. There was comfort to be had if they would just slow down long enough to allow the federal agency to either lend support or shut it down entirely, according to their judgment. Apparently, Morgan didn't care what the FDA thought, and Dr. Golward desperately wished that he did.

The doctor was certain that questioning the suitability of the gadget further would fall on deaf ears, so he tried another argument: "Well, here's the thing, Morgan. What if it works? What if you've created something that would help others? Naturally I'd want this for your son, but you can't expect me to approach this with the same indifference as if I were helping you fix your car. For another thing, if you're asking me to do a favor like this, ethically, I'd need to take this on with the ultimate intention of letting it help humanity, not just Isaac. That requires an IDE to treat him as part of an approved clinical study."

"So, under those terms, how long before he'd get the surgery?"

"Honestly, I'm not sure he ever would. Before approving the study, they must review all the documentation from *prior* studies— laboratory, animal, other human tests—a proposal for how we'll run the study, consent documents. We have none of that. If by some miracle, they approve the request anyway, then there's a good chance they'll impose some serious restrictions."

"There's got to be another way, Ray." Morgan paused awkwardly and then continued, "You know what? Let's not talk about this now. You'd probably like some time to digest it. Come to our house to-night. You've always relied on Rita to keep my head on straight. The three of us can talk about it at home."

Dr. Golward was somewhat surprised by the suggestion because he knew Rita was too level headed for this, and he thought it odd for Morgan to suddenly shift from dogged assertion to being openly willing to bring her into the conversation. It sounded like a safe and perfect way to bring this madness to a peaceful conclusion. "Great. I'll get back to work and then," shaking Morgan's hand he promised, "I'll swing by on my way home from the clinic."

4

STREET BALL
WITH ISAAC

Just before 6:00 that night, the doorbell rang and Rita opened it with Dr. Golward searching her eyes for evidence of camaraderie in his dilemma. As she beamed a wide smile and brushed a brunette curl away from her face, he wondered how much Morgan had already shared with her. Did she know what had been proposed? If so, how did she feel about it? The more he could discern in her eyes before the official conversation began, the more comfortable he'd feel about proceeding. But her deep blue eyes only sparkled with warmth and gratitude for his visit. "Please come in! What brings you by tonight?"

She doesn't know! Dr. Golward couldn't believe it. "Well, Morgan asked me to come by. He said he'd like to talk with you and me about Isaac."

"Oh, of course he did. Let's have a seat in here. Morgan! Ray is here!"

Dr. Golward took off his jacket and clutched it nervously while the three of them sat in the family room, Rita and Morgan comfortably on the couch together, with Dr. Golward sitting not quite as comfortably by himself on the matching love seat. He noticed her unreserved affection for Morgan, clasping his right hand in both of hers as she leaned in, eager to discover the purpose of this visit.

Either she doesn't know, or she's behind this. How alone am I in trying to talk reason into Morgan? Dr. Golward adjusted his glasses. His eyes, keen and intelligent from decades as a surgeon, darted around the room and then back to Rita. Every glance or gesture could be a clue.

Just then Isaac strolled in with a dusty football, wearing a pair of jeans that were a size too big for him, pant legs puckered at his ankles and stacked atop his dingy white tennis shoes because he wasn't quite tall enough for them to hang straight. His voice had a sort of dusty quality to it, as well. Standing behind the doctor's love seat, he looked beyond the guest and begged with a soft and raspy voice, "Dad, can we work on my throw?"

"Hey tiger, you look great! I'd love to, but we're visiting with Dr. Golward."

Isaac apparently hadn't recognized the doctor from behind without his white coat, and probably hadn't expected to see him anywhere but the clinic or hospital room. With the personality of a miniature comedian, he wrinkled his freckled nose and then widened his eyes as he did a cartoonish double take and looked to his parents for a response. He loved amusing them with exaggerated facial expressions and got a lot of mileage out of their chuckles.

Dr. Golward stood up and greeted the boy like a gentleman. "It's wonderful to see you, Isaac. How are you feeling today?"

"Great!" He smiled, while the confidence in his blue-green eyes sparkled like the ocean on a summer day. "And getting better!" The grown-ups laughed again, and Isaac beamed. "Dad says you're going to fix my heart," he held up the football, "so that's why I need to practice. I'm gonna play for Wichita Collegiate!"

The blood drained from Dr. Golward's face and he forced a smile. The doctor's glance at Morgan had the intensity of a thousand eyes. Morgan kept a firm gaze on his son and a superficial smile on his face, but the flush of his cheeks betrayed embarrassment. "Isaac, I'll be out in a bit. Why not see if Kip next door can play until dinner?"

Isaac took a deep, dramatic breath and let out a sigh as loud and forceful as a freshly punctured automobile tire. Having performed the melodrama to his satisfaction, he ran outside to play some football.

Choosing not to go directly to confrontation, Dr. Golward broke the awkward silence, easing the tension in the room with, "He's looking amazingly well. I would not expect this kind of energy in his condition, Morgan."

"He hasn't been this way. Since we brought him home he's hardly gotten out of bed until we finally gave him something to live for."

"And your inspiration of choice was to make a false promise?" Dr. Golward felt his chest tighten and wondered if his hair was turning even more gray than it already was.

"I learned the tactic from you, Ray. You told *me* that you could see him playing football for our school in ten years. You had no more right to make such a promise than I do."

"Yeah, but I never made a promise that relied on someone else to do something against their will, Morgan!"

Morgan sighed and shook his head. "Ray, I'm sorry. I never meant to have you do anything against your will. Isaac seemed to be slowing down and getting more tired by the day, until I started to paint the picture you had given me about him playing football in high school. The way his eyes lit up—well, that's the most life I've seen in him all year." Morgan glanced down and shifted uncomfort-ably. "When he started asking how it was going to happen, I told him about the valve. He just assumed you'd be the one to do the surgery, since you're the only surgeon he's ever known, and I didn't say anything to make him believe otherwise. His symptoms even began to diminish and I didn't have it in me to temper his hope. That's the reason I came to you this morning, because I had to find out in a hurry if I could count on you—before Isaac and I had any more talks about it."

Dr. Golward sat there, gazing at the coffee table in front of him, expressionless. Rita, still holding Morgan's hand broke the silence, "Ray, we can't ask you to do something that doesn't feel right to *you*. I struggled with this myself—but I can't imagine life without Isaac, and maybe I'm crazy, but I see Morgan's vision. I share it. All we ask is that you figure it out in a hurry, one way or the other. Just please don't throw the idea away without giving it serious consideration."

He looked at Rita and remembered back to when she had been on *his* side to talk Morgan into consenting to the first surgery. Now here she was, rallying with Morgan for an experimental one. He thought it ironic for the surgeon to be the one this time with cold feet. "I need to think." Dr. Golward stood up and assured them he'd be back soon, but that he just wanted to take a walk up the lane and get some fresh air. They stood, quietly followed him to the front door and closed it softly behind him.

The knot in Dr. Golward's pit of his stomach was juxtaposed with the joy burning in his heart at the prospect of participating in something so promising and revolutionary. A ground-breaking experience like this is one that many surgeons might only dream about, but it was as good as his, if he wanted it. Why, then, was the elation in his heart so quickly eclipsed by nausea?

Suddenly, his thoughts were interrupted by Isaac's youthful, raspy voice from the neighbor's yard, "Hey, watch out!"

Turning, Dr. Golward recoiled at the flash of something seen from the corner of his eye. Dropping his coat, his arms went up and instinctively caught the ball, immediately tucking it under his arm. Regaining his bearings, he looked from the ball to Isaac and hollered, "Nice throw, tiger!"

"Throw it back!"

The doctor smiled, looking back at the ball again and turned it with a couple inch-high tosses until it was positioned just as he wanted it for the throw. It sailed through the air and Isaac ran into its path, catching it perfectly at his side. At the same moment, his little buddy Kip rammed him from the side, knocking them both to the ground.

Dr. Golward winced, thinking of Isaac's condition, but smiled reservedly when he saw the boy immediately roll away and struggle to his feet. *Good thing he's not on blood thinners.*

Just then the neighbor's door opened and an angry father scolded, "Kip, get in here! I told you not to get dirty before dinner!"

The smile on Dr. Golward's face vanished and in the place where Kip's father stood, was an image—a memory—of his own father calling him in from one of his many boyhood scrimmages. *"Ray, get in here! I told you not to get dirty before dinner. Besides, football will knock the sense out of your brains. Looks like it already has. Get your mind on something worthwhile, boy!"*

Huffing laboriously, Isaac trotted over to where the doctor stood in a daze. "Wanna throw some more?"

Not yet completely present, Dr. Golward looked down at Isaac. The ache from his childhood lingered: to play ball without limits— to throw caution to the wind and do what he loved, but to then be cut short from the full expression of that passion. Sure, while maintaining tremendous grades, he had played well in high school, but when it came time to move into the world of adults, his father said he had *put up with it long enough* and insisted he drop football and go to medical school. Without question, his love for saving lives ultimately transcended the joy of carrying a football through the maze of defensive linebackers across the goal line, but there had always been an emptiness left in the place where there might have been mastery and excellence achieved in his forgotten world of team sports.

"Wanna throw some more?" Isaac huffed again, leaning over and bracing himself on his knees.

Dr. Golward was tempted to decline the invitation and commence his walk. But it was a sudden feeling of rebellion against the path to which he long ago consented that caused him to choose playing ball over thinking about medicine. The decision about the surgery felt heavy; it was just easier to engage in this diversion. He removed his glasses, tucked them safely into his pocket, and running backward, yelled, "let's do this!"

It must have been their cheers and laughter that eventually brought Morgan and Rita outside to see what was going on. Dr. Golward looked up, and grinning, threw the ball abruptly to Morgan. Morgan caught the ball and held it, hesitating, until Rita nudged him. Finally he looked up again, smiling, and yelled to Isaac and Ray, "Go long!"

The two of them ran into the distance and finally turned to run backward a bit, continuing farther than the doctor had originally planned, encouraged by Morgan's gestures to "keep going." They didn't stop until they were near the back of the empty lot across the street. After wobbling its way through the sky the ball landed short, and both the doctor and Isaac laughed at their failed attempts to predict the path of the ball as it bounced to a halt.

Ray finally picked it up, then handed it to Isaac yelling, "Take it to the end zone!" Isaac tucked it under his arm and darted back and forth to dodge an imaginary defense, knocking every obstacle out of the way. It put a smile on their faces to watch his dramatic rendition of the most amazing sprint across the football field anyone had ever seen. Finally, laughter erupted when he slammed the ball to the ground and did a weakly delivered but adorable version of a professional ball player's victory dance.

"Okay, honey, take it easy now. Let's go wash up for dinner." Rita turned to Morgan and, whispered, "I think Ray's heart may be softening. This would probably be a good time for me to leave you two alone to talk. Invite him to eat with us when you're done."

Without a word, Morgan walked toward Ray and met him at the sidewalk. As a knowing smile passed between them, Morgan's face softened and there was a twinkle in his hopeful blue eyes. Ray recognized that look from their carefree high school days, but could he justify providing false hope? The familiar ache in his chest returned.

They were quiet for a time, and Morgan became restless. Finally, he blurted, "What? What are you thinking? Don't leave me hanging like this…"

Dr. Golward put his hands to his face and lifted his glasses to rub his eyes. Shaking his head, he said, "He's a remarkable little boy—and, I can't believe I'm even considering it." Under his breath he continued, almost to himself, "Insurance would throw this out like bio-hazard waste, and I should, too."

"But you know in your heart it's right, don't you? Think of Isaac, and the alternatives."

"You're bold, Morgan. You know that?"

"I'm driven by a cause, Ray. I realize you may not entirely see what I see, but God has spoken peace to my heart and I have no choice but to follow through."

"How do you know this isn't some evil deception, Morgan? Do you have any comprehension of what's at stake here? The ramifications if it fails? We need the FDA behind your device, and we need time to put it into place." Ray ran his hands through his graying dark hair and wiped away the visible line of sweat forming on his hairline. "Maybe your revelation was inspired by your love for Isaac, but really intended for the world? Is it really fair to him that you don't just come to peace with what is, and help him cope by example?"

"Stop." Morgan intercepted the doctor's train of thought, headed straight for images of failure. He could read the doctor's mind and see the headlines about the father who caused the death of his son by using a device not yet approved by the FDA. Raising his voice to drown the haunting mind chatter of doubt and fear, he finally yelled, "Just STOP right there! Stop it! Can't you see? Close your eyes, man." His voice became quiet again, "Can you see him playing football in ten years, *or not?*"

Dr. Golward took a deep breath. "I do, I see it. I know. You've been given a gift—an answer. I feel it as well."

"Then we've got to do this, right away."

"Okay, I'll do it. But I won't hurry the process. I need the agency's support. I see a bigger picture here, and one day you'll thank me that we did it right."

Just then Rita called from inside the house, "Morgan! Come quick! Help me!" The men looked at each other with alarm and ran to the house, leaving the ball on the grass by the sidewalk. After passing through the doorway, they raced to the hall by the kitchen where Rita was on the floor next to her son. She cried, "Morgan! Ray—it's Isaac!"

5

THE LOOPHOLE

Morgan and Rita sat in the old waiting room again, watching for
Dr. Golward to return from surgery. At last, the doors opened and
they stood with eagerness to receive news of Isaac's condition. Dr.
Golward held a manila folder in one hand and kept the other hand
in his coat pocket. "He's resting. All went well, and the device is
performing. He's not yet conscious, but his vital signs are good.
Morgan, I'm optimistic." After delivering the status report, a broad
grin spread across his face and his eyes beamed. "I'm *very* optimistic."

Rita jumped into the air with her hands flying to her own heart,
not entirely sure what to do with the feelings of relief that overwhelmed her. Even though it would be some time before any of
them would know how his body would respond to the device, the
first and biggest hurdle was behind them, and that alone was plenty
to celebrate.

Morgan threw his arms around the doctor, and together they
reveled in the victory. "Thank you. Thank you," Morgan whispered
then pulled away and looked at Dr. Golward intently. "I'm sorry
about the FDA thing."

Dr. Golward shook his head. "My assistant did some research and found a loophole. It's a good thing Isaac collapsed when he did. I know that sounds crazy, but *that* was our loophole."

The doctor opened the file he had been holding and pulled out a document from the U.S. Food and Drug Administration Information Sheets on Medical Devices. Pointing to the text, he read out loud, "The Food and Drug Administration recognizes that emergencies arise where an unapproved device may offer the only possible life-saving alternative, but an IDE for the device does not exist....Using its enforcement discretion, FDA has not objected if a physician chooses to use an unapproved device in such an emergency, provided that the physician later justifies to FDA that an emergency actually existed."

"You mean you can still include Isaac's surgery in the clinical study, even before getting the IDE?"

"That's right. I just didn't feel right about rushing the surgery when there was no real urgent medical reason to do so. His collapse was the best thing that could have happened for him, for you, for me, and humanity at large. I'm not sure you realize this, but under those conditions, your insurance will probably even pick up the bill on everything except the device."

"So, you're getting paid for what you just did?"

The doctor just smiled, and Morgan cried out, "Oh!" as he fell to the couch behind him, and put his hands on his head.

The doctor was also overcome with joy. "Sometimes 'bad' things happen for an even greater good. At least this time, the good was quickly and clearly apparent. Looks like we've just made history, Morgan."

Rita sat down again next to Morgan and their tears fell freely. "When can we see him?"

"How about right now? You can be there when he wakes up."

Dr. Golward led them to the recovery room and Isaac was beginning to stir already. His eyes opened and the doctor welcomed him back. "Hey there, champ. You just won a pretty tough game. Congratulations. Your folks are here, and I'm going to let you have some time alone with them, is that a deal?"

Isaac closed his eyes again and nodded his head slightly.

Patting Morgan on the back, and then giving Rita a quick squeeze on her shoulder, Dr. Golward left the room, feeling strangely, and suddenly uneasy.

6

HEART AND SOUL

Upon arriving at his office, the doctor drew the shades and locked the door. Now that he was alone, he had trouble containing his emotions. There was a mixture of joy, relief, and amazement. However, his grin failed to hold back a brief convulsion of air that escaped, contrasting the composure and professionalism he had maintained during the operation. But now it was done, and he could finally give release to all that had been held in since Isaac had collapsed.

This pinnacle moment in his career would never be forgotten, as he reflected on all the events that led up to this day. Years of medical school and practice flooded his mind. He remembered overcoming resentment that his dad had pressured him into medicine in the first place. He was even grateful for his dad's encouragement, now that he had been privileged to perform this landmark surgery. He thought back to high school and meeting Morgan. He remembered the agony Morgan had suffered through his own surgery, dropping out of school and eventually going to work in an industry that only supported his real passion for saving lives.

He thought it ironic that the degree of Morgan's passion for saving lives exceeded his own, yet Morgan was not the one who had become a surgeon. Even still, Morgan saved a life with his invention. *An invention that could save thousands of other lives, if Morgan would just open his mind to the possibility.*

The doctor could not help but see the potential for Morgan's device. Although, despite the flood of joy that came from performing every successful surgery, there lingered emptiness inside of him that he did not understand. He wished he could *feel* as much passion for saving people's lives as Morgan had demonstrated saving Isaac's. He thought, *Of course I want to save lives with this device, but how do I get my passion to burn as brightly as Morgan's?* Instinctively he knew there was something missing.

What is my passion? What would really inspire me the way Morgan was inspired? What is MY portal to genius? The doctor scoffed when he took notice of the images filling his mind. *Why do I keep going back to thoughts of football?*

He remembered back to his late father's words in grade school after enjoying a little scrimmage: *Football will knock the sense out of your brains. Looks like it already has. Get your mind on something worthwhile, boy*! Despite an unsupportive father, nothing had brought him more energy—nothing inspired him to excel more than the dream of catching a football and running it through obstacles and into an end zone. He could still feel the thrill, the soul expansion, of all the times he did just that for Wichita Collegiate. No surgery had ever brought him the same feeling of exhilaration, not even this one. And that bothered him. *Are my priorities messed up? Shouldn't saving a life feel better than getting a touchdown?*

These questions haunted him, sapping his brain of energy as he tried to understand it, until he fell asleep with his head tipped back against the padded top edge of his office chair.

However, the images in his mind didn't go to rest with him. It wasn't long before he found himself on the ball field, racing to his right where he would be open to receive a pass from the quarterback. The members of the opposing team were, each one, four times bigger than life, and he found it nearly impossible to get clear of their towering presence.

Darting through an opening to the left, he found himself available just long enough to get eye contact with his teammate and receive the pass. *Was that Morgan?* He wondered, but there was no time for a double take. Dodging the defense as he ran, he danced between the diving bodies and fallen limbs of the scrambling opponents in the same way Isaac had weaved across the street just a couple of evenings before.

In the next moment, he realized that even though he was running, and even though the other team persisted in blocking and chasing him, somehow the ball had vanished. *If the ball is gone, where did it go, and what am I running for?* The goal line was in sight and he instinctively kept running, finally noticing the ball tucked tightly under his arm had been replaced with a case of Morgan's heart valves.

The passion flared. He saw giants all around him, and sensed others he could not see, bent on preventing him from accomplishing his purpose. Despite his opponent's obvious intent to pummel him to the ground, there welled up inside of Ray an indescribable flow of determination to get those valves to the end zone.

With superhuman speed, he pulled away from the tangle of giants and crossed the line. Immediately the masses jumped to their feet and roared with cheers, as he spun around doing his own epic victory dance. Looking to the stands, he saw the seats filled with doctors in white coats with stethoscopes hanging around their necks and glistening in the sun. He saw children and adults cheering in hospital gowns. He saw journalists and grandparents, and people from all walks of life; and he saw their eyes. No matter how far away they sat, he saw their eyes conveying deep gratitude, relief, and pure joy that his contribution—his race to the end zone—had brought to their lives.

He found himself in awe, stunned by the impact that such a relatively small feat could have on so many. Not on the *masses*, but on so many *individuals*. Individuals, into whose eyes he had seen: people with histories of their own, with relationships that were real—as real as the relationships he enjoyed with his own family and friends. It overwhelmed him, and the strangeness and beauty of the moment finally gave way to a consciousness that said, "This didn't really happen—people don't play football with cases of heart valves."

His eyes fluttered open and he realized he had dozed off. But he awoke with new clarity of purpose, and passion. It dawned on him that all his experiences had prepared him for this moment in time; his initial purpose in medicine had been fulfilled.

It finally made sense why his enthusiasm for medicine waned, and why football had always held such an interesting place in his heart. He saw a unique blend coming into view of how to take his interests, experience, and passions into a purpose that utilized them all! Morgan's passion and expertise were sufficient to create the valve, and it was time for it to be passed off to Ray—to let him take it to the world! He was going to be Morgan's halfback!

Dad, I CAN have it all! Football DID play a purpose, and I DO have my mind on something worthwhile! Ray could imagine his father being proud of everything he had done as a surgeon to date, and also believed it would have pleased his father to know that his son had ultimately engaged in a purpose that was even bigger than the both could have ever imagined.

From this point forward, everything he did would be for the express purpose of getting the device approved and on the market. The only patients he would see were those who could be included in the clinical study, because the rest of his time would be spent working for Morgan.

Who better to sell the idea to sponsors, investors, and to families facing surgery, than the very doctor who performed the first one? His mind raced with all the things he could do to carry it along the path to global exposure, and it amazed him—the prospect that he could love his work as much as he loved football!

7

OUT OF FUNDS

Present Day – 10 Years Later
Wednesday, 1:54 pm

Morgan heard the phone ringing at Linda's desk down the hall and tried to concentrate on his paperwork in spite of it. Soon the intercom sabotaged his effort altogether.

"Mr. Stillwater, the phone is for you."

"Didn't I ask you to hold all calls?"

"Yes, sir, but I think you need to take this one."

Morgan Stillwater closed his eyes and exhaled through his nose, clenching his teeth. Then, breathing in deeply, he gained composure and finally picked up the receiver. "Hello, this is Morgan."

"Mr. Stillwater, Ed Phillips. I know we've talked, and I realize you've already explained your situation, but I need to warn you that the board is ready to pull the plug on the Simmons deal if you don't show proof of matching funds by the end of the day next Wednesday. Do you understand?"

"Edward," Morgan replied weakly, "why are they pulling the plug so soon? They know I'm good for it. They stand to lose as much as I do. I just need two more months."

"Morgan, you said that last time. They're getting nervous, and they're tired of empty promises. Wednesday, Morgan. Make it happen."

Morgan pulled the receiver away from his head, balanced it briefly in a loose palm-up grip, and then softly hung up the phone.

Standing up and grabbing a short stack of papers, Morgan stepped out of his office and handed them to his secretary on his way to the elevator. "Linda, I'm going home for the day. Please finish up the rest of this before you leave."

8

TIRED OF THE FIGHT

2:35 pm

Hearing the garage door open a few hours earlier than expected, Rita greeted Morgan at the door. "Is everything okay?"

Morgan didn't reply immediately. He quietly stepped inside and put his briefcase on the floor next to the wall. Rita tilted her head to fix her eyes on his, but he was dodging her gaze. Finally, he stood upright and looked at her squarely. "They're pulling out of the Simmons deal if I don't show them the money by Wednesday."

"What? Why? That's only seven days." Rita sat, resting herself on the edge of the marble-topped table near the front door.

"They've just lost confidence."

Gathering her thoughts, Rita replied, "Well, what now?" After a pause with no reply, she continued, "You're not giving up that easily, are you? You need what, $3.8 million?"

"No, it's $4.5 now because I didn't have it before the first deadline. We have a hefty penalty, plus interest owed to the phase one investors."

"It's not impossible, Morgan. You can't give up until you've exhausted *all* possibilities."

"But *haven't* I? *You* tell *me*, who *haven't* I contacted to round it up? Everyone's dry. I'm out of resources."

"Now, wait a minute. You know there's always a way. This is how you've always gotten through. Isaac's experimental surgery ten years ago seemed impossible, too. But the way emerged. You didn't get to the top of the company and build it to nearly 3000 employees by caving under pressure, either. Do what you've always said: See the victory on the screen of your mind, and tell me now, *how would it feel?*" Rita could see her husband subtly shaking his head. She continued, "Morgan, I'm serious. You've *got* to do this, or you'll stay just as blind to the solution as you are now."

Morgan sighed, "Sometimes it's just easier to give up, though. I'm tired of fighting it."

She continued, "Remember, this Simmons deal goes through and you've got the alliance with MedCorp. With that, your heart valves get the status they need to be considered by the insurance companies, and ultimately your valve makes its way into the hospitals worldwide. Just think of it, you're adding a lifetime of family memories to the li*ves of—who knows* how many people."

Morgan started to speak softly, reflectively, "We're so close. Ray's lined up more outlets than we know what to do with, but none of them will make the move until at least one insurance company takes it on. We need MedCorp on our side."

"You've *got* MedCorp, Morgan. They already said they want this! What you want, wants you! This is a minor setback, that's all."

"Yeah, but MedCorp needs Simmons' backing first, and Simmons isn't in until they see my own skin in the game. They don't just want a great product, they need to know that I have plenty to lose, too, if we drop the ball somehow."

"Sure. Like I said, what you want, wants you. It's not like Simmons is trying to keep you out—they *hope* you'll come through. They're not the enemy. The only thing keeping this from happening—something that everyone *wants* to happen—is your blindness to *one simple idea*. Think of it, Morgan; it's only an idea away. Do you realize that? It's just an *idea* that you need."

A grin spread across Morgan's face, and he seemed to relax a little. He'd had at least one good idea before, the valve that sparked into his mind from seemingly nowhere. "You know, for some reason, it seems like it should be easier to come up with a resourceful idea than to come up with $4.5 million dollars."

"That's right, honey; ideas don't cost a thing, but they can be *worth* millions." Morgan's tension seemed to dissipate, and Rita extended her hand to lead him to the family room. "Sit with me, here." Rita sat, turned toward Morgan, who leaned forward with his face contemplatively in his hands. She continued, "So you need an idea. Morgan, remember this whole thing *started* with just an idea?"

"No, it actually started with a hardship." Morgan was thoughtful, "My heart failure, Isaac's, the valve, the surgery, Ray's career change. I'm still amazed at the transformation that came over Ray after performing Isaac's surgery. I don't quite understand what would possess a man to moonlight as a salesman, and then completely leave a successful medical practice to sell the gadget. What in the world drives his passion to do such crazy things?"

Rita just listened. She could tell it would be therapeutic for Morgan to just talk through his thoughts.

Morgan continued, "It's been too long since I was driven by a passion, and honestly, Rita, I'm envious! I'm always happiest when

I'm engaged in a purpose that keeps me awake at night, but under all these current pressures, I've forgotten what it's like to feel that way."

Rita interjected, "As crazy as Ray seems right now, I'm grateful, because Ray's contribution to the company has been tremendous. I love how he brought football terminology into the boardroom to plan and discuss plays that helped you achieve your goals. It's incredible—how he even got the key leadership to speak the lingo."

"I know. It amazed me how the challenges and strategies were so easily tackled when addressed on the blackboard before making the plays in real life. And, because of his passion and energy over the last ten years, there's just one yard left to go, to take these valves into the end zone. If we can do that, it will take the entire business into the stratosphere. The only play left is solving this financial crunch."

"Does Ray know?"

"No, I haven't had the courage to tell him about the company's situation, because I've been afraid to admit this ten-year game may come to an end *without* a victory."

Rita could sense his defeat and refused to let it stand. "You're right, it did start with a tragedy, *and that tragedy had purpose.* So does this one. This tragedy—this threat of financial failure—brings the same ingredients for a genius idea, and I'm not going to let you give up now." She took his chin and turned his head to face hers. "Morgan Stillwater, you listen to me. If it weren't for that valve, Isaac would not be here right now, with a long life to look forward to. I know sometimes you go to work just because you have to, but there's a bigger purpose at play here, *and you'd better get yourself out of the way of it.*"

Morgan listened, and quietly responded, "I'm hoping you can say something to rekindle the spark I've felt before. I've thought of

Isaac and I've imagined what life would be like if he hadn't survived beyond his seventh year." A wave of sobriety washed over Morgan as he closed his eyes in contemplation.

Rita asked, "Now, how many *other* people are at risk *right now*— parents, children, walking time bombs—and *you* have a key to their long life and happiness. The old valves on the market now aren't right for everyone. These people need you to do this, Morgan; and they need you *in time*." Rita had a visual glimpse of what was at stake and placed a hand over her mouth to control a stint of emotion. When she could continue, she admonished him: "Find the solution, honey. *Find,* the solution. It's out there, and you know this isn't about the money. It's about *lives,* and joy, and fulfillment, and kids putting their heads on their pillows at night with smiles on their faces."

They sat quietly, gazing through the glass slider at the edge of the room as a breeze rustled the leaves of the hanging geraniums on the patio.

Finally, Rita deduced the conclusion for him: "I think you need to call Ray."

Sitting up and turning to meet her gaze, Morgan questioned, "*Why?* He doesn't have $4.5 million dollars."

"No, that's *not* why you need to call him, Morgan. Call him, take him to dinner, and remember *why* you do what you do. Get your head back in the game, and think about why you've fought this battle all these years."

"With this deadline, Rita, it's not like I have time to just enjoy a social engagement, shooting the breeze with someone who can't help with the money."

"Morgan, it's *because* of this deadline that you don't have any time to squander *in any other way*. Get back into the right mindset where solutions can come. Forcing them to come in any other mindset will bring you nothing, or even worse, something foolish."

He quietly considered her words, probably because no other solution presented itself. Rita reached for the phone resting on the coffee table and handed it to him. "Call Ray."

9

NEED FOR DIVERSION

Thursday, 6:45 am

At the prodding of his wife, Morgan arrived at work early that day to use the company gym and look over his most impressive test studies while he walked the treadmill. There were accounts of recipients who had initially *not* responded well to the standard valve design, but ultimately found tremendous success with *his* innovative model, the InnoValve. Here in a file were the records of about twenty men and women with newfound life. Morgan's inspiration and Ray's passion had carried the InnoValve from the Morgan Stillwater family into the end zone of these patients' lives.

He pondered the potential ripple effect of tenaciously bringing it to not just these tens, but also hundreds, and ultimately thousands or more. What stories would come out of the collective years of those extended lives? What dreams would be realized? How would the world be better for those recipients having lived completely? Morgan glanced at the only other person using the gym: a man in his twenties, jogging, sweating, and apparently engrossed in whatev-

er was being piped into his little ear buds. He wondered what kinds
of problems this young man faced, and felt pangs of jealousy that
the young man probably didn't need to come up with $4.5 million
dollars in less than six days.

Morgan had nothing wired to his ear. He opted for quiet so he
would notice the spark of inspiration if it came. Despite the tremendous pressure to find a solution by Wednesday, he allowed his mind
to visualize every possible good outcome, hoping it would inspire
him to tune in to the solution, like turning the dial on a radio to
find a desired broadcast. *What if one of my future recipients even lived
to find the cure for cancer? What would it feel like to hear that story?*
So long as his imagination was at his disposal, why not claim it his
privilege to create the most *fantastic* possibilities?

After a few moments, his cell phone broke the silence. He pushed
the button and put it to his ear. It was Ray.

"Hi Morgan, I got your message last night, but it was too late to
call you back. It sounded urgent; everything okay?"

Morgan took a deep breath. He dreaded this moment, breaking
the news to his greatest advocate that they had a serious problem.
"Ray," Morgan glanced at the young man jogging three treadmills
away, who was focused straight ahead and listening to his player. He
appeared to be watching the traffic zoom by through the full-length
windows facing the north side of the facility. Turning his head away
and lowering his voice, Morgan confided, "I don't know how to tell
you this. I need to talk to you. Are you free tonight?"

"What's going on?"

Stealing another glance at the young man, he said quietly, "The
company's in trouble."

"What? Sorry, I couldn't hear you."

A little louder he repeated, "The company—is—in—trouble. Did you hear me?"

"Yes, I heard you; what are you talking about?"

"Listen, I can't talk here. Are you free tonight?"

"Actually, I'm flying out to have that meeting with Solaris Enterprises tonight. I'll be back by four tomorrow. What about tomorrow evening?

"Rita and I are going to the game. What if you join us? We could talk then. Rita's convinced we can get through this, but I need you to help me get the creative juices flowing again. Besides, I'm burned out and think a football game with you would be a really nice diversion."

"It always is. Sure, Morgan, whatever you need."

10

RUMORS

7:40 am

Across town near the railroad tracks was a young father named Richard Goodman, getting ready to leave for his job at Morgan's company.

"Bye, kiddo. See you after work." Richard lifted Matthew into the air and kissed his nose.

"You going to be home in time for Mom's barbeque?" his wife Felicity asked, taking Matthew and putting him back at the table for his toast and scrambled eggs.

"I hope so. Everyone's stressed about the inspection. If it happens today, then I'll be home. If not, they'll expect us to stay and work until it's perfect."

"Well let's hope it happens today, then."

"Felicity, would you rather me fail inspection and lose another job, or have me at your mom's barbeque?"

"Hmmm. Let's see. How about you *pass* today's inspection and then *come to the barbeque?*"

Annoyed by her flippant reply, Richard turned to grab his lunch sack and rolled his eyes out of view. "Then I'd better not waste any more time *here,* had I?"

Felicity pulled the dishtowel off her shoulder and threw it to the sink, annoyed by his sarcastic retort.

Upon arriving at the plant, Richard found a spot in his favorite corner of the lot where he always entered through the side doors. It was the shorter path to his department; the corporation had been kind enough to provide another route so he wouldn't have to pass through the back entrance (derisively referred to as the "cattle gates", first by a few disgruntled employees, and then by even the happy ones with a good sense of humor).

After entering the code on the electronic number pad, there was a rapid beeping sound, but the door refused to open. After striking the metal frame abruptly with his fist, Richard peered through the glass and thought, *It'll be a hot day in Greenland when that fool janitor remembers to unlatch the manual bolt for two days in a row!*

Retracing his steps out of the portico, he followed the outer wall of the plant until he reached the cattle gates.

Shuffling his feet at the pace of the crowd, Richard made his way to the bottleneck where he waved his badge across the sensor and passed through the security entrance. After finally getting to the main hallway, he began his trek to the far end of the building where he'd already be if the first door hadn't been bolted shut. Bart caught up with him and said, "Did you hear?"

"Hear what." Richard's grumpiness hadn't quite dissipated yet.

"The company is in trouble."

Richard didn't stop walking but he did turn his head. "What? What do you mean—how do you know?"

"I saw the president—Morgan Stillwater—in the workout room this morning. He said so, to some other guy on his cell phone. He thought I couldn't hear him, but I could. I was only wearing my earphones for privacy. I do that to avoid conversation; I've got problems of my own to think through, you know."

"So, you think they're going to have layoffs? They've never had layoffs!"

"I don't know. Anyway, I'm using the treadmill a lot lately. Lisa thinks I'm getting pudgy."

"She and I both."

Bart chuckled, "Oh, ho, ho, you've got *yours* coming," as he shoved Richard and then disappeared down another hallway.

Behind him, Richard overheard some others walking to their posts, murmuring about layoffs. They had apparently picked up on his brief and private conversation with Bart.

11

SACK LUNCH

The next morning, Richard woke up extra early to the dryer buzzing in the other room and Felicity was already gone. There was laundry on the bed next to him where she had apparently dumped the clean clothes in order to start another load in the dryer before leaving the house. To go where? He had no idea. With no sign of his family, a puzzled Richard left for work.

As president, Morgan enjoyed interacting with employees at the plant. He'd even enjoyed his lunch hour at the cafeteria like the others on occasion. But on this day, even with employees all around him, he felt alone. He felt heavy with the full weight of his responsibilities. Were any of these employees aware of how precarious their situation was?

Business had been going extremely well with all the other devices, but the clinical study had been financially draining them about four years longer than expected. He realized too late that what had promised to be a relatively short term play (taking the valves to market) had turned into a long-term investment, and they had run out of money to carry it into the end zone. Now the entire company was on the line, with heavy debts to pay and no windfall from the InnoValve, which had consumed most of their energy and resources for the previous ten years.

Sitting, standing, contemplating, poring over the files, pacing the halls, roaming the building, Morgan was restless and couldn't wait until the game and his meeting with Ray that night. So much of the pressure had already been released by just getting a piece of it off his chest over the phone in the workout room. But he knew it was only the beginning.

He prayed that Ray would be plugged in enough to his passion that he could help Morgan see the solution that presently eluded him. There was no productivity to be had that day. He was useless at his desk, so he wandered the facility until he finally ended up at the cafeteria. Taking a seat and pretending to do something important with the papers in his hands, he tried to blend in and hoped nobody would talk to him. A few people, surprised to see him sitting alone at the cafeteria greeted him anyway.

"Hi, Mr. Stillwater."

"Nice to see you, Mr. Stillwater!"

"How are you doing, Mr. Stillwater?"

"*Having a sack lunch today,* Mr. Stillwater?"

With each interruption, he just forced a smile and acknowledged their kind gestures. As difficult as it was to feign happiness, he still felt better sitting there among the people than if he were holed up in his office where he had received the heavy news of the deadline only two days before.

Richard and a few of his peers, Vernon and Shelby, were ignorant of the fact that the president sat just a table away, because they were engrossed in their own gossip. Having been left alone again, Morgan's mind was empty and susceptible to noticing the topic of their conversation, about six feet behind him.

"Well, if they get rid of you, can I have your desk? Mine's a piece of garbage."

"Would they really let anyone go?"

"Companies do it all the time. Greediness at the top does it every time." Richard piped.

"Really?" The newest employee at the table lamented, "I thought if I ever got a job at a big company like this, I'd be set."

"They don't care if you're set or not," Vernon remarked.

"They won't let you go; you've got a degree."

"Yeah, but I've never used it; try getting a job around here with a degree in Political Science."

"I've given them eight years—they'd better *not* let me go, or I'll sue."

"You can sue for that?" Richard asked, "How much could you get?"

Standing and gathering his papers, Morgan slipped out of the cafeteria, purposely passing their table and making mental note of the name badges worn by those who sat there. The lull in his mind turned to agitation from the cafeteria gossip, and he went from feeling numbness to being in a bad mood. *Ingrates*, he thought as the cafeteria door closed behind him.

Returning to his office, he instructed his secretary, "Miss Perkins, contact Human Resources and have them pull up the files of Shelby Ross, Richard Goodman, and Vernon Porter. Add these comments: 'liability, loose tongue, bad attitude' to the supervisor's notes for each file."

"Yes, sir. Contacting HR."

That afternoon, Richard returned home and there was still no sign of Felicity. He grabbed the newspaper, hoping it would calm his nerves about his missing wife, halfway wondering if he'd see something in the paper about her.

As he sat at the kitchen table, a note caught his eye on the refrigerator that had escaped him before. He stood and pulled it off. "Be back later. Matthew is with me. Felicity."

With a sense of relief, Richard put the paper down and went outside to work on the car. For the next thirty minutes he tinkered, positioning himself at the front of the garage to benefit from the cool autumn breeze. If she happened to pull up, and see him sweating over their old clunker, well, that would be okay too. He wondered how the barbeque went the night before, and missed Matthew, having not seen his little guy for nearly twenty-four hours now.

Finally, after another fifteen minutes with no sign of his family, Richard went inside to get some dinner. Grabbing a frozen burrito, he threw it in the microwave and washed his face and hands while it cooked. Drying his face on the dishtowel Felicity had thrown to the counter the morning before, he waited for the *ding*, retrieved his burrito with a paper towel, and turned on the TV.

Not long after, the screen door rattled, and in ran Matthew. "Daddy! Daddy, daddy, daddy!" Throwing his arms around Richard's neck, Matthew exclaimed, "I missed you so much!"

"I missed you too, little guy! Where've you been?"

"We saw a parade! And a carnival!"

"A parade?" Richard glanced at Felicity. "What parade?"

"It's the 150-year anniversary celebration this weekend of the founding of our town. You had to work. I didn't think you'd be interested."

"Oh. Well, I'm glad you had fun. Next time maybe we could go together as a *family* on a Saturday instead." Richard feigned happiness for the sake of Matthew but hoped Felicity had picked up on the dig.

"I grabbed the mail on the way in." Felicity thumbed crossly through the envelopes in her hands. The coldness returning through Felicity's voice confirmed to Richard that there was a conflict coming on. He looked at her, and the message passed between them that they needed to talk.

Felicity walked to the bedroom and Richard changed the channel to keep Matthew's attention for a little while. Richard followed her in and shut the door. She stood by the bed with a stack of envelopes in her hand. Bills, no doubt.

"What time did you get home last night?" Felicity asked dryly.

"About 11:30." Hoping to lighten the inevitable conflict to a mild scuffle, he attempted some civility: "Sorry I missed the barbeque, how'd it go?"

"Mom wondered why you weren't there *again*. She thinks you're avoiding her."

Richard threw up his hands in disbelief, "Avoiding her? Did you tell her I had to stay at work? That we were trying to be ready for inspection? Which, by the way, didn't happen yet."

"Oh? Well that figures."

"Yeah, and it's a *good thing* it didn't. Although, it might not matter after all."

"What do you mean?"

Richard's earlier resolve to bring his best self to this discussion went out the window. *She's in pain? I'll give her some pain.* "Well, looks like whether we pass or not, there'll probably be layoffs. Company is supposedly in trouble."

Felicity's face turned red. "Are you *kidding* me?"

Richard instantly regretted saying anything, especially since it was just a rumor. Nevertheless, it was too late; the damage had been done.

There was silence for what seemed to be an eternity until Felicity finally spoke up. By her next words, he deduced that his last comment, true or not, must have been the final blow.

He braced himself, and out it came:

"Richard, why can't you be more like your brother?" Felicity muttered as she flung the handful of envelopes across the bed.

12

SUPER FOOD

That evening Morgan arrived early at the game, and, wringing his hands, waited at the entrance until Ray showed up. Upon his arrival, Morgan reached out his hand and greeted his friend warmly. He gestured toward the stairs, "Rita's already got a spot at the 50-yard line. Shall we?"

Together they climbed the bleachers and opened their portable stadium chairs, perching themselves comfortably next to Rita.

Ray broke the ice. "So, what's going on with the company?"

Morgan replied dryly, "The board wants to pull out of the Simmons deal."

Rita overheard Morgan's summary and piped in, "No, they *don't* want to pull out, but they will if we don't show the matching investment funds by Wednesday."

Ray's eyes got wide as he shifted his focus from Rita back to Morgan.

"I don't know, Ray. I keep thinking God wouldn't bring me this far to fail now. He wouldn't inspire the new valve if he didn't want it to get out there, right?"

"Of *course,* he wouldn't bring you this far to fail now, Morgan!"

"We've got to come up with $4.5 million dollars by Wednesday or the whole thing comes down, for good. That's it."

Ray leaned back and sighed. "We can't stop now. I have more than 250 accounts lined up, just waiting for the green light. Why are they putting the squeeze on now?"

"I'm not sure, maybe they have some other outstanding accounts receivable and are in a pinch of their own."

"Morgan, if this can do for even *one more person* what it has done for Isaac and the twenty other recipients, then it's worth fighting for."

"Talk to me about what it's done for these people. Help me remember why I'm fighting this battle, because in the last few days it's gotten pretty foggy."

About that time, the whistle blew and the band prepared to enter the field for the pre-game show. Ray didn't reply right away, but after a pause, suggested, "What if we get ourselves something to eat—I think better with fuel in the tank."

"No, I'm good, you go ahead. Rita, you want anything?"

"I brought my drink; I'm good."

"I'll be right back." Ray spoke intently, "Morgan, we're going to get through this. Hang tight for a minute."

"No problem."

When Ray returned, he carried an armload of goodies for all three of them. He figured it would help lighten their mood to enjoy the game with some food. "My treat, to celebrate Isaac's journey to the playoffs!"

Morgan and Rita smiled and graciously accepted some of Ray's generous offerings. Rita agreed, "This *is* worth celebrating. It's been a tough year for Wichita Collegiate."

Still loaded with boxes of stadium food, Ray begged for help so he could return to his seat without spilling everything on the way down. "Hey Morgan, take a few more things. I got plenty for all of us and I don't want it all dumped on the ground! Consider it dinner."

Thanking Ray for the dinner, Morgan took a few more boxes from Ray's arms so he could safely get comfortable while the cheerleaders continued to pose and clap to the music coming from the field.

As Ray adjusted, making sure the food was well distributed, Morgan looked at the contents of the box in his lap, and seeing nachos had a flashback to a day many, many years ago:

"I'm looking forward to the football game we'll watch him play in about ten years. Mark your calendar; we'll eat nachos at halftime."

A chill ran down his spine and he looked at Ray to discern whether the déjà vu had hit him as well. So far, there had been no apparent remembrance.

This moment is a dream fulfilled, he thought. It was a ten-year-old goal come true, even though its realization had come about—almost unnoticed—as part of the regular routine of life.

"Ray,"

"Yeah?"

"We're eating nachos at halftime."

Ray turned, and his eyes met Morgan's stare. As a flood of awareness and emotion crept over him, Ray replied, "You're right. We're eating nachos at halftime, and Isaac's playing guard!" Rita couldn't help but notice the two men, whose behavior had gone from amazed grins to profound laughter.

"What's going on?"

As Morgan's demeanor sobered, he carefully explained, "Rita, one of the reasons I thought of the device was because Ray painted a powerful image for me ten years ago of Isaac playing football for WCS, and of us eating nachos at halftime."

"*Really.*" She stated incredulously. Her eyes widened and she chuckled a bit as she shoved an unruly curl back under her knit cap. "That's *so* cool."

Ray nudged Morgan bringing them back to the present. "Now, you've got to come up with $4.5 million? So, the $250,000 deal I negotiated with Solaris last night doesn't quite cut the mustard."

"Not quite, Ray."

"Look at these nachos. Look at how far we've come. Look at Isaac, playing for WCS. Morgan, your thoughts become things. I don't care if we come up with the money or not; that's not the point here. It doesn't even matter if the company folds, because that's not the point here, either."

"Then, what's the point?" Morgan exclaimed.

"The *point* is the *reason* we do what we do! That's the portal to genius: a reason! The point has always been nachos at halftime! Don't you see? You have a son who nearly died playing football with Kip—it had to happen—because of—nachos at halftime! Ray held up the remnants of the half-eaten nachos like a prized trophy, his words rushed with excitement as the autumn breeze swirled around them.

Remember how his collapse made the surgery possible without ruining you financially? You have a revolutionary device that is only a hair-breadth away from saving thousands of lives and extending the length of thousands more, because of *nachos at halftime*! He looked at the food in his hands and let out a bark of surprised laughter. *How could this be so simple?*

The wind kicked up a notch, ruffling their hair and flapping the lapels of Morgan's jacket, but his eyes, bright with understanding, stayed fixed on his friend. Ray leaned forward, his words tumbling out in a rush, "It wasn't enough that you wanted to see him well, you had to be clear on what 'seeing him well' really looked like, long term! So, if everything we did was, in a way, to enjoy nachos at halftime *today*, and if all the inspiration, breakthroughs, resources, solutions, and *miracles* came because of *this*," displaying the nachos like they were gilded, and looking for the right word he continued, "this '*super food*', then what do we intend to experience ten years from NOW? The solutions have always come when there was a reason that held power for us! We've got to get crystal clear about the *reason* for the $4.5 million dollars! And when we *do*, everything we need will begin to line up again!"

Morgan shook his head in amazement and disbelief as he sat back against the stadium chair. He admitted to himself that the reason he went to work each day was not because he had been driven by a cause that held power for him. No, the business thrived primarily because of the passion Ray had brought to it.

No wonder I haven't been able to derive a solution. I would not have been the one entitled to it, until I tuned in to a higher frequency of thought, discussing possibilities with someone like Ray who does not think from a place of scarcity, who recognizes a purpose bigger than the problem, and who has no fear of short-term potential failure. Why did it take me so long to realize how badly I needed his outside perspective? Without telling Ray about the problem—someone who is committed to the cause no matter what, how could he have ever helped?

He felt a bubble of excitement rise up and expand his chest, filling it with the crisp fall air. With new hope that there may yet be a victory to enjoy after all, he jumped from his seat and began cheering on Isaac with the exuberance of a child.

Instantly he was grateful that Rita had encouraged him to swallow some pride and be authentic with Ray. This was facilitating much more progress than just "looking good and being well composed" had ever produced.

"So, what do we intend to experience ten years from *now*?" Ray finally interrupted his thoughts, "How about filet mignon at intermission this time—at an off-Broadway dinner theater?" The three of them laughed out loud and began to brainstorm with enthusiasm the anticipated details of the future lives together.

"No, how about Hasenpfeffer in Odenthal?" Morgan countered.

"*Hassen-what*?" Ray raised his eyebrows.

Rita leaned over Morgan's lap, "Oh yeah! Hasenpfeffer. It's a traditional German rabbit stew, and you won't find it any better than at a little place in Odenthal, on the outskirts of Dusseldorf. I was there as a foreign exchange student, and Morgan has heard me talk about it for as long as he's known me." Rita got lost in the memory, "I wonder if that little restaurant's still there…."

Ray liked the thought of taking such an interesting trip. "Hasenpfeffer it is. Odenthal—ten years! How about we visit some of our European valve recipients and have them show us around? Let us see what they've been able to enjoy and accomplish, thanks to the device. How about *that*?"

Morgan took a deep breath and let the blustery autumn air fill his lungs. "I can't think of a more wonderful way to enjoy Europe, through the eyes of someone who is just grateful to be alive."

With that, the group sat back in thoughtful silence and with renewed energy, returned their gaze to the team members on the field charging toward the end zone.

13

EVIDENCE OF FUNDS

"Richard!" Felicity followed Matthew and continued to call for her husband.

"Dad-dy! Daddy, daddy, daddy!" Matthew sang, "I'm gonna find you!" Matthew climbed up on a large boulder and turned his head. "There he is, Mommy! I did it! I found him!"

Felicity ran to catch up with Matthew and sure enough, she saw Richard resting under the tree against the rock.

"Is he asleep, Mom? Is that why he couldn't hear us?"

"Yes, Matthew." Felicity was confident. They approached him and Felicity gently shook his shoulder. "Richard, honey, it's time to wake up."

Richard mumbled in his sleep, "Oh, thanks, but I already found a paper...."

"Richard, it's Felicity." Her eyes were moist.

Richard opened his eyes and blinked a few times. He looked at Felicity and then at Matthew and tears of joy came to his own eyes. "Honey, it's good to see you."

Felicity held his face and spoke softly, "Richard, I'm so sorry about what happened and how I acted. I'm grateful for you, Richard, and if nothing were to ever change, I'll be happy enough to just be with you."

"Felicity," he beamed. "Everything is going to be okay. I know for a fact that everything is going to be just fine. Do you realize we have all we need to live abundantly and share a lot!? We're gonna be wealthy!"

Felicity pulled back with a perplexed look in her eyes. "How on earth is that going to happen?"

"I have no idea, but I know where to start. Felicity, what we want, wants us!"

"You know, Rich, it's gonna take a miracle."

"Yeah? Well, Felicity, I happen to believe in miracles."

Only a moment later and about thirty miles away, Ray swallowed another bite and announced to his friend, *"Wait a minute—I just had an amazing idea."*

Morgan turned, curiously awaiting the explanation of this "amazing idea". With his twinkling eyes fixed on Morgan, Ray tipped his head and gathered his thoughts.

Morgan returned the strange look and questioned, "What's that goofy look for?"

Ray's peculiar amusement remained and a warm smile spread across his face. Finally, he said, "It's so simple. It's been right under your nose this whole time."

"What? What's been under my nose? What is it?"

Ray shook his head, with a glint in his eye, as he processed the realization that had hit him so abruptly. "You don't have to come up with the money by Wednesday!"

"Uh, yes, I do."

"No, all this *really* requires is the board see *evidence* of the funds. Don't you see? You could show it to them in less than ten minutes."

"What are you talking about? I can't show it to them if I don't have it."

"But you DO. You already have *all you need* right now."

Morgan glanced at Rita to see if he was the only one not comprehending this revelation. She looked back at Morgan and shrugged her shoulders.

Turning to Ray again he raised his eyebrows as if to say, "I'm waiting...."

"Morgan, how effective is your workforce?"

Morgan didn't answer. His gears were turning but he wasn't quite sure where this was going.

Ray pointed at the WCS team playing on the field. "See those guys? Their coach has an intention to win this playoff, right?"

"Sure."

"And for the last hour, he's observed the opponent and the problems they create for his team, right?"

"Okay...."

"So, after identifying the problems the other team causes, does he go to the NFL rosters and look for some hall of famers to come fight his battle?"

"No, of course not."

"What does he do?"

"He draws from his existing team and arranges them in the most strategic way he can."

"Right. He looks to what he already has, focuses on the objective, and determines the best combinations he can create from the lineup and plays, to match or exceed the effectiveness of the opponent's composition on the field."

Morgan shifted in his seat and sighed, "I think you've lost me."

"Morgan, you've got a problem, just like the coach. You've been hoping for some huge windfall—outside of your present resources, which is like waiting for a hall of famer to come join a game he has business playing. In truth, you already have all you need, because you already have a team to draw from. There are plenty of hidden resources, right under your nose."

Morgan thought about Ray's words, trying to interpret the meaning of his metaphor. Uncertain whether he was on the right track, he timidly wondered out loud, "Layoffs?"

"Morgan, we've done so well for so many years you haven't stopped to really assess the impact of those relatively few individuals who are a drain on the company. Finding ourselves in a pinch like this is exactly what is needed to force us—YOU—to look at your team and reevaluate your strategy."

Morgan shook his head. He felt sick.

Ray continued, "The opponent is ready to take the title and your valves will disappear into oblivion unless you're willing to consider another game plan." Ray paused, showing sensitivity to Morgan's concerns and giving his friend space to think it through.

Morgan sat back against the hard stadium seat and wondered why this hadn't occurred to him in the first place. He had come up from the ranks to become president and during those years he had worked closely with so many individuals in the plant. He was part of them; they were part of him. He considered many of them to be part of his own family.

He felt a cold nip in the air and noticed a dark cloud blowing in from the east as he remembered the employees from the cafeteria.

He knew there were those who were unappreciative of their jobs, were emotionally divested, and were unintentionally bringing the company down, thus, hindering his ability to carry the valves into the end zone and save lives.

He hadn't wanted to see it before, but now the need had arisen and strangely enough, so had an unexpected solution: *Restructuring*.

14

NEVER SO HANDSOME

After his dream in the woods, Felicity had never heard Richard talk so optimistically about their future and wondered if she herself was dreaming. "Richard, what in the world has happened to you?"

He hesitated, grasping for adequate words to convey the journey he had just traveled. As Richard spoke of the impact of each bizarre encounter with those on the path, and explained how he had learned to find and catch rabbits—and even get them to follow him—Felicity's interest faded into skepticism. "Rabbits? What are you *talking* about?"

"Felicity, just trust me. I'll explain as we go. I need to write a book; I'll call it *The Jackrabbit Factor*."

Laughing, she did a double take to see if he was serious. "Oh, so now you're going to be an author?" Seeing he was not kidding, she tempered her levity and turned her head, fixing her eyes on his and furrowing her brows. "You really mean that, don't you?"

"You have no idea what just happened to me; I'm not the same person I was when I left."

"That's becoming apparent." Felicity liked where this was going but had no idea what it meant. If what she sensed was true, she believed they may have just turned a significant corner and were on a new path to something wonderful. *I hope this change isn't temporary. Look at that fire in his eyes; he's never looked so handsome!*

As they walked back to the house, Richard's words and demeanor continued to exude confidence. Felicity had to know, "What does this mean for our future, Richard?"

"Everything's going to work out like never before, I just know it," he promised with confidence. These final remarks as they paused at the screen door put a smile on her face and a hopeful glint in her eye.

15

HONOR THE SPARK

The emergency Executive Committee meeting was called first thing Monday morning, and Morgan mustered the courage to speak matter-of-factly, having decided ahead of time he would not be flustered by the myriad of responses from those who were learning about the trouble for the first time.

The concerned looks on their faces expressed varying degrees of heaviness; after all, their livelihoods were at stake. Some handled it cool-headedly while others reacted with bitter accusations under their breaths that certain people at the company must be to blame.

Naturally the committee members had already been aware of—and were eager supporters of—the heart valve project, but the sudden deadline and firm ultimatum was the unexpected blow nobody seemed quite ready to hear.

Through a tense debate, it was concluded that for the company to survive, they had no other choice but to let a certain percentage of the employees go. For those who remained, there would be pay cuts, even for the committee members.

After the group dissipated, Morgan was left alone with Ray. Ray stood by the window and Morgan tilted back in his chair and took a deep, cleansing breath. Finally, he spoke: "I hope I'm doing the right thing; I think we're actually going to pull through. I just wish there was some way to do this without putting people in a tough spot."

Ray smiled, "Remember: Hasenpfeffer in Odenthal."

"Yeah, but hasenpfeffer anywhere is not reason enough to hack these employee's salaries."

"I know, Morgan. This isn't about hasenpfeffer; it just represents the ultimate reason for doing what we must do. We're not cutting salaries for hasenpfeffer; we're restructuring to carry the valves into the end zone." He continued, "You know what drives me? The eyes. All those eyes in the stadium from my dream after Isaac's surgery. Those were real people, Morgan. Somewhere they're out there, needing this valve. When it all comes down to it, it's more important we offer life, than pay more than necessary for certain people to keep jobs they aren't doing anyway. If cutting back here allows someone else to live long enough to raise their kid, don't you think it's the right thing?"

"I suppose."

"And those who suffer will ultimately be okay. They'll adjust or find something else, or they'll reinvent themselves and find something they're more capable of doing and becoming." Ray stood, pushed back his chair, and planted his palms on the table. Even as angst filled the room, his tall form was still. "I believe," he continued calmly, "in the human spirit. There is a divine spark inside of each person that can be fanned to a flame if it doesn't remain hidden under complacency or dependency on external forces. It's there, and sometimes it takes a shake-up before it can be discovered. Remember? You thought *your* life was over when you had to take a new path away from medical school. If you hadn't been forced to do that, you wouldn't have been led to work with devices and understand them well enough to come up with something to save Isaac. What seems 'bad' always has something good to be found in it, and the people who suffer will have the choice to find the good or not. It's within *their* realm of control to decide how they will respond. I choose to believe in these people."

"I suppose," Morgan replied quietly.

"You don't need to agonize about this. It will all work out just as it should."

That night Morgan couldn't sleep. It was all he could do to keep his mind on the *purpose* for the cutbacks. He thought about Isaac and tried to imagine the future recipients, and the families who would be affected if he failed to do the hard thing.

But then he thought about the families who would be presently affected by the cutbacks. These were families he knew, faces he could see. People he had laughed with at the company picnics and Christmas parties.

How can I possibly have more loyalty for families I've never met, than for the families I've associated with all these years?

Ray's voice was in his head. He could hear the words in his mind as clearly as if Ray was delivering them himself:

"What's your passion, Morgan? Are you in this business to provide jobs? Is that your purpose? Or are the jobs there to support a bigger purpose? The bigger purpose, Morgan, is to save lives, and to honor the spark of genius delivered through you ten years ago. Don't let that spark die, Morgan." His heart clenched as the truth of the words ran through him. *"Honor it. Don't forget the exhilaration we felt after*

Isaac's surgery—the compelling desire to offer the same relief and joy for others who experience what you've been through."

Morgan got lost in the memory of those early days. He relived the moment when Ray had returned from surgery with the news of their victory. He replayed the family excursions they had enjoyed with Isaac over the past decade. And he envisioned the stadium Ray had described from his dream, full of all the people who would be impacted by their victory. Adrift in his thoughts, Morgan Stillwater finally fell peacefully asleep.

On Tuesday morning, with just one day to go before the Simmons people were expected to come knocking, Morgan awoke with a contradictory blend of agony and hopefulness. "At least," he thought, "the process has begun." He imagined his team in the huddle the day before, and today engaging in the strategic play. He knew what he needed to do, and he had weakly come to terms with it.

In his heart, he said a prayer for those in his company who would be hurt the most from this shakeup. *Please help them adjust, or find a better, more profitable job, so they can ultimately be grateful that we had to initiate these changes....*

16

DRAGON SLAYER

Richard, on the other hand, awoke that morning full of enthusiasm and excitement for life. Remembering his words, "I happen to believe in miracles" and the feeling that accompanied them, he *knew without a doubt* something wonderful was about to happen. "Felicity, this is a perfect day. Let's kneel and give thanks for all God has done for us."

"Perfect? It's hardly begun."

"Yes, it's going to be a perfect day; I can feel it."

Felicity agreed, so they knelt and Richard expressed heartfelt thanks for their home and family, his job, and the love they had for each other. The impact from his experience in the woods had not worn off, so for the time being, Felicity felt lighter, too.

After standing again, he described with enthusiasm the beautiful home they would live in, in the suburbs of Wichita closer to work. He particularly favored Andover where the schools had a reputation for being among the best. Felicity allowed herself to be carried away in the moment, and together they enjoyed the manicured landscaping in their minds, and the playground they'd create in the back yard for Matthew and other children they may have.

His passion was contagious. Felicity fixed him an extra special breakfast and prepared his lunch to send him on his way to "slay the dragons."

She had no idea how their dream would happen, but Richard made it clear the first thing they must do is become resolved about the desired outcome, and feel it as though it was already theirs. He convinced her that doing so would have some kind of influence on people and situations in the world around them, until ultimately everything would come together on their behalf, and all they wanted would become their reality.

The whole idea of it fascinated Felicity as Richard described how it worked and why. Put into words from his perspective made it easy for her to understand, and inspired her to participate in the process. If hope is a poor man's bread, she had never before enjoyed such a feast. She felt as though she were floating six inches off the ground. Life was good; they were successful, because Richard's words helped her *feel* successful!

As Richard approached the plant that morning, he looked at it with new eyes. A wave of gratitude washed over him that at least *he had work*. He thought of all the people in the world who didn't have jobs, and while it wasn't his favorite thing to be doing, at least he had one. Though not quite sufficient, it supported his family while he could begin his search for a way to create a better life.

Making his way to the side entrance, he approached the door and entered the security code. A series of beeps sounded, but the door refused to open. Initially, the feeling of upset toward the janitor began to build, but he caught himself, and instead, chose to be grateful he'd get just a little more exercise that day.

Maybe this delay will be the reason I get to talk to someone who has an answer; maybe I'll meet someone who has an idea that'll lead me to the solutions we're seeking.

He was certain he was now—finally—a student who was ready for the teacher to appear, and he eagerly watched for the right one to show up. Somewhere in his world was someone who would mentor him, and help him to achieve his goals. The way it worked had been so clearly illustrated in his dream; when individuals seek to advance, and come to the end of all they know and understand, a teacher appears to help them get to the next level. He looked forward to it.

So now that he had made a firm commitment to achieve the goals outlined with Felicity, and now that he was at the end of all he knew to do, he had no doubts the right person would show up to help him get to the next level. He just didn't know where that person would come from, how long it would take to recognize him or her, or how that person would show up in real life.

At the cattle gates, he was cheerful and personable to everyone. He was committed to maintaining a positive, expectant attitude and keeping the images in mind of the outcomes he intended to pursue and achieve. He thought *that* would be the best way to remain receptive to the unseen influence, which would direct him unconsciously to do or say the right things. That would be important, he believed, so he would be ready to receive all the resources he needed as they came.

Arriving at his workstation, he organized some papers that were strewn across his desk and took a few minutes to spruce things up. He noticed his sack lunch on the corner and it made him smile, remembering that even though he envisioned catching a "rabbit," (a goal worthy of his focus and energy), the "sandwich in the bag," (his meager paycheck) was sufficient to keep him going another day, and he was grateful.

His work environment had become a little more important to him, and he thought it would be a tremendous idea to add some inspiring images to the dividers and wall next to his desk. He found some images in an old magazine in his drawer that he believed would inspire him to stay focused and think positively about where he and Felicity were headed. After tearing a few of them out, he carefully folded the edges straight and pinned them on the tiny bulletin board fixed to his right side cubicle wall.

Within the hour, his supervisor arrived at his workstation, and he didn't look cheerful. "Richard, I need to give you this." He handed Richard a paper and then continued, "I'm sorry."

Richard looked it over and his heart sank. Across the top of the slip was the company letterhead and a letter addressed to Richard A. Goodman—a little too formal for an invitation to a company picnic. He read:

"Due to an unforeseen financial deficit within the company, and a broad review of individual performance according to documented supervisor feedback over the previous year, it is our regret to inform you it has become necessary to cut your monthly salary by 25% effective immediately. Details and additional restructuring measures will be discussed at a company meeting today at 11:00 am in the cafeteria. Attendance is mandatory by all day-shift workers." It was signed, *Morgan Stillwater, President.*

Richard felt his face drain of blood and he looked to his supervisor for an explanation. Confused, he said, "Jeff, *what* supervisor feedback?"

"Honestly, Richard, I don't know. I've never submitted anything derogatory, but when I challenged them on it, they said there's something in there from Morgan Stillwater himself. I'm really sorry."

"What? I've never even talked to the man!"

Jeff shrugged—keeping his shoulders lifted longer than customary to not treat the blow dismissively. Finally, he reached out, gave Richard a squeeze on the arm, and returned to his post.

Richard sat bewildered. Remembering his conversation with Felicity on Saturday, his mind was in a spin. *"I thought everything was supposed to go BETTER when we dream, imagine, and design our life. Not worse! What the heck am I going to tell Felicity?"*

He began to picture the conversation, and the argument that would probably ensue, based on years of patterns which had become well established in their marriage. He pictured her saying, "I knew it was too good to be true," and imagined her chalking this setback up to additional evidence that he was still the deadbeat she had long since determined he was.

He felt sick and closed his eyes, sliding down and resting his head on the back of the chair. To lull his mind in the agony, he twisted the chair side to side, trying to gather his thoughts. *"What am I going to do?"*

As soon as he opened his eyes, however, he found himself facing one of the images he had posted on his wall: a house in Andover, and a playground for Matthew. Gazing upon these images interrupted the doomed thought-train, stopping it in its tracks.

While the picture replaced the image of Felicity's disdain in his mind, it didn't shift his *mindset* immediately, but at least it got his attention. Had he really been determined to make it happen? He wondered. He wondered if he had the mental stamina to hold the image in his mind, an image contrary to appearances, long enough for their dreams to be realized.

He imagined Randy Mollup from his journey on Friday, and could hear a reminder in his head, *"Visualize the outcome, and the right people will do the right things to help it happen...."*

He found himself talking back to the memory of Randy's voice. "But I did, and this *isn't* the outcome I visualized!"

"...Express gratitude and get excited because it means something better is on its way, or it isn't what you would have wanted after all, or it isn't yet the right time. It's all good, and thinking so will help attract as much good to yourself and your family as you are capable of enjoying."

Richard took a deep breath, pursed his lips together and exhaled forcefully, puffing his cheeks. He next imagined Andy Zauff, also from his Friday journey, telling him, *"When you go as far as you can go, and reach what appears to be a roadblock, that is where you must expect to find the way around it."*

Determined to keep his forward momentum, Richard made a decision. *This doesn't matter. This cutback has nothing to do with my ability to win. I still choose to believe.* And with that, Richard took a few moments to remember the images he and Felicity had painted in their minds over the weekend.

He imagined pulling up to their house in Andover, and parking the car in front of the walkway. Brick was stacked decoratively around the mailbox at the edge of their property. Opening the back door of their new, rugged vehicle, he lifted Matthew out and set him down on the sidewalk at his feet. Felicity climbed out of the front seat, radiant. Reaching for her hand, and holding Matthew's, the three of them walked up the steps and then Richard pushed open the heavy, tall wooden door which flaunted a beveled, decorative glass inlay.

As the door opened, he could see beyond the breezeway through the back slider window to the grassy knolls in the back yard with the massive fort, swing and slide contraption Matthew couldn't wait to conquer, climb and claim his own.

"Hey, meeting time." Jeff's voice interrupted the daydream, and though he felt disappointed to be yanked from that wonderful place and brought back to a drearier experience, Richard nevertheless had renewed commitment to *somehow* turn lemons into lemonade. He stood resolutely, pushed his chair under his desk, and followed his supervisor to the cafeteria.

This was the first time he had ever seen the company attempt to address the entire day shift at the same time. There was a shortage of chairs, so the lunch tables had been pushed to the back and employees were invited to sit on them. Some remained standing around the edges of the room and everyone murmured with apprehension for what was coming.

Morgan Stillwater took the podium that had been carried in previously from the smaller, adjacent meeting room. He tested the microphone and after a piercing whine, he tapped it twice and said, "Is this working? Okay, great." After a moment, while he appeared to be gathering strength, he continued, "I'd like to thank you for joining us today. I'm sure you're wondering what this is all about; some of you have probably heard some things that may or may not be true. I'm here to set the record straight, explain the situation, and help you understand what it all means to you."

The people in the cafeteria were quiet. Morgan had their attention, and the fading color in his face indicated a wave of adrenaline had just surged through his body.

His humble tone carried more than just words. Morgan's authenticity captivated and calmed the anxious minds of those who listened. Even though the news was unpleasant, his delivery appeared to be void of ego or excuse. It became obvious to Richard that the man who stood before him was not greedy. He was a real man with a tremendous responsibility, like a captain willing to go down with the ship if that's what needed to happen.

Morgan gripped the podium and took a deep breath. Using his usual football jargon, he painted a vivid picture of the company mission so those who had only ever come for the paycheck could begin to feel the importance of the broader cause. He reviewed the history of the company and described the events surrounding the development of the valve. Richard deduced that until this moment, many, if not most of the employees, had no previous interest in what significant events had been taking place in the offices of their plant.

The room was quiet. There was a long, emotional pause, and Morgan turned his face to the wall at his right. Isaac stood there, red-faced and brimming with emotion, leaning coolly out of the way. Morgan raised his eyebrows slightly, as if to ask, "You okay?"

Isaac tipped his head down and blinked a confirmation. Then he quietly pushed off the wall and made his way to the front.

Morgan stretched his arm toward Isaac as he approached the front. "This is my son, Isaac. I want you to meet the young man who was my inspiration for the valve in the first place."

There was a rush of whispers, as some of the employees appeared shocked that a teenager was about to address them at a company-re-structuring meeting. Richard relaxed as if he had been drawn into the Stillwater family living room, in contrast to the more sterile, threatening atmosphere of the factory.

Isaac wasn't eloquent, but he did speak from his heart. His words effectively brought a deeper meaning to the work that was performed there, day in and day out.

Richard scanned the faces of his coworkers in the room. Many appeared thoughtful, as if a strange new sense of purpose had come over them, and Richard predicted that their menial tasks would feel more significant, and of greater value than they had previously realized.

Richard also saw the bigger picture, and had a growing feeling the company had something important to do; and if it could just get through this predicament, it would flourish. Without question, the long-term prospects would be tremendous for the entire organization, if they could just hold it together through this final playoff.

Morgan returned to the microphone and regretfully explained that while pay cuts were a temporary fix, to keep the cause alive, the company would also have to let up to 20% of their workforce go. He extended an opportunity that if anyone was willing to leave voluntarily, a modest severance package was available. "If you feel this is a viable option for you, please speak with Human Resources before you leave."

Richard listened and was tempted to look around the crowded room and roughly calculate his odds of being let go. His mind returned to Jeff's words that the president himself had made a negative remark in his file. *What did I ever do to him?* He looked to the guy sitting at his right. *If they had to choose from the two of us, I wonder which one they'd keep?*

Taking notice of his thoughts, he sat up straight, and stretched his back. He forced himself to tune out and reject the details that caused feelings of scarcity. *There's more than enough for everyone. I choose to believe,* he repeated to himself. *There is no competition. There has to be something good that can come out of this.*

He had trouble comprehending how these mantras could possibly be true, but he *relied* on them to be, and reiterated in his mind the affirmation: *when I have a choice, I choose to believe.*

Mr. Stillwater continued, but Richard had already tuned him

out. His gears were turning as he searched resolutely for an idea that would allow him to come out on top, despite all the existing evidence of impending doom.

He thought, *There are about 600 people in the room, and 20% of them will probably be out of work by the end of the week. I've already been pegged as a slacker, and even if I stay, my salary is now 25% less than what we could barely live on before. And I still have to break the news to Felicity. Her belief in me is already so fragile....*

With these facts stacked against him, it was all he could do to keep from suffocating from anxiety. *Breathe, Richard. Breathe....*

The extra oxygen to his brain had a relaxing effect and opened a way for him to look for an upside to what he had to work with. *What I do have going for me is a dream, and the determination to find a way to accomplish it.*

But that's about it.

With just that much, and with a question solidly anchored in the forefront of his mind, waiting for and expecting an answer, Richard wondered: *What do I have to offer that would make them want to keep me, and even allow me to serve in a more important capacity?*

Such a bold question would have never even crossed his mind, except his recent choice of counter-intuitive thoughts had all the right ingredients for producing an ingenious idea. Remaining tenaciously hopeful despite the odds, he was prepared for it when it came, taking him by surprise.

The number seventeen flashed in his mind, and he wondered where it had come from, and what it meant (if it meant anything). His gears continued to turn until he finally identified a connection between that figure and a file folder that also popped into his head labeled Financials. Piecing it all together, the potential solution gradually came into focus like a Polaroid.

Then he saw a flash of light illuminating a few more details in full color—but just as suddenly, they vanished again. After pondering the images for a moment—long enough to become completely conscious, but short enough to avert potential misgivings—Richard jumped to his feet and threw up his hand.

Morgan's face showed alarm and the interruption halted his message, mid-sentence. Richard's energy was commanding and Morgan couldn't ignore it. "Uh, yes?"

Richard spoke loudly enough for everyone to hear. "I have a retirement account with about seventeen-thousand dollars in it. If I give it to the company, can I stay on and have partial ownership?"

Immediately the blood rushed to his face and he wondered where in the world those words had come from. He coached himself to breath, rejected the fear, and chose to believe he had nothing to lose. *Be strong, Richard, stand firm! You have nothing to lose by asking!*

Morgan was speechless. He turned to his Chief Financial Officer sitting at his side, whose eyes widened, but who didn't offer any on-the-spot counsel.

Another man stood, "I have nine-thousand, I'd like a piece of the company, too."

Morgan left the podium and leaned over to confer with the CFO again and a few other officers who sat in a short line next to him.

"I have twelve!" Another man announced.

Employees continued to interject one-by-one until they began to stand in clusters, individuals bravely declaring their offer. When the commotion settled, there were more than *two hundred employees* standing.

Not everyone was enthusiastic about the idea. Those standing only represented a minority, but it was enough to shift the direction of the meeting off its predicted course.

Richard could hear the critics. One lady muttered under her breath, "Pshh. Like I'm going to give up my retirement for these executives."

One man leaned to his friend and said, "How do you even know if you have a 401K?"

Another said, "Is it legal to use the money before you retire? How does that work?"

Someone else said, "How do you know how much money you've got?"

In a room with six hundred people, every possible reaction was represented.

Finally, Morgan returned to the podium and asked those who stood to stay in the room, while those who remained seated were invited to return to their workstations.

After about ten minutes of clamor, everyone remaining found a seat. During the shuffle, Morgan instructed the department heads to pass out blank half-sheets of paper.

Once everyone had a sheet, he returned to the microphone and said with feeling, "Thank you, for sharing our vision for this company, for the good it can and WILL do for families across the world. You're part of a movement. We appreciate the gesture and are pleased to explore the possibilities it may offer. Please put your name at the top of your paper, with your employee ID. Beneath your name, state the amount of money you are potentially willing to contribute in exchange for preferred stock in the company. Then pass it to a supervisor, so we may review the numbers and determine whether this is a viable option. Submitting this information does not commit you, nor the company, to such an agreement now. Thank you."

There was new energy that lifted all who remained in the room. A few were tearful, shaken by the upset, but also present was a tremendous sensation of fulfillment for being a potential part of the solution.

As the crowd dispersed, several fellow employees slapped Richard on the back, and he realized he had never experienced anything like this before. It felt amazing to have been a catalyst for change that would positively impact others.

Smiles of gratitude passed between the employees, thanking each other for making such an interesting solution possible at all.

Richard's mind immediately projected forward to a hopeful vision of Felicity being awestruck that he had finally faced and conquered his first big dragon. However, the image was unusually difficult to hold with any degree of clarity. Something wasn't right. Despite his premonition that all was *not* well on the home front, he assured himself Felicity would be nothing but fascinated by his part in this courageous battle that had just been won.

17

BIG NEWS

That evening, Richard came through the door of his home beaming with pride and with a glint of gratitude in his eyes. Felicity sensed something good, and greeted him with a smile. "So, what's up, handsome?"

"Oh, you would *not believe* what an amazing day I've had!"

Felicity didn't know what to expect, but his enthusiasm was infectious. "Try me!" she blurted.

Richard took her elbow and pulled her from the entryway. Both plopped down on the low profile avocado green couch, and Matthew ran in and started climbing on his back. Looking over his shoulder, he ruffled Matthew's hair and said, "Hey, sport!"

Felicity's patience was wearing thin. "Richard! Get on with it! What's the big news?"

As he quietly retraced the events of the day in his mind, something dawned on him. "Actually, the day didn't start out all that great." The look on his face went from excited to perplexed as he thoughtfully continued, "I got to my workstation and Jeff brought me a letter that said my paycheck was getting cut 25%, and..."

With a jerk of her head, Felicity's face turned red and her eyes flamed. "What? What did you just say?"

Richard smiled and shook his head, "No, wait—it's all good—just let me finish."

Felicity was no longer enthusiastic, but on-guard, and prepared to scrutinize everything else he had to say from this point forward. She sat back and folded her arms until Matthew climbed onto her lap requiring her to move them out of the way.

"So, I was all stressed and confused, wondering why the principles weren't working. I never expected things to get *worse* when goals were set, but then I stopped and remembered I had to think contrary to appearances, and I decided we could still achieve our goals, and the setback was something I could turn around, somehow. But I didn't have any clue how to do it. All I could do was hold the images of life the way we want it on the screen of my mind and trust somehow it was changing *me*, so I could respond the right way."

"Mm, hmmm," Felicity tempered her reaction and waited for more details.

"And then we ended up in a company-wide meeting where the management said they *were* in trouble just like I thought, and the workforce was going to be cut by up to 20%. But then, as I forced myself to expect a solution, and refused to get all worked up like most everyone else in the room, I had a thought and it made me jump up and offer our retirement for a piece of the company!" Richard beamed like a puppy dog that had just proudly eliminated in his master's slippers.

Felicity was stunned. She wasn't sure she heard right, because she couldn't fathom how any of this information could possibly be anything but disastrous. Finally, she spoke: "Wait a minute. You did *what*? You gave them our *retirement*?"

Hesitant, Richard replied, "No, not yet, but—I'm sorry—I left out the details that would have explained the reason *why* this is such a good idea." The rest of his comments were spoken more to himself than to his wife, and he felt there was something deep and unexpected rising to the surface of his consciousness. "You know nothing of the company vision, and how *moved* I felt to support their cause. You know nothing about the images I've put up around my workstation, or how they inspired my actions..."

Felicity's eyebrows were raised, as she leaned in and waited for a better explanation, already having decided one couldn't possibly exist. All she could see was that things had started out bad, and then had progressively become worse. They hadn't just lost 25% of their income; they also lost their whole retirement in one fell swoop. This man had inconceivably given it up voluntarily, and to top it off, he was proud of himself for doing it. She concluded he must be insane.

Before Richard had a chance to find the words to put her mind at ease, she blurted, "Tell me this. How do you see this playing out? You're giving up all you've worked and saved for; by putting it into someone else's company to help *someone else* get their dream. Where does that leave us? Richard, this is madness!"

Little Matthew sat quietly on her lap, touching her cheek as if he hoped his tender caresses could help her feel better and calm down. She knew that was what he was trying to do; after all, she had many times utilized the technique with him herself.

"Felicity, they explained what their company mission is. And I *get* it. I am proud to be a part of their cause and feel like I should do whatever I can to help them succeed. I imagine helping them succeed and I believe the success will spill over into our lives, too."

"Great. So where are we going to get what we need to pay *our* bills while you're gallivanting around in their business?"

Richard's head was already shaking before the words finally began to flow. "Felicity, I'm sorry, but I'm done listening to you gripe. I've finally spotted a rabbit, and if you think all this barking and jumping is insane, so be it. You obviously don't see the rabbit. But it's there, and I'm not going to let this one get away. I've got to do what I need to do to provide for this family."

Shocked by the sudden edge in his voice, Felicity didn't know quite how to respond. He had never stood up to her like this before, and she didn't know whether she liked or *hated* the spark she saw in him now.

Richard finally broke the silence. "You know what, Felicity? *I love you.* I'm sorry this doesn't make sense; that's my fault for not explaining it better. But there's no question in my mind I'm doing the right thing. Everything is going to be okay—I'm not sure how, but I can *feel* it."

His decisiveness reminded her of the day she found him in the woods. He had been so confident, so assuring. As crazy as it all seemed, his certainty in this moment also had a strengthening effect on her. She wanted to believe, but she was afraid of yet another let-down. Closing her eyes, she took a deep breath and exhaled slowly. "I think you're insane, Richard. I can only hope you're doing the right thing."

"You know what's so disappointing here? I thought you'd be proud of me for dodging a lay-off today. I guess that was just too much to hope for."

Before falling asleep that night, Felicity pulled out her journal. She hadn't really touched it since their engagement, but now she felt she had nowhere else to turn. In the past, talking to her family had only tainted his reputation with his in-laws (damage not easily undone), and talking to her friends had never accomplished anything except making her feel angrier.

Felicity *wanted* to feel good about him. She wanted to be an unconditionally loving, constantly supportive wife, but didn't know what else to do with the angst that consumed her. She hoped that expressing herself in writing would help clear the heavy, dark clouds away from her heart:

I just don't know what to do. I think he's flipped his lid, and I'm worried. Maybe I'll just have to take things into my own hands, but how? What am I supposed to do, get a job or something? What about Matthew? How bad does it have to get before he wakes up to this insanity? How can he be so irresponsible? It's intolerable! Maybe I need to just go find a way to bring in some extra money, or I seriously fear we may never get out of this mess.

Exhausted, she closed the book. Gently she laid her cheek on her pillow, pulled the comforter next to her face and gazed out the side window. Freely giving release to a buildup of tears, she silently pleaded, *Please dear God; take me out of this nightmare.*

18

TEMPORARY REPRIEVE

First thing Wednesday morning, the leadership reconvened in the boardroom to receive the report from the accountants who had stayed late crunching numbers the night before. The CFO gathered the final count and reviewed the report quietly while the other committee members held their breath. When he was finished, he pressed his lips together and shook his head. Everyone in the room leaned forward, eager to hear the outcome. Rather than opening his mouth to hastily state the result, he offered meaning and context around the numbers:

"We have 253 submissions here, representing 8.4% of the company. The average balance in each retirement plan is a little more than $19,000. With the penalties they will pay from those funds, we would receive nearly $17,000 per person, yielding $4,265,000. That's only $235,000 shy of the $4.5 million needed."

Ray piped in, "And I just landed the Solaris deal on syringes—$250,000."

The room erupted with cheers and clapping, and Morgan called in his secretary, smiling at her as she arrived. "Linda, please make an appointment for me to speak with Edward Phillips on the phone." He turned to his CFO and said, "I need you to check with our attorney—make sure we do this properly."

"Sure thing."

Before his secretary was out of sight, he called to her again. "And Linda?" Linda grabbed the doorframe and spun around, raising her eyebrows and leaning her ear toward Morgan. "Find out who that was," he continued, "the first man to stand and offer his retirement at the meeting."

"Yes, sir."

Ray beamed in the glory of victory, until a moment later when a wave of sobriety flowed through him. "Morgan—I think it's important we still take a good look at the current workforce. I feel like this resolution is just a temporary gift—one that should not be taken for granted. We have a serious responsibility to preserve the good health of the entity. It's been given an extension, but we could blow it if we don't learn the lessons this near-failure has taught us."

"What do you mean?"

"I mean, remember how this crisis forced us to step back and evaluate the effectiveness and efficiency of the workforce? I think that awakening really needed to happen. Until the crisis, we had become careless and unaware of the efficiency of our staff. Remember, we're not in business for the sole purpose of providing jobs—the jobs are a *byproduct* of our purpose. Just because we've 'found' enough money to keep going in the short term, that doesn't mean it's the wisest thing to keep the current staff."

One man across the table piped in, "I agree. I think a small reduction in workforce may still be necessary. They're expecting one anyway. Besides, the better we do, the stronger foundation we lay, and the more people we'll be able to employ in the long run—and for long term."

"But what about the company morale?" another committee member wondered. "It could do more damage overall, letting people go, than it might cost to just keep the less productive workers."

An older gentleman spoke from his chair, "Yeah, you've got to think about the tradition of this company—we don't lay people off. We never have."

A younger man piped in, "Hey, there are no sacred cows here. We have to do what's responsible, even if it ruffles some feathers."

A woman interjected, "And company morale can suffer anyway, if you keep an employee around who isn't doing what they've been hired to do."

Again, Morgan was sickened by the thought of letting workers go, and a little disappointed that the relief and joy of this victory were so quickly replaced by a reminder of heavier matters. But he had come too close to losing the game. In his mind, he vowed to do the right thing—no matter how hard it would be—to fulfill the purpose for which he and Ray had worked all these years. He thought about hasenpfeffer in Odenthal, and visiting with survivors who lived because he did the hard thing *today*.

Finally, he spoke: "We're not out of the woods until the valves are on the market saving lives, and the company is profitable and solid. You're right, Ray, it's our stewardship and responsibility to be wiser than we've been in the past. Certainly, we don't need to reduce our workforce by 20% as we originally thought. In fact, I don't want it to be a pre-determined percentage at all. We're not looking for a certain amount of revenue to reclaim anymore, anyway. We just need our efficiency and productivity to be at its maximum." After a thoughtful pause, he resolutely tapped one finger on the table four or five times for emphasis, then continued: "So here's what I want to do: let's have the managers take a good look at their teams and find potential holes in productivity. Bring 'em in for a pow-wow. Give these folks a chance to improve their game before we issue a *single* pink slip."

Morgan was relieved and somewhat surprised when everyone nodded in agreement that it was the most sensible thing to do.

He continued, "And if anyone does need to be let go, let's real-locate *those* salaries and give a raise to those who remain—so we build or at least *preserve* some company morale through this. We must remember our people are the real assets in this company. We couldn't do what we do without them."

Turning to a woman from Human Resources at the far end of the large conference table, he posed a final request. "Betty, make sure that as we review employee performance, we're careful to be legal in how we deal with those who may be falling short. Ladies and gentlemen, I think enough has been said for one meeting."

Betty nodded and made a note in her planner.

Just then, the CFO appeared in the doorway and announced, "Spoke with the attorney, we're all compliant."

"Excellent. Thank you," Morgan replied.

As the meeting adjourned, Morgan expelled a cleansing breath. Ray stood, squeezed his shoulder and leaning in, whispered, "Only one more play to go, and it's a touchdown, man."

"Play?"

"Yeah, Morgan, we're nearly to the end zone." Ray winked, slapped him on the back, and left the boardroom.

Emotional exhaustion threatened to overcome Morgan, but he still had one more critical thing to do. Pushing the intercom on the phone, he checked with Linda, "Do I have an appointment to speak to Ed Phillips?"

"Yes, sir; he's ready as soon as you're ready."

"I'm ready now; just give me a chance to return to my office."

Within minutes, Ed was on the line, and Morgan was pleased to give him the update that the funds had been found, pending proper paperwork, so the deal could be structured legally. There were several pieces that needed to be finalized, of course, but Mr. Phillips seemed convinced that the board would be satisfied enough to proceed. Ed seemed additionally impressed that Morgan had been the one to call, instead of waiting for Ed to initiate their deadline-day conversation. "This shows pro-activity—I'm sure the board will be grateful to get a phone call from me today. I'll let them know right away."

"Thank you, Ed."

"Have a great day, Morgan."

While on her way to the copy room, Linda heard Morgan hang up the phone and leaned into his office, "Mr. Stillwater, about that gentleman from the meeting..."

"Oh, yes. Did you figure out who he was?"

"It's Richard Goodman, from Shipping and Receiving."

"I'd like to meet with him. Will you please send him up to my office? Let's see if we can catch him before he clocks out for the day. I'm dying to ask him a question."

19

AS GOOD AS DONE

Still reeling from the effects of his disconnect with Felicity the evening before, Richard was instantly nervous upon word that he was expected in the office of the president. No company-wide announcement had yet been made regarding the outcome of the board's deliberation, and last he heard there were negative remarks from the president himself in his file.

Richard forced himself to set aside his worries and to think only on the images posted around his workstation. He relied on the hope that keeping them on the screen of his mind and pretending they were part of his reality would somehow put him in the right energy to think on his feet and make the *most* out of whatever was about to happen. Arriving at the secretary's desk, he quietly announced, "I'm Richard Goodman. Mr. Stillwater asked for me?"

Linda pushed the button on her phone and stated, "Mr. Stillwater, Richard Goodman is here."

Morgan's reply came through the speakerphone, "Send him in."

She pointed the way and Richard walked pensively down the hallway behind her desk and into the double doors at the right, which were already propped open for him. Morgan stood and extended his hand. "Richard...."

Shaking his hand Richard replied, "Mr. Stillwater."

"Please sit down."

Richard stepped around two small black chairs to face Morgan who sat in a more impressive high-back leather chair.

The president said nothing for what felt like an eternity. Richard, seeing the blank-faced president and still fearing the worst, tried to keep his composure, but naturally his face exuded concern.

Becoming aware of the furrow in his brow, Richard immediately wiped clean the visual data of the president's face from his mind, and envisioned himself in the den of his new home in Andover. For just that moment, he sat in his own office full of exquisite furniture and imagined Mr. Stillwater visiting *him* in *his office* for a meeting as his equal.

As a result, the concern on his face melted away and was replaced with a joyful glow. Morgan reflected the transformation with a smile.

"Richard, do you have any idea why you're here?"

With the fear set aside, he spoke freely and honestly. "Well, sir, you've either brought me here to lay me off, or to let me take stock in the company. I suppose it could go either way."

Morgan chuckled, "Lay you off?"

"Actually, sir, I believe you want me on board, for the contribution I believe I can make to the cause. I only mentioned the possibility of the layoff because I think there's a derogatory remark in my file. However," he paused, "there must have been some mistake, and I hope it can be resolved." Richard fearlessly held his gaze with the president.

"Ah. Yes." Morgan paused, and then continued, almost unconsciously, just to fill the silence, "I'm sure it was a mistake."

Richard was a little surprised to be spoken to with such respect, but then again, he wasn't. He had felt different all day, simply from exerting mental strength to keep his thoughts solution-oriented, and surprisingly, this conversation was feeling rather "normal." He was proud of himself for speaking confidently, yet without arrogance. It astounded him, when he thought about it, that he could interact so naturally with someone like Mr. Stillwater and for once in his life *not* feel inferior. Somehow, and almost inconceivably, he felt like a peer. "Thank you, sir. But truthfully, the remark, whatever it was, was probably right at the time."

"Oh?"

"Well, I'm not the same person I was even just a week ago. I've come to realize I have the ability to do more than I've been doing, and I am looking for opportunities to achieve and contribute more."

"Richard, you did something incredible yesterday. The effect it had on your coworkers was inspiring. Have you ever held a leadership position?"

"Leadership?" Richard searched his memory for anything he had done that could be considered leadership-like. "Team captain for dodge ball at recess in sixth grade. That's about it." His smile turned to a smirk as he delivered his answer in good humor. Consciously he knew this solitary example wasn't much to be impressed about, but deep down he knew it didn't matter. With a dream and a purpose burning brightly throughout his soul, he had more going for him than anyone with even ten pages of credentials, but who lacked a dream.

"Well, it sounds like perhaps you were just never given the chance. There's something about you that has me really intrigued, but I can't quite put my finger on it. I feel like you need to be doing something different here, and I hoped that having a conversation with you would help me know what that might be. Remind me; where are you now?"

"Shipping and Receiving."

"Do you enjoy it?"

Richard's pause was apparently answer enough, because Morgan immediately continued.

"What are your interests, talents, ambitions? I mean, if you were to create your own position at the company, what would it be?"

Richard leaned back. He hadn't expected a question like that. He knew clearly what he wanted his *lifestyle* to look like, but he hadn't quite identified what service he wanted to perform to achieve it. *Interests? I want people to know what I learned in my dream.* Unsure of how Mr. Stillwater would respond to something so abstract, he chose his words carefully. "I'd like to inspire others to get better results."

"That's interesting. How would you do that?"

"Honestly, I'm not sure. I've decided to write a book, but I'm not sure that's anything that will be useful to your company any time soon."

"A book? About what?"

Now that was a tough question. *How in the world do I sum up what my book's going to explain?* "Well, I suppose it's going to be about getting clear on the reason you do what you do, and how much of an effect it has on the outcome. It's about being on purpose, instead of just jumping and barking at air."

"Jumping and barking?"

Richard chuckled. "I'm sorry—it's from a dream I had. Pursuing a goal without first seeing the outcome in your mind's eye is like a dog jumping and barking at air, thinking the activity alone some- how will produce the jackrabbit it hopes for. In reality, the activity *without* the clear objective in sight tends to repel the object of one's pursuit. I call it the *jackrabbit factor*."

"Hmm. That's deep. Have you started on it yet?"

"No, not yet."

"You know, I'm intrigued by the analogy—it makes me think about some recent conversations I've been in about the company's purpose, and how genius ideas have only ever seemed to show up when we've had a passion for and firm commitment to a purpose. In fact, you know what? I've got someone I'd like you to meet. Ray Golward, VP of Sales, is my long-time friend who actually performed the surgery on my son Isaac about ten years ago."

"Sales? He was a *Surgeon*?" Richard couldn't fathom why a surgeon would ever end up in sales. "Did he lose his practice or something?"

"No, he just found his passion." Leaning forward with his hands clasped together on the desk in front of him, Morgan continued, "I think what you have to share about being clear and on purpose is critical. I think you'll also discover that combining your purpose with doing something you love holds even greater power." Leaning back in his chair he spoke directly. "I'd like to help you discover your passion and see if it can be utilized here in our company. The kind of initiative you showed in that meeting is rare, and I know good blood when I see it. Will you meet me at lunchtime, say 12:30 here tomorrow? I'll have Ray join us; he may have some good ideas. He's been known to have quite a few in the past."

"Wow. I'm not sure what to say. I guess—Thank you, Mr. Stillwater. I'll come back tomorrow at 12:30."

"Please, Richard. Call me Morgan."

Richard stood and shook his hand. Hesitatingly he responded, "Mr.—Morgan. Thank you. See you tomorrow."

"Wait," Morgan pulled a green book from his shelf. "Take this and read it. It'll help you get into the right mindset for this transition."

Richard took the book, raising one eyebrow at the picture of the cow on the front, and he couldn't help but wonder what cows have to do with any of this.

Morgan smiled, "It'll help. Trust me."

Gliding past the receptionist, Richard waited for the doors to close behind him before he allowed his elation to bubble up and spill out through his expression. He romped past some workers, running and sidestepping those in the way, and floated to his corner of the building.

Upon arrival at his workstation, he fell into his chair and spun it around to face the images on his wall. *Surely what has just happened here will finally bring the peace of mind that Felicity needs so desperately.* As if to quote himself from his own dream, he grinned like he had finally caught his first rabbit, and whispered to himself, *"Felicity, I'm coming home."*

20

CONSCIOUS COMPASSION

That night, as he pulled into the driveway, Richard found it difficult to stop thinking about what had transpired on their couch the night before. He really hoped Felicity had had a chance to cool off. Before cutting the engine, he pictured himself putting his head on his pillow that night with a feeling of gratitude, knowing he had communicated his vision well and that somehow, in time perhaps, their relationship would ultimately thrive.

Walking from his car through the evening darkness and taking a deep breath, he turned the knob and pushed the front door open. The yellow bulb above the kitchen table filled the room, spreading a golden glow in all directions. Felicity was somewhere in the back of the house and apparently didn't hear him enter.

"Felicity—I'm home!" Richard called.

The door to the bedroom opened and Felicity came out, obviously forcing her friendly smile. "Welcome home. Matthew is having a late nap. He'll probably be up all night, but he was just so tired he couldn't stay awake beyond 4:30." Leaning a hip on the kitchen counter with her arms folded, she asked politely, "How'd things go today?"

Believing it would be best to ignore the fact that her warmth was obviously artificial, he simply replied, "Progress. Good progress. I feel like my mind is expanding at an incredible rate. I was reading a book during my afternoon break that the president let me borrow, and one part validated that we're on the right track. It said if you need more "financial capital", you have to stop clamoring for the money and focus fearlessly on doing the things that *bring* the money."

"Like what? And what do you mean by 'capital'?"

"You know, 'capital' as in 'resources'."

"Oh, got it."

"So anyway, it said financial capital is always a *by-product* of mental capital and relationship capital. In other words, rather than spending all my time worrying about the money, I should spend my time and energy focused on the other side of the equation."

"How are you supposed to do that?"

"Well the good news is that it's what I've already begun to do without even knowing it. And as crazy as it seems, there's something inside me assuring me that the things I feel like I need to do are exactly the *right* steps to take." Richard stopped and realized he was rambling. Apologetically, he returned to her question. "So, your question was about how I'm supposed to do that. According to this book, I do it by building mental capital—studying the principles I learned in the dream, or by learning a new skill or trade. Education. Investing time and maybe even money in myself is how I build mental capital. I suppose if I were a stock on the stock market, then my value—my ability to command a better income—increases when I build on my knowledge."

"Okay..."

"And then the other part of the formula is 'relationship capital'. That's where I put focus toward building relationships, and seeing where I can make a meaningful contribution to help someone else. See what people need, and look for ways to fill those needs. When you're completely out of ideas on how to *get* more money, staying focused on building mental or relationship capital supposedly keeps you in forward motion and leads you to opportunities that, if taken, will ultimately affect the financial side of the equation. In fact, the author said if you focus too much on the financial side of the equation, quite often it creates a withdrawal on your relationships, and can even result in a neglect of mental capital, and then it's no wonder the money becomes elusive."

Felicity looked thoughtful, and her countenance began to brighten. He could tell she was beginning to adopt his enthusiasm when she finally said, "You know, that reminds me of a story I heard once of a guy during the Great Depression who was looking for work but couldn't find anyone to hire him. But he couldn't stand to be idle, so he went to the railroad line—I think it was part of Roosevelt's Works Progress Administration thing—and he just started helping. He figured, he can either sit around doing nothing for no pay, or he can be useful and help someone for no pay. At least by helping, he felt better about himself as a person. Well, as it turned out, the foreman noticed and questioned him about why he was there and made sure he knew he wasn't on the payroll. The guy responded that it didn't matter; he just wanted to be useful. And then it turned out the foreman liked him so much, he ended up getting the job after all."

"Exactly! That's what I'm talking about. That's what I've been learning. And in fact, that's sort of what I've been trying to do—by offering the retirement fund. Something like your story happened at the plant for *me* today, too."

Felicity did a double take. "What do you mean, 'something like that' happened for you?"

"You remember how I offered our retirement funds, right?"

Her fragile countenance fell again. "How could I forget?"

Again, giving no energy to her jab, he continued, "Turns out that because I did that, more than one hundred employees stepped up and offered the same thing. We all hope the company will get through this pinch, because they're onto something huge. I could see it, as they explained where they've come from, and why they do what they do, and I saw I could help. Well, this afternoon, the president himself called me in, and I thought he was maybe going to let me go, but instead he offered to keep me on and let me *create a position of my own design!*"

Felicity's eyes widened. "Are you serious? I've never heard of such a thing! What did you say? How much are they going to pay you?"

"Actually, we just talked a lot about a bunch of things. I thanked him for his offer, and now I'm supposed to go back for lunch tomorrow and meet his VP of Sales for a brainstorm session or something."

"So, what's it going to *pay?*"

"Felicity, *I don't know*. But this is exactly what I'm talking about. For once in my life I'm not focused on the money and what I can *get*, but instead I'm focused on what I can *give*, and I'm telling you, it's already begun to open doors! It was amazing to be in that office with the president of the company, and literally be treated as an equal. It felt like I belonged. I felt like a valued contributor. I can tell I'm going to learn a lot from him, and probably from this VP guy, too." Richard stopped long enough to review the events of the last two days in his head and then continued, "I went to work the other morning, fully expecting to find a mentor. I thought someone would just show up. I had no idea it would be the president! And it only happened after I got a cut in pay, and after my job was threatened entirely, and after I decided to think contrary to appearances…"

Nodding, Felicity's eyes began to glisten with amazement, and Richard gratefully recognized she was quietly allowing him to continue expressing the flood of thoughts that poured into his mind.

"You know, something else I heard once really stuck with me. It was an Einstein quote that said something like, 'The significant problems we face in life cannot be solved at the same level of thinking we were at when we created them.' It dawned on me that for years we've tried to fix our situation without first gaining more knowledge. No wonder we kept getting the same kinds of results. Now, I'm having the chance to associate with people who think on a completely different plane, and as I learn to think like them, I know I'll be more capable of finding solutions to our financial problems, long term."

Gradually, Felicity's wonderment was replaced with another question. Richard sensed she really didn't want to dampen his zeal by the way she posed it so cautiously: "Richard, honey, this all sounds so wonderful, but we still have bills to pay. Didn't they say *anything* about your salary?"

Richard pursed his lips together and regretfully replied, "No. It didn't come up."

"Is your salary still cut by 25%?"

"I'm not sure."

"So, really, you're telling me you're getting an unknown position doing unknown things; nothing was said about salary increase, and you're really excited about it. You know, Richard, I'm happy for you. But for me, I'm having a hard time with it. I didn't experience the same transformation you experienced in the woods, and just hearing about your dream has not quite been enough to shore me up against the disappointing realities when they show up. It just seems to me it's the normal thing to do: that salary would have been the *first* thing discussed, or at least the most *important* thing brought up before leading the president to believe you would actually go along with it."

Richard was saddened, but couldn't blame her for feeling that way. If he had been in her position, he probably would have had similar trouble understanding his enthusiasm. He had spotted a rabbit and was actively in pursuit. Felicity, however, didn't see the rabbit. That was clear.

Then he remembered the hope of ending the day with putting his head on his pillow, believing their relationship was going to get through this and ultimately flourish. With that choice of thought, it wasn't hard to feel an increased measure of compassion and patience for her and her fears.

Making his way to the couch, and with a gesture inviting her to sit by his side, he maintained his composure. "Honey, I think I understand. I don't blame you for how you feel. I wish I could just show you what I saw in the dream. I know it would help you feel differently."

Felicity remained standing. "Yeah, well, I wasn't there, so how can I be expected to see the good in it without a stitch of monetary evidence?"

Tenderly, he pleaded: "Felicity, I need you to have faith in me. But you know what, whether or not you do, I'll still succeed. I'd just rather you enjoy the journey with me, and not be so worried!"

Felicity was quiet. Finally, she responded delicately, "I really don't want to be negative, but how can I help it when—when you're being so—*impossible?*"

Richard rejected the temptation to strike back. Taking a slow, controlled breath he replied, "I might not have the entire picture, but I know what I need to do in the *moment*, Felicity. There's something inside me driving me to follow where this is leading, and I've never been more at peace with our future."

"But it's never looked scarier."

Richard grinned mischievously. "I know! Isn't it crazy? Felicity, I don't expect you to feel the way I do—although, of course, it would be nice if you did. But I'm convinced there's a direct correlation between the way we choose to think and the results that are going to show up for us. Didn't you say you and Matthew found me in the woods only after choosing to believe everything was okay, even though you had zero evidence that it was true?"

Felicity softened. "I know; you're right; I just have a hard time believing I would be expected—that *anyone* should be expected—to consistently and habitually do something *so difficult* to have a respectable life! How can anyone think something so entirely contrary to overwhelming evidence? Why does it have to be *so hard?*"

"I don't know. Maybe the more we practice, the easier it gets. I can only hope."

Later that night, Felicity pulled out her journal and wrote:

> *I'm still wrestling with my fears that Richard is all talk and no results. I've concluded with certainty that regardless, I'd better start doing something to help with the finances, just in case his plans don't materialize. I*

really want to believe in him, but I need to do some-
thing so my own peace of mind isn't so dependent on
what he does or doesn't do. I can't control his results, so
I've just got to do what I can do. I hate feeling helpless
and upset. It's not fair to him.

Closing the book and setting it on her nightstand, she rolled over and waited for Richard to return from locking the doors and turning off the lights. As he climbed into bed, she hesitated, unsure of how to broach the subject. "Richard, I need to talk to you."

"Okay."

"I think it's amazing what you're doing—I don't understand it, but I can tell you're on purpose, and I like seeing you that way. It's just that I worry about the money. What if I just get a part-time job or something, to help out until your stuff pans out?" She wouldn't have suggested such a thing unless she was sure his self-perception of being a poor provider was gone, but apparently, it was not. His edgy response took her by surprise.

"What? Felicity, to hear you say that feels like a dagger in my gut. What about Matthew? We agreed long ago that it's best for *you* to care for him, not some babysitter! That's what *you* wanted!"

Felicity never intended for her question to cause him pain. Although the idea originally stemmed from her desperate need to have some financial stability, in the moment she was suddenly inspired to spin it in a way that preserved his self-respect. "Richard, your work is going to pay off big, I'm sure of it. We just don't know how long it will take, so just think of this as a temporary season of imbalance. Maybe I could find a job that lets me bring Matthew with me, the way Shannon gets to bring Brittany to the daycare where she works. Then, when things get a little more stable, I'll quit. We can do *anything* for a short period of time, if we know it's temporary, right?"

Richard sighed and shook his head. "I don't like the idea, Felicity."

"Honey, sometimes I go stir crazy around here and wish I had somewhere to go, just to break up the monotony. I miss having adult conversations," Felicity lied. It was true she had felt that way on occasion, but by and large she loved being at home and it made her sick to think about going to work and figuring out what to do with Matthew. She agonized over the time she'd miss with him, but the pain of allowing life to stay the same had finally come to the point of exceeding the pain of change—so she was now ready, and even longing, for that change.

To Felicity, the thought was surprisingly tolerable, but only because she planned for it to only last a short time, and *only* because she knew it would help them get on top of their bills and retire some of their debts. "I need something to change. So, I plan to start looking for something tomorrow. Would you support me in this?"

Richard didn't respond, at least not out loud. She *thought* he had said something, but if he had, she was entirely unable to decipher it. Halfway annoyed at his departure from consciousness, and halfway relieved that the conflict was melting away with his fading presence, Felicity shifted on the creaky bed, causing him to rouse briefly, and squeeze her arm affectionately while slurring the words: "Can we talk about it later?"

Before she could reply, he was sound asleep.

21

CHAMBER OF GENIUS

In the morning Felicity slept in, and as Richard arrived at the plant he thought about their conversation the night before and was uncertain of how it had concluded. He could only hope it had ended on a good note.

At 12:20 pm Richard's stomach had already been grumbling for nearly an hour. He was used to taking his lunch break at 11:00 am and was trying to stay busy to keep from noticing the complaints coming from his stomach. Checking the clock, he closed the folders on his desk and stacked them neatly to the side. Jeff sauntered by and noticed Richard getting ready to leave.

"What's up? Going somewhere?" Jeff wasn't an obnoxiously demanding supervisor, but he clearly prided himself on staying in the know of all that took place under his watch.

"Yeah, actually. Mr. Stillwater is expecting me upstairs in a few minutes."

"Mr. Stillwater? What for?"

"He's asked me to come meet with him and Mr. Golward. Not exactly sure why, but we'll see." Richard downplayed the event, shrugging his shoulders, to avoid the need to explain any further the grand opportunity he knew was developing behind the scenes. He was certain this would result in a vacancy in Jeff's department, but he also felt certain that it wasn't his place, and it wasn't the right time, to disclose that information.

Remembering there had been something derogatory in Richard's file from the president himself, Jeff prepared for a vacancy in the department anyway. Suspecting the meeting would be about his discharge, and not wanting to reveal his knowledge of the probable blow, Jeff downplayed the event with a cool frown and a nod, and casually strolled away from Richard's cubicle.

By the time Richard reached the president's office, Ray and Morgan were already there. They were loading their paper plates with cold sub sandwiches from a six-foot board stationed in the corner on a shallow table.

"Richard! Welcome. Get yourself a plate."

Richard smiled and thanked the president. As he loaded his plate, Morgan introduced the two. "Richard, I'd like you to meet Ray Golward. Ray, Richard Goodman."

Awkwardly shifting a few items out of his right hand and balancing them on the plate in his left, Richard extended his hand to Ray and they exchanged a hearty shake.

"Pleasure to meet you, Richard."

"You too."

"Come sit down," Morgan invited the men to his desk where they both unloaded their food. After everyone was settled, he didn't waste any time getting down to business. "Richard, Ray is the engine behind this company. His vision has carried it through several crises, and I wanted you to share what you explained to me about the—the jackrabbit effect. As VP of sales, I think he may find the analogy helpful with the rest of the sales force."

"Oh, of course, the jackrabbit *factor*," Richard's correction was subtle. Then, feeling relaxed and appreciated in their presence, Richard rehearsed the idea as he had the day before, this time also including an explanation of the circumstances around the revelation, and Ray was noticeably intrigued.

"You know, Richard, I believe I've operated by the principles you've described for years but I've never heard anyone really put them into words. Maybe it's been instinctive for me, I've not been aware others can really struggle to think that way. I can see though, that having a conscious understanding of these concepts would be a tremendous advantage for my sales force. There are men in the sales department who struggle to operate with expectation of success, and as a result, their paychecks are less than what I know is possible for them."

Richard was amazed that his little experience appeared to be valued so genuinely by this incredible person who sat before him.

Ray continued, "Richard, would you be open to teaching a class for my sales force? Take what you learned in your dream—which, was an amazing dream, by the way, totally inspired—and create a course from it? Some people might think this information is unconventional, but experience has taught me that you're right on."

"I—I'm not sure..."

"Well, Richard, I'm in agreement with the president: there's a spark in you that deserves to be fanned into a flame, and I know this company will surely benefit when it happens. One thing I know for sure is that genius ideas show up when you're working on something that holds passion for you. You're clearly passionate about this. If you let yourself believe in the possibilities here, not only will you have tremendous satisfaction in your work, but also, you'll get inspired ideas along the way. It's just how it works; when you're living your purpose, there seems to be an unseen force working for you, more so by far than when you're *not* living your purpose." Ray smiled, "I get the sense that your purpose is *not* shipping and receiving, but teaching."

Morgan piped in, "And, you'd be getting paid to do what you love."

Richard was amused that they seemed to be selling him on the idea—an idea on which he was already sold. However, the comment about getting paid reminded him of Felicity's words the night before, and temporarily shifting the focus of the conversation, he ventured to get more information on the pay—for her benefit.

"Well, sir, actually, things have been a little tense at home because I haven't been able to tell my wife what all these changes will mean to the family. I haven't known what to tell her. Believe me, I see a tremendous opportunity here, and I am *really* excited about it, but, I haven't wanted to jinx anything by bringing up the question of salary, to be honest." Richard was suddenly embarrassed that he had so freely disclosed his thoughts.

"What do you make now, Richard?" Morgan asked.

Richard replied matter-of-factly, "$28,000 per year," then added, "Actually *that*—was last week. I think this week it's down 25%."

Morgan shook his head and replied, "Hmmm. Richard, how much do you *want,* to continue with the company in this new responsibility as, say, a trainer?"

Richard was feeling even more uncomfortable now. He hadn't expected this question and wasn't prepared to reply judiciously. *How much do I need; or how much do I want? How do I possibly put a lid on how much I want? It'd be nice to get enough to pay off all our credit cards in a single month, but certainly that isn't reasonable. What do I say so I don't sound greedy, but so I also don't cut myself short of what it could possibly be? What if I ask too little, and Felicity gets mad? What if I ask too much, and they think I'm off my rocker?*

The long pause eventually became uncomfortable for all three of the men, so Morgan compassionately broke the silence. "Well, Richard, that's not something that has to be decided right away..."

Richard panicked. *But—no! Here's my chance to tell Felicity that I got a raise today!*

Somehow Morgan must have picked up on Richard's concern for Felicity because he promptly continued with, "...So just let your wife know that for now, you've been given a *25% raise.*" Looking embarrassed as if the proposal might have been insulting, he added, "With potential for more. And, when you've had some time to think about your desired base pay, get back with me and we'll talk about it. I think there may even be a way to put you on a sliding scale, based on the results we see in the sales force."

Richard was grateful for the raise, although he was certain it couldn't have represented the maximum it *might* have been, had he felt justified and prepared to ask confidently for more. He determined to take some time before the end of the day to get in the right frame of mind, to pick the right figure, and request it fearlessly.

The sliding scale idea was new and unfamiliar to him. He wasn't sure he liked the idea at all. In a way, it seemed too vague to mean anything, and he was certain Felicity would have suspicions that it was nothing more than the president's way of getting more work out of Richard without imparting additional compensation. Very quickly he determined that for now it would probably be best to just keep that piece of information entirely out of his conversations with Felicity.

Not wanting to be ungrateful, but secretly doubtful that the best possible outcome had been realized, Richard politely agreed. "Yes, thank you Mr. Stillwater. That would be appreciated. I'm sure I'll be ready to speak with you about it again soon."

"So now," Ray jumped in, "let's talk about where to go from here. I recognize it will take you some time to gather your thoughts and prepare the class. Morgan, do you have a quiet spot where he could work? Someplace with the right environment for creation: no interruptions, an inspiring view. I'd like to see something put together—an initial introduction, perhaps—by the beginning of next week."

Richard's mind was in a spin. Life in shipping and receiving had never moved this quickly. *Next week?* His heart started to pound and his face began to feel pale. *Breathe, Richard, you can do this. This is the opportunity you've been waiting for!* Richard knew these changes were good for him and his family, but physically he was feeling ill.

Morgan nodded. "Oh, sure. We've got a room down the hall not far from here. It's got a great view and the fountain is just across the hall—you can hear the water from there."

Ray must have noticed the glaze that had appeared over Richard's eyes because he stopped to ask, "You okay?"

When Richard smiled and nodded to silently convey, "Yeah, of course," Ray assured him: "You're going to do great. I've got a good feeling about this. Just prepare a simple two-hour presentation by next Tuesday, and we'll give these sales guys a recharge."

"Sounds good." Feeling nauseated, Richard forced a smile.

With that, the men stood and Richard realized he hadn't yet had a single bite to eat. The other men's plates were empty except for crumbs, and he wondered at what point during this conversation they had managed to ingest their lunch.

Apparently, the others hadn't noticed the status of his plate either, or they probably wouldn't have rushed him along by standing up and ushering him toward the door. But he felt satisfied that all was just as it should be; he was anxious to get out of there anyway, so he could privately recover from feeling like he was in way over his head. Discreetly he slipped half of the sandwich into his jacket pocket and said, "Where should I go?"

"I'll show you the room. We'll get word to your supervisor of the change so he can delegate your duties to someone else. You can get your things after you see where your new chamber of genius is," Smiling warmly, Morgan slapped Richard's arm and led him down the hall toward his new office.

Weakly, Richard smiled politely at Ray who excused himself to return to his own office. Turning to follow Morgan out of the room, Richard's hearing began to fade and the indistinguishable office chatter started to echo as if coming through a tunnel, while darkness slowly began to close in on his view of the blurring hallway. Feeling sudden peril, he abandoned all pride and feebly and unnoticeably attempted to appeal to the man he was following for rescue. Reaching for the president's arm he slurred something that he himself found inaudible and collapsed to the floor.

At least in the blackness, all was peaceful and his sensation of nausea was finally gone.

22

RELATIONSHIP CAPITAL

That night, Richard came home again to an empty house. "Felicity? You home?"

Upon hearing no answer, he retrieved a tube sock from the bedroom and filled it with ice cubes. Putting it to his head he fell onto the couch and kicked up his feet. As weary as he felt, and as much as his head throbbed, he couldn't prevent the smile from spreading across his face as he thought about the good news he was eager to share with his wife. *I wonder where she is?*

Twenty minutes later, Felicity opened the door and put her purse on the counter. She looked in Richard's direction and her eyes widened. "What happened to you?"

"Where's Matthew?"

"Mom's bringing him home in a little bit. I just got back from the book club. Now, Richard—what happened?"

Still smiling, Richard lied, "I was mugged at the gas station after work."

"What? Are you okay?" Felicity ran to his side and pulled the sock from his head to inspect the wound. "What happened?"

"Oh, a couple guys jumped out of their car and threatened to beat me up if I didn't give them my wallet." Richard didn't really know *why* he was feeling this irresistible urge to take her for a fictional ride, but maybe it was the victory of the day that put him in a playful mood. It became his self-imposed challenge to see how far he could take this with a straight face. "So, of course I told them they couldn't have it."

"Honey! You should have just given it to them! What happened?"

"Well, they were surprised I stood up to them and looked like they didn't know what to do with that, so while they looked at each other like I must be crazy, I took off running."

"You RAN? But there were two of them! What made you think you could get away? Where did you go?"

"I don't know what it was, I just felt like I had to get out of there and I headed toward the street. I figured if I could get across the road I could lose them somewhere in that apartment complex."

"Are you talking about the gas station on Lakeview?"

"Yeah, that one."

"And you ran across the street? That's a busy road!"

"I know; I nearly got hit by a big white church bus. It had to swerve to miss me, and ended up hitting the curb and blowing a tire."

"Richard!"

"I know—but see, the guys were still on my tail so I couldn't stop to help. I disappeared behind one of the dumpsters and just sat there, waiting. I didn't know where they were at this point. But eventually, they ran past and that's when I thought I saw one of them holding a gun in his hand."

Felicity's hands flew up to her mouth and the terror in her eyes was too much. Richard knew he had taken it a step too far, so he quickly added, "But when I looked closer, I realized it wasn't a gun. I don't know what it was, maybe a flashlight or something."

Felicity relaxed, and Richard looked for a suitable conclusion that would somehow put a smile on her face. He wondered, *how can I possibly keep her in a good, playful mood? How can I tell her about my fantastic news, in a way that she can't possibly spin it negatively?*

"Well, then what?" She urged him to continue.

"Well, they just kept going, so when they were out of sight, I made my way back to the gas station. But before I got to the car, a package of frozen baloney came flailing through the sky from the direction of the church bus and it nailed me in the side of the head." Richard remained expressionless and waited for her reaction.

Felicity's eyes remained locked on his, and her mouth seemed ready to say something but nothing came out.

Richard waited, straight-faced.

She scoffed, and smirked at him through narrowed eyes.

He just smiled.

"Baloney?"

"Yes, sweetie, a bunch of baloney."

Felicity stood up with hands on her hips and jaw jutting forward. Finally she huffed, "You're such a jerk."

Richard knew that depending on his response in this moment, the conversation would either turn into one of the most fun and memorable moments of their marriage, or one of the worst evenings in the history of the Goodman family. Carefully choosing his stance and beaming with good humor, he replied, "Guilty as charged."

Scoffing again, Felicity backed up and exclaimed, "I can't believe you just did that! You are *such* a *jerk!*"

Richard just grinned and noticed that as much as she wanted to be angry, she couldn't help but smile back instead. Finally, he spoke, "Felicity, I'm sorry—I couldn't help it. I was just in such a good mood about some things that happened today, I guess my playful side got the best of me."

"Well, how did you get the bump on your head then?"

"I blacked out and hit my head on the wall after the president gave me a scary challenge, a raise, and a new executive-style office."

"You *what*? He *what*? What scary challenge? What raise?"

Felicity seemed to have already forgotten Richard's prank, and with hidden relief for the miraculously smooth transition, he responded, "Yeah, they asked me to do a presentation for their sales team next week—and they're giving me a 25% raise."

"Wow." Felicity sat on the edge of the end table and looked thoughtful. Before long, she grabbed a pencil from the table and started scribbling figures. "Okay, does that mean 25% above your original salary of $28,000 bringing you to...$35,000, or 25% above your salary *after* the 25% cut, which would be something more like...$26,250? Huh," Felicity sneered, "if that's the case, then that isn't a raise at all, and not even back to what it was before!"

Richard's head fell forward and shook from side to side. Bringing it back upright he whined, "Oh, for heaven's sake, Felicity."

"No, I'm serious! How do you know if this is really a raise? What if they're just yanking you around? How much are you really going to be making? It's probably only the $26,250, huh."

No longer interested in trying to keep the conversation positive (since it never seemed to do any good anyway), he faced her squarely, audaciously leaned forward, and frankly declared: "I—don't—know. *Deal with it!*" With that, Richard stormed out of the front door and let it slam behind him.

Watching the door hit the frame and jumping with the sudden crash of some silverware falling into the sink, Felicity began to cry. Running to the bedroom, she pulled out her journal and wrote:

> *Why did I do that? He brings home a "raise" and I can't even offer my congratulations. Why can't I get it right? He needs support, my unconditional love; I'm behaving horribly but I don't know how to "just be okay" with these pathetic announcements of good news, which are never good news at all! AAAARRRRGGGHHH! Am I going crazy? I must be crazy. I don't even know whether I'm angrier with him, or just mad at myself.*

Richard drove toward Andover, trying to pretend his wife was proud of his accomplishments. Before long, he was rolling up to the home they hoped to live in one day. It was amazing how difficult it was to pretend everything was okay when all the evidence pointed to a relationship in serious trouble.

He breathed a heavy sigh. *Something isn't right about trying to imagine this. I can't pretend she's okay—she's NOT okay. She's really struggling, but I just don't know how to help her.*

He pondered the situation for a long time in front of the stranger's house. Refusing to let go of the hope that he and Felicity could be happy together, he rejected the intruding thoughts that pointed to irreversible relationship failure. Fortunately, his desire to be happy was stronger than the temptation to entertain defeat. His determination to win swelled up in his chest and mixed with the residual anger he felt toward Felicity, resulting in a magnified rage of passion toward conquering the dragon that threatened to destroy everything he cared about. The problem? He found it difficult to identify exactly what this intangible dragon was.

Thoughts from a past conversation returned. *Mental capital... relationship capital. I'm building great relationship capital with my boss and the team, but what for, if I have a miserable relationship with my own wife? Is it worth it—to be so focused on my work? Is it right that all I have for Felicity is a seemingly eternal promise that things are going to get better, when no matter how good things get, she keeps finding something wrong with them anyway? What else am I supposed to do?*

Relationship capital, Richard repeated in his mind. Then he admitted it to himself: *I'm in debt. I'm in debt with my most important relationship. I keep thinking my success at work is what will solve my relationship with Felicity—but if I'm in debt with her, and if financial capital is nothing but the byproduct of mental and relationship capital, then I'm really in trouble.*

Richard's thoughts bounced from optimism to discouragement like a birdie in a badminton tournament.

But it isn't like I haven't been trying! I've been bending over backward to make sure Felicity's complaints are satisfied, but no matter what I do, it's never good enough!

Back and forth, Richard argued with himself until well past eleven. There was a strong temptation to end the evening angry, feeling completely justified for how he had spoken to her; but a purer part of him wanted to be able to just cherish her the way she was, even if she didn't cherish him back. No, more accurately it was that purer part of him that wanted to *want* to cherish her the way she was. Deep down, he knew that's exactly what she needed from him, but did he really have it in him to serve it up without condition?

When Richard slipped in the door just before midnight, he stopped at the kitchen counter to write a personal message in a card he picked up on the way home. His time away and feeble efforts to think right had helped it be just a little easier to see Felicity with a small measure of unconditional love, compassion and patience. Ironically, though, buying the card wasn't the *result* of compassionate feelings; it was simply a *choice* that helped him *develop* the compassion he was hoping to feel.

> Dear Felicity,
>
> I'm sorry about tonight. I know you deserve better than this. You're a great mother and a wonderful wife. Thank you for being patient with me. I know I'm not perfect; I'm still a work in progress. Please forgive me for not being more of what you need. I believe in our future—and am sorry it hasn't already arrived. Please just don't give up on me yet.
>
> I love you,
>
> *Richard*

Felicity was already fast asleep, so Richard tucked it under her journal on the nightstand and quietly climbed into bed, counting on the hope that even the smallest, most pathetic gestures would eventually add up to make a difference in their relationship. Something inside told him that patience and compassion were what she needed, but he wasn't sure he was even doing it right.

At the very least, even without a positive response from Felicity, and even without evidence that his gesture would do any good at all, he fell asleep feeling just a little bit better about *himself.*

23

CHOOSING A SALARY

Early in the morning, being careful to not stir Felicity, Richard gathered his things and headed back to work. He felt she needed time to discover the card and think things through on her own, so leaving the issue behind for now, his next task was to figure out how much of a salary he should ask of the president.

Chuckling as he drove, he shrugged and sarcastically muttered out loud, "No big deal. It's just my *marriage* that hangs in the balance, depending on how I do this today."

Feeling the constant burden of the task heavy on his mind, he arrived at his office and collapsed into his chair, burying his head in his hands.

After regaining some emotional composure, he sat up with his mind still full of anxiety. Pulling out a notepad from the top drawer of the desk, he roughly calculated their household expenses, added an extra $300/month for miscellaneous unknowns, and came up with nearly $32,000.

But then he glanced at one of those images on his wall: the one of the gorgeous brick home in the suburbs. He paused to take it in, to fool himself into believing it was his reality. Suddenly $32,000 didn't seem all that big. No longer did it feel like a skyscraper to be looked up to, but like an appliance box to be looked down upon.

He figured the house alone could easily cost an additional $23,000 per year just in mortgage payments. *Holy cow, that's insane!* Recalculating his expenses, the new figure needed would be more than double to $65,000.

$65,000! What would that feel like to see that much in a year? Richard tried it on for size. It wasn't easy, but the more he worked on coming up with an experiential answer to the question, "How would it really *feel?*" the more believable it felt. He was getting good at the imagination thing because he ultimately managed to conclude: *Humph. $65,000 is not that big of a deal.*

He had begun to suspect that in effective goal setting, feeling the victory ahead of time wasn't really the hardest part. He began to realize that the hard part was *holding on to the ideas* long enough for them to materialize *without* kicking them out as preposterous.

But then he thought that perhaps even *harder than that* was taking whatever action steps were required, no matter how scary or absurd, so the success *could* materialize. With his recent experiences at work, he was becoming well acquainted with feelings of discomfort that he suspected might always accompany the process of breaking out of a comfort zone and moving into better conditions.

However, in this case, thinking on the $65,000 was not really a conscious effort to obtain it; it was just a playful exercise of his imagination. He only regarded it as a fantasy. In fact, he had no reason to doubt the image because he had no expectation for it to come true this soon in his career, anyway. That would be for another season to come.

For now, $32,000 was feeling like just the right amount to ask for—to push him out of his comfort zone. It was certainly a step up from the $26,250 he assumed he had since his recent 25% pay cut. With that in mind, he'd be thrilled with thirty-two grand.

Approaching Linda's desk, Richard rubbed his hands together and took a deep breath. Linda looked up and he asked for Mr. Stillwater, assuring her that he was—*sort of*—expected.

"I was supposed to come back when I was ready to answer one of his questions."

She pushed the intercom announcing Richard's arrival, and Mr. Stillwater said, "Send him in."

Richard entered his office and noticed Ray was there, too. "Hey, you feeling better after your fall?"

Smiling sheepishly, he greeted them both with a nod and a "Yes, thank you," and shook their hands. Assuming it was okay to bring up his salary with Ray there, since he had been there when it was discussed before, he sat and began, "I've thought about the salary thing."

Morgan smiled, "Oh? And what have you come up with?"

Ray stepped from the wall where he had been leaning and moved to where he could more easily see Richard's face. In a moment of unexpected anxiety, Richard's face turned pale and his brow suddenly furrowed with concern. "Um, can you excuse me for just a minute?" Putting his finger up and standing from his chair he said, "I'll be right back."

Before the men could ask if he needed help, and without waiting for anyone's permission, Richard disappeared down the hall to the restroom where he barely arrived in time to hurl his partially digested breakfast into the first stall.

As the men uneasily waited for his return, Morgan broke the awkward silence. "You think we need to go check on him?"

Ray replied, "No, I think he's fine. Let's preserve his dignity and give him a little more time. I have to be honest—I'm really enjoying watching Richard peel away his cocoon. That boy is wired for success, and it's only a matter of time before he'll be doing amazing things. You know it, don't you? I get the sense he is a rare and valuable asset to our cause."

Just then Richard returned with an embarrassed grin, and parked himself back in the chair he had left only a few minutes before.

"You okay?" Morgan showed concern.

"Yeah, yeah. Fine." Richard took a deep breath through his nose, so it wouldn't be so obvious he still needed the extra oxygen. Holding resolutely to images of his family life with more freedom, he responded. "I'm ready to talk salary."

"Okay," Morgan patiently waited for Richard to continue.

Nervously, Richard continued. "I've decided to ask for thirty-two..."

There was a long pause, and Morgan and Ray glanced at each other saying nothing.

Richard had trouble reading their blank stares. He had obviously said something off base, but didn't know what. He thought that asking for $32,000 would be a reasonable jump from the $26,000 he thought he had now, but something about their response left him convinced that his proposition must have been out of line.

Morgan raised his eyebrows and looked at the table with a brief chuckle, but still said nothing. Ray simply grinned and nodded politely as if he hoped someone else would be the first to speak.

Have I asked too much? Do they think I've asked too little? Richard was perplexed. Then it hit him. *Maybe my pay cut never took effect! Maybe Felicity was wrong, and my salary was already $35,000! Oh, no! If that's the case, then asking $32,000 makes me look like an idiot!*

At a complete loss for how to recover gracefully from his blunder, suddenly the same audacity that swelled up inside of him during the meeting in the cafeteria returned. Knowing his current salary worked out to be under $20 as an hourly rate, he felt that if he asked for $32 an *hour*, whatever it worked out to be annually, at least it wouldn't be a pay *cut*.

So finally, he relieved everyone in the room by speaking up. The men listened intently as he completed his unfinished request of "thirty-two" with the grammatical modifier, "*...an hour.*"

The men relaxed. Morgan smiled politely and did some quick calculations on a device he pulled out of his pocket. "Thirty-two dollars an hour? That works out to be about sixty-five thousand annually." Ray and Morgan passed an embarrassed glance at one another.

Again, the blood rushed to Richard's face when he realized how audacious his request really was, yet he responded courageously with, "Yes, that's right."

What have I just done? Sixty-five thousand? Breathe, Richard, Breathe! He coached himself.

Morgan replied, "Well, that's a little steep for our company right now, especially until the valves hit the market; but would you be willing to take forty? I realize it's not even close to what you've requested, but we could include in the agreement that if our sales force generates more revenue after taking your training, you could get a percentage—like a commission. Depending on their results, your salary plus commissions could reach as high as seventy thousand or more."

Richard was still spinning from what had just occurred, a little embarrassed for asking so boldly. But with Mr. Stillwater's reaction came tremendous peace and gratitude, because he *had* asked largely, and the achieved results were much better than he originally expected. *Better to shoot for the stars,* he thought, *and hit the moon, than to shoot for the moon and miss it completely!*

"Now, how about you go finish up your preparations for the presentation on Tuesday." Morgan smiled. "We're all looking forward to it."

Richard's elation instantly fell like a ball of lead; there couldn't have been a quicker way to destroy his glorious moment of victory than to remind him of the looming responsibility to now prove he was, indeed, worth the higher compensation.

24

THE COMPANY VACUUM

While the fifteen members of the sales team had been struggling to meet their goals, Richard's exposition at the training on Tuesday convinced them that next quarter's sales *could* literally shoot through the roof, and in fact, *probably would.*

To Richard's gratitude and amazement, the team unanimously agreed that the training was a tremendous success. The elation he felt when it couldn't have been more opposite to how sick and nervous he had felt for the twenty minutes prior to Ray's glowing introduction.

Before leaving the room, Ray patted him on the back. "Richard, you did a tremendous job. I realize it'll be some time before we know what these seeds will yield, but I honestly haven't seen this kind of enthusiasm in the sales force in years. Their energy is better, and that can only be good."

"Thank you, sir; I enjoyed myself so entirely—I can hardly believe it—it almost seems wrong that I get paid to do something I love this much. I wouldn't even call it work."

"I know—that's how I felt when I switched from medicine to valve sales. And remember, if these guys really produce like I think they will, you've got a better paycheck coming than you know."

Richard chuckled, "Funny, I completely forgot about that."

"Let's not go too long before holding another training. I could tell that having just two hours was restrictive; how long would you need to prepare for a full, two-day workshop?"

"Oh, I don't know; maybe by the end of the month I could have something put together."

"Plan on it. We'll get it on the calendar and invite a few more department heads to join us. I think it will filter down and make an impact on the morale of the entire company. This is powerful stuff."

"Thanks, I agree."

Richard spent the next two weeks holed up in his office, organizing his thoughts to come up with a logical structure for the two-day workshop. Most of his time was spent just sitting there, thinking.

Something taunted him: *Who are you to think you can make a difference here? You're overpaid. They're paying you and you're just sitting around. This can't last forever; one day they'll find out you're a fraud and you'll be out on the street. What will Felicity think of you then?*

Fortunately, the wall images placed strategically around his office provided a constant reminder of why he was doing what he was doing. They helped him remember the value of the knowledge he had gained in the woods. He had brought in additional pictures of his family, so his environment would naturally help him focus on the things that kept him inspired and on the things that really mattered.

When doubtful thoughts returned, he focused on one of the images—and answered the question, "What will it feel like, when..."

As before, only a feeling could ever be the answer, so his task of staying focused always translated into feeling passionate about where he expected his life was going. *That* was his toughest work, and it was one of the hardest things he had ever done. Knowing his thoughts and feelings were what would determine his results, his primary objective became *to live in gratitude and continually exercise an active imagination for good.*

He constantly coached himself through each day. *The hardest work happens in the mind. Thinking is the toughest work a man can ever do.* These were the thoughts that kept him feeling worthy of his paycheck. Fortunately, the ideas and words he'd been using to coach himself were easily utilized as workshop content every time he committed those guiding words to paper.

Near the end of the month, Ray peeked around the doorframe. "Hey, man, you ready for tomorrow? Our sales guys are really looking forward to it. They loved your first one."

Richard sighed. "I don't know—I hope so. There's just so much to convey, I'm afraid I might leave something important out, and then only remember it after it's already over."

"Don't worry about that; you'll say just what needs to be said for those who will be there. Relax. Do your best and just trust it's good enough. If you forget to say something, then it probably just didn't need to be said."

Smiling, Richard nodded. The philosophy was believable, based on all he'd learned so far. Whether or not it was true, he chose to believe it, because he knew it would help him stay in the right mental space to be effective with the workshop participants.

When the second workshop was finally behind him, Richard realized that all the agony and turmoil during his preparations had been for naught. Although he wasn't entirely pleased with his performance and wished he had felt a little more comfortable in front of the group, the participants didn't seem to notice and soaked in every bit of information he had to offer with enthusiasm. The information was so unique and empowering they scarcely even noticed the messenger.

Months later, the real measure of their success became obvious when the sales for that quarter turned out to be *double* what they had been in any other quarter since the company began. Mr. Stillwater was particularly amazed, and Richard and Felicity enjoyed a nice performance bonus of a little more than $8,000, just in time for Christmas.

Stopping Richard in the hallway one day, Mr. Stillwater said, "How would you feel about letting *all* of the employees attend your training?"

"What for? They're not in sales. How would that help the company?"

"Company morale. Based on the principles I've been learning by sitting in those trainings, I've concluded that if *everyone* in the company could feel empowered to think and do better, the entire company will *do* better. I'm not sure how it all works, but I believe that the happier the workforce, the more profitable we'll become. I think it has something to do with my stewardship and responsibility. If I can inspire the employees, and help them get what they want, it will come back to me multiplied, don't you think?"

Though he had never seen the principles applied quite this way before, it seemed to make sense. So, Richard consented to train the main body of employees.

The training was received with enthusiasm, and created a buzz among the employees that lingered at the plant for weeks. But rather than doubling or tripling their sales that quarter, the company instead experienced a *mass exodus* of employees, and was struggling to keep up with the work left behind for the employees who remained. They couldn't get good help hired fast enough to keep up with the inexplicable loss of manpower.

"What happened?" Morgan spoke to Ray and the rest of his key leadership. "I thought this training would create *more happiness*, and that it would translate into *more revenue* for the company!"

One of the supervisors spoke up, "Sir, I think I know what happened. Richard did such a good job of helping them feel like they could have whatever kind of life they wanted, they set some goals. As a result, some are finding greater fulfillment in their present position, while others discovered new opportunities that were better suited to them, so they left."

Another supervisor piped in, "I can confirm that, Sir. Quite a few who left my department were really excited to leave. They found something that paid more, or something that was more aligned with what they loved to do. Those who remained seem more focused, and overall production *is* up."

Morgan was baffled. "So, what are *we* supposed to do? One thing's for sure; Richard won't be taking the entire staff through his training again. We can't hire good people fast enough to replace the ones who bail! It's hurting our bottom line because we can't keep up on orders and we're starting to lose some of our larger accounts. The salesmen who are still with us are increasing sales like mad, but now we can't fill the orders fast enough." Morgan was baffled. He wasn't sure whether he should thank Richard, or fire him.

The head of Human Resources spoke up, "I'll get in touch with the local temp agencies and get the positions filled as soon as possible." Cautiously she continued, "Sir, if I may offer my opinion?"

"Go ahead."

"I think you can look at what's happened here as a *good* thing; we've weeded out a few of the people who were not happy. Remember, the training was meant to help the employees be happier and more fulfilled; and although we expected them to be happy and productive *here*, the truth is you accomplished exactly what you intended for those in your stewardship. *They're happier.* And we didn't even have to fire anyone to clear out at least some of the underperformers. Honestly, I think many of them were under-performing because they were simply uninspired. Now that they're inspired, they've found places better suited to them."

She continued, "As for us, you've simply created a vacuum, and since according to Richard, 'nature abhors a vacuum', you can expect nature won't allow us to be without what we need for very long. The right people will come, and the company will be all the better for it in the long run. Frankly, I think Richard deserves to be thanked. In a way, he's made *my* job a whole lot easier, because most of the employees on probation ended up leaving of their own free will!"

Morgan sighed. "You're probably right. Okay, then," he slapped the table, "let's get busy finding the right people. Supervisors: make a list and set the intention to fill your positions with people who have the qualities on that list. If you've forgotten how to set an intention, go talk to Richard. I don't want HR wasting time interviewing anyone without your intentions solidly and effectively in place first. Now, let's go fill the company vacuum."

25

FELICITY'S UNREST

Thrilled about Richard's raise, Felicity enjoyed seeing the bills get paid quickly and completely every month. But old thought-habits returned and prevented her from getting too comfortable with the good fortune. Rather than worrying about where the money would come from to buy groceries, now she worried about how much it was going to take to get into a decent home and eventually retire. So, sadly her concerns remained, and the restlessness she felt to *do something* to help them reach their goals *faster* simply wouldn't leave her alone.

What if something happens to Richard? What if he loses his job? How will we send Matthew to college?

As she actively explored various moneymaking ideas, the sense that she needed to contribute financially kept giving way to her fears of returning to the work world. Her anguish over leaving Matthew in the care of someone else caused her to wrestle with the questions: *Should I go to work? What about Matthew?*

She felt trapped between the habitual fear that enveloped her when new bills showed up, and the anxiety that paralyzed her each time she casually looked for work outside of the home. She hadn't worked a regular job for more than five years and struggled to believe she had any skills worthy of compensation.

Richard's fulfillment in his new career helped him feel peace of mind about Felicity wanting to do something more. "I just want you to feel alive and keep your thoughts in a creative, happy place, too," he told her one Saturday afternoon. "Whatever you need to do, just follow your heart. Matthew needs you to be excited about life."

She was amazed when he stopped responding as if *his* self-worth depended on having her staying home 100% of the time. He instead had begun to encourage her as if he just wanted her happy and fulfilled; and, without either of them knowing how that would be accomplished, his feelings about it at least were no longer in the way. She freely began looking for and chasing a few rabbits of her own.

Reflecting on the card she found on her nightstand many months before, she remembered his note. Her heart was again touched, and she sat on the bed contemplating the remarkable transformation that had been taking place in her husband that year. A piece of her was envious of his happiness and fulfillment. She was confused as to why she could still be so worried about their future, even when he was providing so well. *I should probably just get a job, if for no other reason than having less time to worry about so many things!*

Over the next few months, Felicity explored at least twenty different kinds of jobs. However, before anyone could offer to hire her, she repeatedly decided that none of them seemed quite right.

Am I just too darned picky? What's wrong with me?

She wasn't even sure what she was looking for; but she was undoubtedly restless and feeling a curious urgency to do *something*. If she had any inkling about what she was looking for, she was certain it would have been a whole lot easier to find.

Then one day as she and Matthew walked down Main Street enjoying an ice cream cone together, a dance studio caught her eye that she hadn't really noticed before. The sign in the window said, "Help Wanted" so she decided to go see what they needed.

Matthew tagged along but didn't mind the diversion. Approaching the receptionist's desk, Felicity said, "I'm here about the sign in the window. Are you hiring?"

Smiling, the girl replied, "I'm not sure. But here's an application." The girl behind the desk didn't seem to know much of anything important, so Felicity deduced she was there because she was probably just good at answering the phone cheerfully and taking messages for the boss.

Felicity took the form and thanked the girl. She looked around and was flooded with memories of the lessons she took in her younger days, and of the exhilaration she had always felt from being in the lights when the curtains opened.

That night she wrote in her journal:

> *Something strange happened today; I stopped at a dance studio, and something about it made me feel like I was home. I picked up an application and I am going to turn it in tomorrow. I have no idea where this is going, but I'm kind of excited to find out. The strangest part of it is I'm not even concerned about what it might pay. I just want to be useful, and I feel like I'm supposed to do something there.*
>
> *WOW, I think I'm starting to sound like Richard.*

26

INTERNAL CONFLICT

Over the next two years, Felicity worked at the studio, utilizing skills she had originally developed through her first and only year of college. Her love of dance was rekindled, and she was given ample opportunity to work with the children and even create some of the choreography.

At first, Matthew was allowed to play with toys in the corner for an hour until Grandma got off work and could take him home with her. After that, he was in school and only needed supervision for a few hours by a neighbor friend until she got home.

During the third year, she became pregnant with twin daughters, and it forced her to take an extended leave of absence. Part of her was grateful for a good excuse to step away from the studio, as she continued the internal wrestle about whether she was doing the right thing by working at all. The conflict kept her up at night, but she just couldn't give it up. There was more to be accomplished, and she felt responsible to see it through.

When she was helping the kids at the studio, she felt alive. When she thought of Matthew being at Grandma's or the neighbor's house, she felt sick. *Why do I love being at the studio so much?* It worried her;

she felt guilty for enjoying work and could see how easily mothers could get pulled into careers despite their family's needs. At the studio she felt appreciated, valued, and enjoyed gratification knowing she was adding value to the lives of the youth who learned from her. She compared it to how she felt before taking the job: bored, haggard, and starving for adult interaction.

If motherhood is supposed to bring some of the greatest joys, what am I missing? Why can't I feel this good just being Mom, raising Matthew and taking care of the home?

These questions haunted her. Richard was supportive of whatever conclusions she came to, because frankly, he just wanted a happy wife. In good humor, he often quoted aloud one of his favorite mottos: "*Happy wife, happy life.*"

The time away during her pregnancy was a good opportunity to make sense out of her feelings. While she was on bed rest, she watched some TV to pass the time. One day as she was flipping the channels, she came to an old black and white show and it caught her attention. The wife in the show was picture-perfect, wearing a dress, high heels, and pearls as she dusted the living room. When it was time for dinner, the tablecloth was spread beneath elegant china with complimentary silverware. The family arrived, sat down and praised her for the wonderful dinner spread of mashed potatoes, roast beef, and fresh vegetables from her very own garden.

Felicity remained glued to the episode and watched the son, who was Matthew's age, practicing his piano lessons, and the father being sent off in the morning with a kiss and his briefcase. Of course, by the time hubby left for work, the wife was already gussied up with well-set hair, a light-colored dress, apron, and *high heels*.

Matthew isn't in piano lessons, and I'm a lousy cook. Why is our family so dysfunctional that we can't be like these people on TV? But then, why would I want to wear high heels to clean my house? Who in their right mind would ever put on high heels to do manual labor?

Felicity couldn't take it anymore. She flipped the channel again and came to a documentary about early America. In some ways, she felt like she was finally seeing reality. The women were always busy doing something to keep a functioning household. They worked the fields and even built dwellings with their husbands. There was no lap of luxury, and they appreciated simple things. It seemed so romantic: a different kind of romantic than sending the husband off to work with a kiss in heels at 7:00 am.

What am I supposed to do? How am I supposed to think? Do I hold onto the hope that I might become the domestic goddess I want to be? Or do I throw it away to pursue something else? If I just knew what God really wanted me to do, I'd do it! Why does life have to be so complicated?

Felicity did a lot of soul searching. She looked to her scriptures for guidance she could trust to help her come to a comfortable conclusion. After a heartfelt supplication in prayer, asking for help finding and feeling right about the path that was right for her, she noticed a gratitude journal that her grandmother had given her sitting on the shelf. Letting the journal fall open on the bed, it landed on a page with a message derived from Proverbs thirty-one. Instantly drawn in, she read:

> Who can find a virtuous woman?
> For her price is far above rubies.
> She works willingly with her hands.
> She brings her food from afar.
> She rises while it is yet night,
> And gives meat to her household.
> She considers a field, and buys it.
> With the fruit of her hands she plants a vineyard.

Her merchandise is good,
Her candle goes not out by night.
She stretches out her hand to the poor,
Yea, she reaches forth her hands to the needy.
She makes fine linen, and sells it,
And delivers girdles unto the merchant.
Strength and honor are her clothing,
And she shall rejoice in time to come.
She opens her mouth with wisdom,
And in her tongue is the law of kindness.
She looks well to the ways of her household,
And eats not the bread of idleness.
Her children arise up, and call her blessed,
Her husband also, and he praises her.
Many daughters have done virtuously,
But thou excel them all.
Give her of the fruit of her hands,
And let her own works praise her in the gates.

When she finished, she shut the journal and fell back onto her stack of pillows, stupefied.

Surprised at the heightened awareness that accompanied her new thoughts, she reflected with awe, *women have ALWAYS worked. Since when did it become our culture—or at least my perception of it—to think I'm only a good mother if I'm wearing high heels and dusting the piano all day?* Although she knew her internal sarcasm was an exaggeration of the real issue, her choice of word-thoughts did indeed reflect how impossible her self-expectations had been.

Not completely prepared to draw a solid and final conclusion, her deep-seated expectation remained: that her days should be spent cleaning, cooking, and playing with or teaching her son. But as much as she tried to deny it, something inside persistently compelled her to do more, to make a meaningful contribution to humanity at large.

She spoke out loud in an attempt to bring herself back to her senses, reminding herself of a tenet she valued with all her heart: "Felicity, raising your children *is your contribution* to humanity at large. *The hand that rocks the cradle rules the world.*"

Nothing could make her feel otherwise. Not even scripture. She knew there was always the possibility of interpreting scripture incorrectly anyway. She felt that anything that threatened to change her mind about her role must be regarded as deception meant to undermine her family.

So, if there truly was more for her to learn, she'd do her best to be open-minded, but *only* if it fit well within the parameters of certain standards she already, unquestioningly, believed to be true.

Okay, then, what about this "virtuous woman"? She seems awfully busy and involved in a ton of things, including a lot of activity in the community—for profit. Maybe this is why my soul expands and feels joy when I do those sorts of things, too, and why I feel like I'm withering when I don't. I would expect doing the right thing should bring the sense, or a feeling, that I am, in fact, doing the right thing...

As she pondered the problem, her mind opened to answers she hadn't ever considered before. It was as if someone was speaking to her mind, because the words came clearly and quicker than she could have invented them herself: *Society changed when technology brought time-saving tools like the dishwasher, the washing machine, the automobile; these inventions were inspired and given to humanity to free up time for more meaningful pursuits. What are YOU doing with the time you've been given? Are you feeding the hungry? Clothing the naked? Lifting the hearts of the weary? Helping children discover the worth of their souls?*

The final words struck her heart like a mallet on a huge gong, and the vibrations reverberated through her soul.

Felicity's eyes brimmed with tears. Reviewing her experiences of the past several years, she recalled that she truly did find great joy making a contribution to others, as with her own family. She could feel God's love flowing through her when she would notice the little dancer whose feelings had just been hurt, and when she'd pull her aside to remind her of how special she really was. In fact, she felt the same joy when she'd glance at Matthew in the corner of the studio, and see he was watching her every move, beaming with pride that "Mom" was so engaged with, and admired by the other kids.

Something deep down assured her that by her example Matthew was learning principles of service, production, and contribution. *Maybe I really am being a good mom after all.*

She concluded her interest in dance was perhaps not necessarily a *career*, but it was unquestionably a meaningful *contribution*.

Hers was a family working *together* for a common purpose; and if she conscientiously strived to fill her inborn role as nurturer, she believed that following her own passion would indeed keep her on a good and worthy path. *Why else would God plant this passion for dance in my heart? I feel his love, acceptance, and assurance when I pursue it; it HAS to be part of his plan for me. How could it NOT be?*

During her leave of absence, while maintaining bed rest, Felicity worked on concept and choreography, and developed programs with the primary purpose to draw the best out of the kids and introduce them to their great self-worth. They would learn to be confident and poised, and to have a strong and graceful presence.

Her little girls' arrival infused an even greater drive and passion to create programs that would liberate *their* little spirits, too. She wanted her girls to discover the beauty inside of them, and to rely on their spirits and personalities to help them realize how special and worthwhile they were. The dance programs she developed for these great little souls took on a powerful essence because of the genius ideas that inspired them.

By the time she returned to the studio, Richard was doing well enough that they afforded a mother's helper to care for the twins on site. She was grateful the owner was accommodating; although she worried it might not last. The babies cried most of the time, and eventually she had to change the plan to have the caregiver keep them at home.

Plans change.

In fact, returning to the studio after nearly a year and a half was not what she thought it would be. During those months away, she had concluded it was where she belonged, but upon her return, the glory of serving children was replaced with disgust and frustration. In her absence, a new director had been hired and the programs had taken on a completely different feel. The music to which they danced delivered a heavier beat and brought out exaggerated sassiness, which, according to the parents of the preschoolers enrolled, was nothing but adorable. Compared to how classy the operation had been before, the costumes were tasteless. The movements were suggestive, and Felicity was devastated.

After trying to reason with the owner to make recommendations and express her opinion, the owner replied, "We've never made so much money since we changed our approach. Parents aren't into the classics anymore. They want what's popular."

Felicity's heart fell. She couldn't fathom sending her girls to the studio now. And she couldn't imagine carrying out the owner's expectations under the new program, either. Her passion for teaching inner beauty and self-worth would not survive in that environment, and she finally had to respond with sadness, "I can't do this. I'm sorry—if anything changes and you want me back for what I know I can do for these children, give me a call."

The owner watched her walk out the door and muttered, "Humph; *whatever*," shaking his head and getting back to work.

27

A SCARY OPPORTUNITY

Richard continued to be hot on the rabbit trail: developing his programs, completing his book, and occasionally contracting his services to other local companies in the evenings. The money that came in was spent to pay the bills and improve their lifestyle to an extent, bringing it close to the pictures he had placed on his wall at the office. Except for the house in Andover. Over the years, investing in his mental capital always seemed to take priority over spending the money to afford the house.

This became a source of frustration for both him and Felicity, because he had built a career around helping people get what they want, but after all these years, they still didn't have all *they* wanted. Every time it came to the moment of decision between investing in the home and investing in his career, they repeatedly concluded it was more important to nourish the goose that laid the golden eggs than it was to eat the goose for dinner.

"At what point do we get to start enjoying the fruits of our labors, Richard?"

"When we've made enough, I suppose."

"What's *enough*? When is it ever going to be enough?"

"Honestly, I'm not sure. It's got to feel like the right time, and something inside just keeps telling me to *be patient*."

Felicity sighed. Over the years, she had learned to trust that instinct of his, and in fact, deep down, her own instinct was telling her the same thing.

Then one autumn day Richard received an interesting phone call:

"Richard? It's Charlie Reynolds from Leadership Academy, Inc."

"Yes, what can I do for you?"

"I've been hearing about what you've done for Stillwater Technologies, and I want you to come work for us."

Richard's mouth dropped and nothing came out. He had wanted to do something with Leadership Academy ever since attending one of their trainings (one of those investments that took priority over the move to Andover). Eventually he gathered his wits about him and replied, "Uh, I don't know what to say; what did you have in mind?"

"Well, I'd like to incorporate your materials into our programs, help you get your name out there a little better. I think you know you can only go so far as a trainer in a medical devices plant."

Richard knew he was right; it was something that had been on his mind now for several months. "What are we talking about, salary-wise?"

"Oh, there would be no salary. You'd be paid a percentage of the seminar fees we collect for the classes you teach. It would probably be approximately $15,000 a month for three months. Our company has a good market hold, and we do pretty well at filling the rooms every time."

"Three months? Full time?"

"Right. All our trainers come in as contractors. We're putting these upcoming events together and will probably only need you for the three months, but maybe more, depending on the corporate agenda at that point."

"So, no insurance, no retirement plans..."

"Oh no, you just go get those on your own."

"For three months, that is."

"Right."

"What about after the three months? If I leave my job for a short-term contract, what am I supposed to do when it's over?"

"Richard, I think you need to look at this as an opportunity to take your career to the next level. You've been moonlighting long enough outside of Stillwater Technologies, haven't you? Don't you think it's time to spread your wings a little and go out on your own? You've established an incredible reputation as a speaker, and this opportunity will give you exposure to participants and leaders of other corporations who will be flying in from all over the world. Imagine where it could go from there. If all goes well, we may even have you hold your workshops at our annual conferences in Canada and Southeast Asia."

Richard's mind was racing, and he needed to think it through from all angles. In one sense, it was perfect. In another sense, it was insane. "Can I give you a call next week?"

"I'll look forward to it."

28

HEART PEACE, GUT SICK

"It feels right, Richard. I don't understand it; but it feels kind of exciting. Is that weird?" Felicity stood, bouncing little Sadie gently to help the babe stay asleep against her shoulder.

"I feel the same way. I think it's what I'm supposed to do, but it's only guaranteed for three months. I don't know how *you're* feeling so peaceful about it; you don't go to the studio anymore, and this would mean paying our own insurance and setting aside our own retirement."

"I know; that's why this is so bizarre. Strangely, I feel peace. I think you need to just do it."

"Yeah, I feel the peace in my heart, but I feel sick in my gut. What am I supposed to do with that?" He declared with a sigh.

"Richard, if it feels right in your heart—if you feel the joy you expect to feel from the freedom it could mean when you *consider* it in your heart, then you can also *expect* to feel anxiety on a physical level when you go to take action on it. Remember? You've always taught that the anxiety is often just a physiological response when your subconscious mind is dealing with two contradictory ideas, which have both been accepted as truth. Like accepting 'I am broke' and 'I am wealthy' both as truth, simultaneously. It doesn't know how to handle that, so it simply shows up in the body as anxiety. Actually, the physiological response is just evidence that you're *this close* to claiming the new reality."

Richard chuckled, "You sound like me."

"So, let's just look at the anxiety as a good thing; it often means we're only one more step away from our next big breakthrough."

Smiling, Richard wondered at the transformation that had been taking place in Felicity over the recent years. "Honey, do you know how much I love you?"

Felicity just smiled. Neither of them was completely comfortable with the decision, but their peace of mind and the anticipated possibilities simply overshadowed the scary details. At least they had managed to set aside almost six months of income in savings. Taking the leap was a little more palatable with a small reserve in place.

Richard arrived at work the next day with mixed feelings. He worried about how Ray and Morgan would take the news, and what they would do without him. Would they bring in another trainer? Maybe he could come back as a contractor when the three months was up. Above all, he didn't want to cause any hard feelings or burn any bridges.

Surprisingly, Ray beamed at the news. "Oh, man, this is great! What a tremendous opportunity; you'd be crazy not to take it!"

Richard was perplexed. "You *want* me to go?"

"Heck, of course not; but I always knew this day would come.

You've outgrown us, brother, and it's time to spread your wings and fly!" Ray was uncommonly supportive because his had been a similar transition nearly fifteen years prior, back when he left his own career as a doctor. "You're lucky that the leap you're about to take is doing the *same kind of work*; at least you don't have to switch careers entirely like I did. Either way, when your soul is compelled to a purpose, you've got to go for it!"

"You don't think I'm crazy to give up a secure job with benefits?"

"You know, Richard, we're programmed to believe we're not *good* enough to provide for ourselves, and that security is only available by doing well what we're *told* to do in a job. The truth is, security is best found in following your purpose and believing you will be supported in it and shown the way. That can happen in a job for which you're perfectly suited—like I feel about mine; but if it's not a perfect fit, then maybe there's something better for you to be doing. Have courage. If you're doing what your passion drives you to do, then the fear can rightly be dismissed."

"Why? Why can the fear 'rightly' be dismissed?"

"It's because you'll *know* you're finally and unreservedly magnifying your gifts and making the contribution that you're divinely and uniquely endowed to perform."

Richard was quiet. Life was about to become a daring bold adventure—even more so than it already had been since his dream in the woods. He was nervous about it, but excited at the same time. "What if I fail, Ray? What if I leap into the unknown and end up crashing and burning?"

"Let me share something with you that helped me take the leap fifteen years ago." Ray reached for a book on the shelf behind his desk and opened to a page near the front.

He read aloud:

A little acorn wanted to become all that its blueprint promised it could be. It was meant to become a grand and mighty oak, but for now, it was only a simple nut dangling by a stem.

It hung on the parent tree and reached high, wanting to see the grand views and sweep the vast sky with broad branches. It wanted to experience the fluttering of leaves and the swaying of limbs, but alas, it could barely feel the breeze slowed by the shelter of its protecting parent.

Finally the parent heard its cry and said, "Yes, little seed, I have great plans for you. You will scrape the sky and sway in the wind, and the view will be glorious. You'll provide a home for many creatures, giving shelter and food. Your friends will be many, your influence will be vast, and you'll be great and happy."

The little acorn's heart swelled with excitement as it stretched its rigid shell upward to receive its promised reward, but instead of enjoying the exhilaration of greatness, it was shaken from the tree and took a long, hard fall, landing with nothing more than a slight thud. In fact, there was no apparent compassion or understanding, since its terrible fall seemed to go unnoticed. Its very world seemed to have crashed down, and yet time marched on for everything else around it.

The tiny acorn soon found itself trampled upon, with dirt kicked rudely upon it. Eventually, it was completely buried, in the dark, and alone. "Have you forgotten me??!" He cried, but there was no answer, no explanation, no reprieve. Instead of rescue, the rain began to pour and at once the buried seed believed it just may drown as well.

It tried to throw its weight one way and then the other to force its way out of the ground, or to find its way back to the tree. But nothing changed. It seemed as though it was trapped and could not escape its doom. Weary of the fight, it surrendered to its fate. Holding still with a sigh, the elements around it took notice of its calmed demeanor and began to respond to its mere presence there. In fact, without any more futile struggle, it began to notice there was a subtle change taking place within itself.

It discovered that as it remained calm, it actually ALREADY had all it needed, right there in its immediate environment. It hadn't perished from being cut off from its parent, as it feared it might. Though the fall was frightening and terrible, there it remained, as alive and as well as before.

No, it had not perished. Rather, it had sprouted new parts of itself from within that it didn't even know it could sprout, and the little seed began to experience the joy that always accompanies growth and soul-expansion. Though it hadn't achieved its ultimate goal, it felt good enough just to grow.

After that temporary period of loneliness and fear, soon the seedling broke through the crust of earth and could finally saw the goal again—though it had never appeared to be so far away as it was now.

However, in truth, it had never been closer.

Be patient, little seed; you were created for the great-ness that is in store for you. Allow yourself time to de-velop roots, and keep reaching for the Sun. Trust God, and success is inevitable. All you need to accomplish the goal will be yours in the right time.

Remember: Peace, be still.

Closing the book, he continued, "Richard, you may get to the point of feeling buried and forgotten, but stay calm and don't give up. You were put here to do amazing things; don't shrink from your calling. Do what brings you that deep and profound inner joy. That's God's way of letting you know you're on the right track. Follow that divine inner guidance toward your life's purpose. Trust it—and the money you need will come as you need it; sometimes not as quick as you *think* it should, but always in the right time."

29

VICTOR

5 years later

"Honey, Victor's on the phone and he doesn't sound good," Felicity whispered with her hand over the receiver.

Questioningly he looked at Felicity and reached for the phone. Whispering back, he asked, "My brother? I haven't talked to him since he left for Europe."

Felicity looked worried and leaned against the counter to listen to Richard's half of the conversation.

"Hey, Victor, what's going on? Yeah, I have a minute. You what? Where are you, I'm having a hard time hearing you. Sure. No, that wouldn't be a problem." Richard covered the receiver and whispered to Felicity, "Okay if Victor comes and stays for a few days? Something's wrong."

Felicity nodded, uncertain and worried about the unknown news.

Richard continued speaking with Victor, trying to be cautious and sensitive because he had never known his big brother to be in anguish over anything before. He couldn't imagine what horrible thing might have happened to cause Victor—his invincible big brother Victor—so much grief.

Carefully he asked, "Victor, what happened? Uh, huh." Richard suddenly looked sick and moaned, "Oh, *no*." After a deep breath he continued, "*I am so sorry.* Yes, come to our house. When will you be here? Okay, we'll make a bed ready."

After he hung up, Felicity had to know but was almost afraid to ask. "Richard, *what's wrong?*"

Richard looked at the floor and his face was pale. Finally, he looked up and explained, "There was an accident—Victor was driving too fast and his snowmobile clipped the corner of a stump. His machine flipped into the air, and it collided with Michelle's, with Christopher on the back." Richard was shaking. He could scarcely get the words out as the tears welled up in his eyes, "His wife—and Christopher—they're gone." He convulsed, "It took them both."

Felicity threw her hands to her face and quivering, the tears flowed. "*Oh no!*" Her legs buckled and slowly she sat on the floor burying her face behind her knees. Richard sat with his arm around her, until they managed to regain their composure. Even when the tears flowed no more, the heaviness crushed their hearts and they eventually went quietly to bed for a fitful night of sleep.

Victor's flight arrived late the next day. With the help of the American Embassy, the bodies had been transported on the same flight and were met by a special attendant to be taken to the morgue to await burial.

Victor stayed with Richard and Felicity the rest of the year, because he couldn't deal with being home without his family. The arrangement to be in the company of his brother's family was only supposed to last a week, but he continued grieving and could scarcely pull himself out of bed, and Richard especially couldn't imagine sending him on his way any sooner than he was ready.

Felicity was concerned, too. Behind closed doors, she gingerly asked Richard the questions that wouldn't leave her alone. "Honey, how long will Victor need to stay? Doesn't he need to be going to work or something? Doesn't he still have a mortgage to pay and everything?"

"His business has done well enough that he doesn't have to show up for it all the time. The business partners have been keeping things going during this unscheduled sabbatical. But it won't last forever; he let me know the other day that some of his partners are starting to lose confidence and have redirected certain deals away from his interests, not to mention that some of the client's needs have not been cared for by his team quite as well as when *his* charisma and leadership were holding everything together. Victor's always been the magic in his business. Now, with the magic gone, things are slowly beginning to fall apart."

"I'm trying to be patient, Richard; but it's getting hard having the children's beds in the living room so Victor can have a place to mourn in peace. I'm telling you, that home in Andover is starting to seem less like a dream home and more like a necessity."

"I know. I just don't know what to do about it."

"But maybe it's something worth figuring out?"

That night Felicity's thoughts were recorded in her journal:

...

I really do love Victor; I'm glad we've been able to help, and I feel guilty for thinking this is getting old. I feel bad he's in so much pain; but is he ever going to pull out of it? It's putting the wedge back in my relationship with Richard. I resent this tiny home. I need more space! Even if Victor wasn't here, we're already bursting at the seams with the twins and Matthew.

Dear God, please get us out of this two-bedroom house. Would it be too much to ask for the home in Andover now? It feels like we're coming home every time we drive up to it; it's the same feeling we had before Richard took the leap to Leadership Academy. It's the same feeling you gave me when I stepped into the dance studio. Please give us a better home; if it's not the one in Andover, fine. Just please guide us to the right one for our family—one that won't strap us financially, and please hurry.

She closed her journal and put her head on her pillow. She couldn't get the home out of her mind. *Who are you kidding, Felicity; the home is occupied. It's not even for sale.*

As she lay there, she couldn't tolerate the feeling of helplessness—she had to do something about this. If Richard's work wouldn't make it happen fast enough, she'd have to do something herself.

Glancing to the side, she noticed that on the dresser sat the folder of her dance programs she had created when she carried the twins. They had been collecting dust ever since she walked away from the studio. Her passion for dance had never vanished; she just never quite knew what to do with it.

Determination boiled up from deep reservoirs she didn't know she had. Her life had once again become utterly intolerable, so she resolved then and there to create the change she needed. She sat up, grabbed the folder, and began to thumb through the programs, reminding herself of how inspired she felt when she created them. Grabbing her journal again, she wrote:

I was given these programs for a purpose, and I am determined to put them to use!!

What I need:
A studio
A new home

Felicity paused to contemplate the list and wasn't sure what else to put. There were a lot of things she needed but didn't quite know how to write them so they would hold the kind of power that Richard said was possible. Feeling like she had to do it perfectly, but not knowing what 'perfect' looked like, she put down her pen, rolled off the bed, and fell onto her knees. Taking a deep breath, and trying to imagine there was someone there listening, she prayed:

"Dear Father, I don't know what I'm doing. I know there's a right way to set a goal and some not-so-right-ways to do it, but I get stuck with fear that I'm going to do it wrong and that it won't work." She took a deep breath and sighed. *"All I know is that I need a bigger house. I feel that you want me to do something with these dance programs. I want to help Victor."*

Pausing again, she remembered being a child in church and learning that she needed to express gratitude, and not just complaints. So, she changed her focus long enough to consider the quiet reminder. *"Thank you for all you've done for this family over the years; I know you've been there, helping us along the way. But I've been left wondering whether you still care. Have you forgotten us? Have you abandoned Victor?"*

Felicity stopped talking for a minute because she still didn't feel like she was saying the right things. She sighed again.

"I do believe you're still there. I do believe you care about us, and that you're carrying Victor through this difficult time."

Subtle warmth washed over her, and she felt a confirmation that the words she had just uttered were true. Then after a few quiet moments, the words *"just ask"* came unexpectedly into her mind, and she determined it was just her imagination.

"Just ask." Almost imperceptibly it came again.

She opened her eyes and sat back on her heels. Could God be trying to tell her something? *Am I important enough that God would speak—to me?*

The words didn't return at that point, but the memory of them lingered. She wondered: *would it really be okay to ask such a thing? Could it finally be time that we move into the home of our dreams?*

"Just ask." This time, the barely noticeable, subtle thought took her breath away.

Catching her breath, she sighed, and pictured herself walking to the front door of the home in Andover, holding the key, and pushing open the tall, heavy wood and beveled glass door. She saw herself walking to the kitchen and putting down a bag of groceries. She saw the girls run in and clamor for the contents. Matthew was in the back yard climbing all over the fortress with a neighbor friend. And Richard snuck up from behind, wrapped his arms around her waist and kissed her behind the ear.

She began to cry, and her heart felt as though it would burst. Lips quivering, she closed her eyes again and continued her prayer:

"Oh, Father; I feel your love. I know you are mindful of this family and our needs. I have wanted that house for so long that I struggle to believe it can be ours; but I also feel your invitation to ask. Please help my

unbelief. I'm doing the best I know how and need you to make up the
difference, where I might not be doing this perfectly. As a loving Father,
I believe you can. Now I'm asking—dear Father—will you please—give
us—the house? I can be happy without it, but if it doesn't matter to you,
please grant my request."

Felicity then created an image in her mind of a loving and glorious Father figure, smiling upon her, pleased with her courage and
belief. She was suddenly consumed with a love like nothing she had
ever experienced before, and felt compelled to express one last thing
in a whisper before closing her prayer:

"Thank you for the house."

After a peaceful night's sleep, Felicity awoke with awe at what had
transpired the day before. She felt to keep it sacred and not talk
about it with anyone—at least not yet. She wondered if the witness
she felt had actually happened, but it had left such an imprint on
her heart that it *had* to have been real, and she knew she would
never forget it.

Not knowing exactly how her request would come about, she felt
responsible now to reject all doubtful thoughts that threatened to
derail the process, and do whatever she could think of to help it
happen.

However, the only thing she could think to do was to get
Matthew off to school, load up the twins, and go to the house.
Victor remained asleep in his room with the door closed all day, so
she knew he wouldn't notice or care when she left.

As she approached the house, the feeling of coming home returned, and it put a smile on her face. She had never been inside,

so she could only imagine how nice it would be to spread out and enjoy the space it obviously had to offer.

She set the brake and got out of the car. Walking up to the front door, her heart began to pound. She didn't know why she was there or what she was going to say, but it was something she just had to do. Ringing the doorbell, she glanced back at the girls to make sure they were okay. Just then the door opened and a lovely lady greeted her with a questioning look.

Felicity smiled, "Hi, my name is Felicity—I just wondered if your house might be for sale?"

The lady looked surprised and chuckled a bit. "Actually, we were just talking about that last night. We decided to put it up for sale but it isn't on the market yet."

"You know, I've wanted this house for years, and felt like today was the day I needed to ask about it. I'm not prepared to make you an offer; I don't even know what we could afford. But if there was some way we could work something out," Felicity just shook her head and couldn't find the words to finish her sentence. Her eyes began to fill with tears, and she could no longer see clearly the lady who stood listening to her.

"Well, dear, I don't know what to say; my husband handles these kinds of matters, but I'm sure he'd be happy to visit with you about it."

"I'd like that. Can I come back with my husband to talk with him about it?"

"Certainly."

The ladies exchanged phone numbers and promised to speak again before the weekend.

Felicity returned to her car full of emotion, not entirely sure what just happened, but knowing she had done what she was supposed to do. Now she just had to talk to Richard about it and find a way to buy the house.

30

HOME

It pleased Richard to hear about Felicity's ambition, because he knew she was always happier when she was engaged in a cause. But this ambition also created an instant sense of panic. "Now? Honey, how will we afford a house like that?"

"I don't know, but I know there's a way, and furthermore, I feel like it's where we're supposed to be."

Richard shook his head. "Okay, but here's what we have to work with: I'm not an employee with a predictable monthly income, and my business hasn't been running long enough to show the kind of track record we'd need to get a loan."

"I don't think any of that has to matter."

"Okay then, what do we do?"

"Let's just go talk to them. At least we'll get to see the inside of the house. What could it hurt?"

The meeting was cordial, and the Davenports seemed to be just as glad to meet the Goodmans, as the Goodmans were glad to be inside their house. It was as beautiful as Felicity expected, but not so ostentatious that their kids couldn't be themselves there.

Mr. Davenport explained they had not yet contracted with an agent, so if they were serious about the house, they might be able to make a deal and save some transaction fees. Richard frankly explained the situation with his work, and how even though they *could* narrowly afford the property, they had reservations about using their reserve for a down payment on a house, and they probably wouldn't be able to get a regular bank loan because of his "unemployment."

"What is your line of work?"

"I'm a trainer. I help companies achieve sales goals, and individuals achieve personal goals. And I'm an author."

"An author? What is your book?"

"*The Jackrabbit Factor: Why You Can.*"

Mr. Davenport got a big smile on his face and turned to his wife. She just shook her head, stood up and walked out of the room. Richard thought that was odd until Mr. Davenport explained, "Yes, we know that book. That book is the reason we're moving. Because of what we learned from it, I was finally able to retire and now we're going on a service mission to Africa."

Mrs. Davenport returned with a dog-eared copy of the book and set it in front of Richard. "Would you mind signing it? My kids aren't going to believe we actually met you," her eyes sparkled.

"Richard, what if we did this: let's forget about the bank; your book changed our lives, and I know you'll be good for it. I'd be willing to carry the loan under these terms…" Mr. Davenport scribbled some figures on the paper in front of them. "If you can just put $2000 down and send us $1500 each month until you can secure a regular mortgage for the balance; you can have the house. It's not the going market rate; I'm sure you know we could ask closer to

$2000 per month. But I've been hoping to avoid the headache of getting the home on the market, showing it at odd hours for weeks or months, etc. We're ready to go, and don't want anything else delaying our trip to Africa. All we really need out of the house for the next few years is $1500 a month. Would that work for you?"

Richard and Felicity were speechless. Looking at each other, with that unspoken assurance settling over their minds and hearts that this home had been prepared for them, there was no reason to question it. Felicity nodded, and Richard held out his hand to Mr. Davenport. "You've got a deal."

They shook hands and discussed meeting at the title company to handle the paperwork in the morning. Felicity gave Mrs. Davenport a heartfelt hug and they were on their way.

As they ran down the walkway from the front door, Richard gave Felicity's hand a squeeze. She was struggling to contain her emotion. The thought that this long-awaited dream might be materializing was surreal.

31

MEET THE LAWS

By the time they came home, Victor was watching a movie with Matthew and the twins were still napping. Victor could tell something was up by the way they bounded through the door.

"Hi Vic; thanks for watching the kids. Everything go okay?"

"Yeah, girls slept the whole time. Matt and I had some burritos."

"Vic? How would you like to go for a drive?" Richard felt a sudden urgency to get Victor out of the house. Maybe he'd finally be ready to talk about things, get some of his pain out in the open where it could be faced and dealt with.

Even though the new house would comfortably accommodate his brother, and even though having him move out would mean they'd lose the convenience of that extra on-site guardian, Richard ached to see him happy again. While he couldn't pretend to comprehend Victor's pain, he searched continually for ways to help him discover the joy life still had to offer. At forty-five, he could feasibly live another life just as long as the one he had lived so far. It broke Richard's heart to see his big, heroic brother exist as though he were already dead.

Victor literally hadn't been out of the house more than five or six times that year. But Richard's energy was magnetic and had an uncanny influence on his brother in that moment. Something inside of Victor hungered for the happiness Richard radiated. Surprising everyone in the room, he responded, "Alright."

Victor labored to get up from the low-profile couch that seemed to hold him in its cushy space like a suction cup. Richard extended his arm to help him win the tug-of-war, and after succeeding and turning towards the door, Richard's eyes briefly met Felicity's and widened to say, "Can you believe this?" Felicity just smiled and wished them a good time.

Victor sat in the passenger seat and didn't say anything. Richard put the car into gear and pulled out of the driveway, wondering how to break the ice—or whether he even should.

Finally, he said, "So, what were you watching?"

"Oh, you know, that football movie you guys got last week."

"Matthew's idea?"

"No, mine. I thought it would be a big rowdy sports show."

Richard was silent. He knew the movie delivered a more meaningful message than just the winning of a football game and wondered about the effect it had apparently had on his brother. They sat in silence for another fifteen minutes. Both seemed to be dealing with too many thoughts to know which ones, if any, should be expressed aloud. Richard continued to drive through the countryside and simply let the headlights lead the way.

Surprisingly, Victor was the first to speak. "I was convinced God had abandoned me, that He was angry, or that maybe he just didn't exist at all." There was a long pause. Finally, he continued, "But I've slowly begun to see things differently. That movie—I didn't realize what I was in for. I do know he's there, and that he loves me," Victor shook his head. "But I don't understand it, and I still don't know how I'm going to carry on. I always just thought everything would work out for me. It always has. Everything used to come so easy. Lately, when I've forced myself out of the house to talk to clients or partners, even when I say and do the things I used to say and do, things just fall flat."

Richard was astonished at Victor's open sincerity. He had never heard Victor talk like this before and wasn't sure what was more difficult to bear: the chronic silence of the last twelve months, or these verbal expressions of his deepest struggles. What complicated matters was that Richard felt he could offer some philosophical answers to bring him comfort but wasn't sure they'd be welcome or appreciated.

That is, until Victor shifted in his seat to face Richard more directly. Pleading, Victor begged to know, "Richard, what am I supposed to do with what's happened? Michelle and Christopher were my life. I was stupid. Drove too fast." Victor paused, leaned again into his seat and his chin quivered. Slowly he reiterated, "I was—*so*—*stupid.*"

Richard's own throat tightened and he didn't know what to say. He took a deep breath, and after holding it for a moment, let it escape with the emotion that swelled up from his heart. The message of sorrow and compassion was conveyed without a word.

After another long mile of silence, Victor seemed to feel safe enough to continue. "You know, I used to think everything would go my way, and so it did. Now, I try to regenerate that confidence, and it's just gone. I just don't feel like I deserve happiness anymore. My wife, my son—*are* gone—*because of me.* I think of her family and can't tolerate the thought of facing them again. The funeral—I don't know; I'm just afraid I'll run into one of them, and won't know what to say. I can't give them their daughter back. They've lost their grandson."

"They've tried to reach out to you, Vic. I wish you'd return their calls. They want to heal, too. They know it was an accident. You're still a son to them—seeing you grieve so deeply only reminds them of their loss all the more."

Victor unexpectedly whimpered and quickly cut it short.

"Vic, all those years you did so well, had the world at your feet, *I struggled to believe in myself.* I was envious of your success and wanted to be just like you. Heck, *Felicity* wanted me to be like you."

Victor burst into a chuckle with sudden comic relief.

Richard continued, "I had to take some tough steps to overcome the relentless self-doubt that held me back from the happiness I wanted. It was *not* an easy climb, but I did it; and I know *you* can do it. It wasn't a sudden tragedy like yours that stripped me of my confidence; instead I wrestled with a *lifetime of evidence* that I was no good." Speaking freely, with emphasis he made a daring point: "Honestly, I'm not sure *which* of the two would be harder to conquer."

Victor rubbed his face and rested his hands again on his lap. Without interruption from Victor, Richard felt the need to keep going. "I realize now that *back then* you applied the laws I've been studying without even knowing it. It was natural for you. Your success *was* your evidence and therefore it always bred more success. I'm talking about the success in your business as well as in your family and personal life. You had it all. But you didn't even realize *why.* Now that you're dealing with the accident, you're questioning *for the first time ever* whether you *can* come out on top. Before this, you always knew you would."

Victor spoke softly. "It started with Dad. He taught me—and I didn't recognize its significance. I took it for granted."

"Vic, I don't know everything, but there are a few things I'm *pretty* sure about. First of all, it could be that our personal growth is more important in the long run than anything. The victories are sweetest that come at a great price. Secondly, I believe you'll be with your family again. You know, I kind of look at our trip on this planet like going away to school. In the eternal scheme of things, when all is said and done, I think we'll look back on it and feel like it was a pretty short semester. I think you'll see your family again at the end of it. Thirdly, we haven't been left without a way to understand and cope with the challenges life throws our way. In fact, I think there are more answers than we have room or capacity to receive them. Maybe our heartaches and challenges are nature's way of carving out a place in our heart to make the necessary room. Sometimes it isn't until we have a crisis that we start finally asking the right questions."

Victor's eyes were red and tired. He wanted answers desperately but was afraid the answers would be insufficient to fill the void that sat where his heart belonged. With no hope for real relief, he lacked the strength and desire to do what it would take to find out. "I don't know, Richard; I want to believe I can be happy again, but part of me feels like it'd be a betrayal. I don't deserve to enjoy life—it's my fault these two other precious, innocent people aren't enjoying the lives *they* deserved to live."

"Would you let me share a few thoughts?" Richard spoke softly. "I don't know if it will do any good, but whenever I face heartache or difficulty, I reflect on some things I've learned in the last few years—some ideas—that always help me feel better. They don't always take the pain away, but at least they help me cope with it. Then I find the strength to put just one foot in front of the other, and in time, the pain is always replaced with joy. The more pain I feel, the more glorious the joy tends to be on the other side."

"But, how do you get to the other side? I've nearly forgotten what 'another side' might look like."

"You haven't read my book yet, have you?"

"No," Victor was a little embarrassed, "sorry about that. I've been meaning to get to it."

"Oh, no, Vic. This isn't about me; and really, it's okay with *me* if you never read it. I just wondered what you already knew, so I could know how much to say, and where to start."

"Well, no. I guess I'm sort of starting from ground zero," Victor admitted.

"Okay, then." As Richard struggled to know where to start, he finally relented, "Actually, I *would* recommend starting with the book." Richard smirked, uncomfortable with the self-promotion of his comment since he was still just Vic's baby brother.

Vic chuckled and waved his hand, "We can all take turns learning from each other, little brother."

Richard smiled, "But until you get a chance to read it, I'll tell you about the seven laws. I like to think of them as 'heaven's astonishing help with your money matters'; or, help with *any* kind of difficult matters—for that matter."

Richard's play on words broke a secondary level of tension that had been lingering and they both chuckled. Something about their conversation had been growing increasingly light, replacing the heavy despondency with which they had begun. Finding humor in the little things, they became increasingly comfortable expressing the thoughts and feelings that had been suppressed for so long: Victor's need for understanding, and Richard's desire to remedy it. This occasion of liberating their pent-up thoughts was having a cathartic effect on both of them.

Richard proceeded, "The Universe operates in a lawful way, Vic. Just like with the seasons, and the way the planets move according to a perfect balance of natural laws, our very lives are governed by invisible, natural laws as well. When we live in alignment with them, things go better than when we don't. As with gravity, we don't have to see it or even believe in the law of gravity for it to have an effect on us. Understanding the law, or at least becoming aware of it, allows us to consciously *cooperate* with it, and avoid unnecessary pain."

"Right," Victor agreed so far.

"So, what I discovered is that there are *other* invisible, natural laws governing my life, and so much of my pain in those early years was unnecessary, and went away as soon as I started consciously cooperating with those laws."

Victor was silent and wide-eyed as his brother peeled away the dark film shrouding his mind, one thin layer at a time. Life had finally and effectively created a space in his heart for the answers that would help him know how to live up to his name, but this time, *consciously*.

Richard explained, "I believe God wants you to get answers to your questions, so you can ultimately re-create, in *some* way, *another* life of success, maybe even better than the one you once enjoyed."

Victor shook his head, "I can't accept that. Not where my mind is right now. I can't believe there could possibly exist a life any better than what I had; especially because no matter how good it might be, it would always include the memory of what was lost. My life could *never* be so good that it compensates for the hell that follows me everywhere I go. *Nothing could be that good.*"

Richard didn't reply right away; the lighter mood had vanished again and Victor's pain was beginning to resurface. Unnoticed, the car drifted to the edge of the road where the grooved pavement caused the tires to moan their warning. Gradually correcting his course so as not to alarm his brother, Richard determined to also proceed more cautiously in his conversation with Victor to keep from losing the ground that had been gained in the previous twenty minutes.

Rather than calling attention to the last interaction, he proceeded with the information he thought would help: "The Law of Perpetual Transmutation. That's the first one I should probably mention. Everything: every situation, every event, every object in this world is either coming into form, or moving out of form. Like vapor trans-muting into a cloud and then to rain and ice. At any point along the way, the process can reverse. Not all clouds result in rain. Not all rain turns to ice."

Just then the car passed through a wet spot on the two-lane coun-try road where some water had crossed to the other side. The tires swished over the asphalt and then went silent again.

Victor was nodding, so Richard continued. "When we think of an *idea*, so long as we believe in it, circumstances are shifting; resources are lining up. *The idea-cloud is beginning to gather.* Something unseen orchestrates all the elements necessary for our idea to become reality. As we believe, the processes remain in forward motion. When we begin to doubt, those processes reverse. By our belief, the things we want and need are drawn to us, but of course we must take action to receive them.

"So, if I had an idea..." Victor's head drooped, and he stared his hands. "...an idea about somehow, someway, healing just a little bit..." his voice broke and he swallowed, "I would move closer to that reality?" His gaze lifted to his brother's face. Richard nodded and the brothers let the quiet hum of the car fill the silence.

"The real problem," said Richard, breaking the silence in a gentle voice, "is that we generally are careless with our thoughts, and let them wander, and we change our minds too often. If we could focus with determination on any one particular outcome, and maintain it long enough, we'd succeed. We don't know our thoughts are having any effect on the world around us, so it's easy to wish for something and then give up before the idea has had a chance to fully mature."

In the darkness, between the sporadic street lamps along the wooded road, Richard did not see the road damage before they were already upon it. Their conversation had to wait until the noise beneath them finally subsided nearly a half-mile later.

Victor reflected, "So all those years I did so well, I was cooperating with the law and didn't even know it? I'd set a goal and get to work, and just *know* it would all work out, and it always eventually did. Even when something got in the way, I had nothing but expectation that I'd *ultimately* win. But now, I go to check in with my clients or catch up on issues with my partners, and—I'm practically useless."

"Hm." Richard paused thoughtfully, and then offered an evaluation: "Ever since the tragedy, a piece of you seems to stop the process before it can all come together. You might've set a goal, and had the expectation, but you've been reversing the process every time you saw yourself as undeserving of anything good. Vic, try to be a little *kinder* to yourself; accept the tragedy for the *accident that it was.* What other choice do you have? As hard as it is, it's better to honor their memory with joy than to continue to disintegrate behind a closed door, Vic." Richard was growing bold, and surprisingly, Victor was allowing it.

As the light of the near-full moon gently broke through the

woodland canopy like a strobe light, Richard encouraged him, "Forgive yourself the way you would have forgiven Christopher if *he* had made a terrible, but *unintentional* mistake—and don't allow those self-doubts to interfere. Let the Law of Perpetual Transmutation do what God designed it to do. He always said, 'Ask and ye shall receive.' But he also required that people 'ask in faith, nothing wavering'. I believe he's up there, ready to shower us with the good blessings we desire, but he requires we first pass the test of our faith. We have to believe *long enough* for the law to do its job."

"Actually, Rich, over the last year I've been thinking a lot about what might happen to me if all my money runs out and the business completely dries up."

Richard didn't comment. He let Victor draw his own conclusion about what that could do to his ability to financially endure through this tragedy, in light of the Law of Perpetual Transmutation. Before long, Victor shook his head and groaned, spreading his hand across his forehead.

Richard interrupted his brother's self-loathing. "And then there's Polarity. The Law of Polarity promises that in every adversity is the seed of equal or greater benefit, as Napoleon Hill put it nearly a century ago. I don't think he called it 'polarity' per se, but it's the same concept. So, if something is *just a little bit bad*, then the potential benefit connected to it is only *just a little bit good*. If something is catastrophic, then simultaneously there is contained within it the seed of something equally phenomenal. When you really understand this law, you'll find the people with the greatest challenges are really the 'luckiest' people in the world."

"If they find the benefit, that is."

"Right; *if* they find the benefit. This law only assures the benefit *exists*; it doesn't automatically guarantee the benefit will be realized.

It's our job to find it. It's a conscious choice to go looking. The natural thing to do is to wallow in our misery. The uncommon thing to do is look for a way to turn the setback into an asset of some kind."

"That doesn't sound easy."

"It's not easy, Vic. But that's why the rewards for co-operating with this law can be so extraordinary." Richard continued, "Law of Vibration. Everything in the world is in a state of vibration on a molecular level, including you, including cars, including restaurants, including anything you can think of. Once your vibration is compatible with the frequency of the thing or circumstance you want, then you'll resonate with it and come together. If not, you will repel it. You change your vibration by changing how you feel. You change how you feel by changing your thoughts. If you want to make the sale, you need to see yourself accomplishing it, and let yourself *feel* it as though it had already happened. That's because it's the way you *feel* that determines your vibration. So, if you have more energy on the disaster you're hoping to avoid, than the dream of how you want things to be, then your vibration will repel the success and attract the disaster. The people involved will *not feel right* about doing the things you hope they'll do—and they probably won't even know exactly why. It's a subconscious thing. One analogy that helped me understand this one is that of an acorn. If I hold an acorn in my hand, according to the Law of Perpetual Transmutation, is it in a state of growth, or decay?"

"Decay, because it can't grow without soil."

"Right. It isn't in a compatible vibration with your hand. But in the ground, it naturally begins to resonate with the elements in its immediate surroundings, and bonds with the ones that support its pattern plan. It doesn't have to scramble around, digging and clawing for what it needs, it just holds itself in a vibration and naturally connects to everything in its immediate environment that it needs, one element at a time. We're the same way, Vic. Everything we need is already in our immediate environment: the people, the resources, whatever. But until we change our vibration to be compatible with the vibration of what we want, our life remains as it is."

He continued, "Here's another one: The Law of Relativity. All things that happen in our life are neither good nor bad until we compare them to something else. What happens just is. It is what it is. But then we decide to attach either a positive or negative meaning to what happened, and according to our choice, our vibration is affected. Based on our vibration, we either resonate with, or repel, the things we need. If we struggle to attach a positive meaning to an event, then we use the Law of Relativity to help us see it in a more positive light. I know we're grasping at straws to come up with something to help us see the loss of your family in a positive light, but maybe we instead recognize you could have lost them many years earlier than you did. Or, maybe we can be grateful it happened during a time when you were all creating a wonderful memory, which is better than if you had lost them in the middle of something unpleasant. I don't know, Vic, like I said, I'm grasping. But however we do it, this law guarantees we can put *any* difficulty into a positive light, and in fact, we're expected to."

Richard perceived Victor didn't have words, just an aching heart. He hoped these ideas were bringing comfort like salve, and since Victor looked like he wanted more, Richard kept going.

"Law of Rhythm is pretty useful—*I rely on this one a lot.* Just know with this law that all things in this world are cyclical. The seasons come and go, the tide flows in and out, the sun rises and sets, and so also goes the rhythm of our lives. When things seem bad, this law guarantees an upturn. When we know this, and things are bad, we can begin to watch for evidence that things are improving somehow. Then you can see how the Law of Transmutation facilitates the upswing perhaps a little sooner. 'To everything there is a season,' as the Good Book says, *not permanence*."

"My loss is pretty permanent, Richard. Seems like the Law of Rhythm just doesn't apply to me."

"No, it still applies. It just means you can know you won't have to feel the pain you feel now, forever. One day, your wounds will have healed enough for you to have the capacity for joy again. Sometimes the season can seem to last forever, but it doesn't. It won't. In time, you're going to be okay, so allow yourself to look forward to that day. It's not a question of if there will be potential for joy, but a question of when."

Victor's thoughts turned inward and Richard allowed some time for the ideas to be absorbed.

"You're saying I can expect joy even if I don't deserve it." To Victor the thought was ludicrous.

"You may be more deserving of it than you think. I think the desires of your heart are good, so there's mercy that *can* bridge the gap between who you are and who you wish you were. I've seen amazing things happen when I move forward with nothing more than a *hope* that that's true in my life. But you must rely on that divine power that's bigger than both of us, and just believe. There comes a point when you really have no other choice anyway."

"I'm at that point. If something doesn't change, I feel like I'll self-destruct." Victor leaned his head back on the automobile headrest and rolled it side to side as if it might rock his agony to sleep.

"Law of Cause and Effect. When you make the effort to take a step toward the life you want, the life you want takes a step toward you. Step back, and it steps away as well. A friend of mine once called it a 'cosmic dance'. Sometimes we think it'll take Herculean effort to effect significant changes, so we don't even start; when in reality, it only takes one small, simple step at a time. You don't have to 'go the proverbial distance', you'll only have to go halfway, meeting the success in the middle. Just remember that every effort you make is bringing the things you need a step closer to you, too."

Victor gazed into the distance—although he couldn't see very far—and pondered the significance of what he was learning.

Richard paused, then added, "This law also states that whatever you want more of is what you must give. If you want happiness, then you'll more likely find it by helping someone else be happy. If you want money, you'll more likely find it by developing a spirit of generosity with others." Parenthetically, Richard included one more thought, "Investing in yourself can increase your ability to serve others more extensively."

"So essentially, you're saying, 'if you're not growing, you're decaying'." Victor admitted, "Yeah, I feel like I've been decaying."

Richard nodded understandingly and then went on. "Law of Gestation. All things in nature must evolve over time from seed to fruition. The same is true with our ideas. If we want things to be different in our life, there is a *finite* period of time—a gestation period—for our idea to go from conception to maturity. This law guarantees the harvest will come *so long as you nourish the seed and don't yank it out of the ground*. If it doesn't come as fast as you want, that doesn't mean it's stopped developing, unless *you decide it has*. This law helps me be patient, and then the Law of Perpetual Transmutation helps me remember to hold onto the idea, even long beyond the expected due date."

Victor's eyes closed. Clenching his teeth he took a deep, cleansing breath, then stared at the dashboard and shook his head. Richard could sense his gears turning, and suddenly when the gears shifted, Victor (with lips still pursed) began to nod instead, resolutely.

His next declaration required every ounce of energy he had, from out of the deepest corners of his soul. Victor didn't realize he had this much will until he opened his mouth and began to speak. "Richard," he began, with a tone of disbelief, "I've got to go home. Somehow, I must find peace in my own home. You and Felicity have put up with me long enough."

"Vic, you *don't have to go*; that's part of why I brought you out here—I wanted to tell you we're moving. And it's a big house with plenty of room for you to stay."

Victor's eyes widened and he leaned forward in shock, "You're moving?"

Richard nodded and tempered his excitement.

Sitting back again, Victor muttered, "Wow..."

"So, you *can* stay with us, until you're sure you're ready to move back home."

"Well, it's behind on payments. But I do want to go back. If what you're telling me is true, then it may not be too late to save it. I had no idea I was being so un-cooperative with the 'law'. I guess this time around, I can put the laws to work consciously, on purpose. I'll just have to put them to the test; it's not like I have anything to lose by trying." Victor smirked sadly.

Richard reached over and squeezed his brother's shoulder. After a tender pause he suggested, "Let's go back. Felicity is probably is getting worried." Richard smiled, "And I wouldn't want her troubling the police again about a *missing husband.*"

32

TENDER MERCY

At the title company, the Goodmans and the Davenports completed the paperwork, and eventually the keys were passed off to the proud and grateful new owners of the home in Andover. It was on the drive to the new home that Felicity mused, "Do you realize, we never even took a tour of the place?"

Richard nodded. "I realized that while we were sitting there; while you stepped away to take Matthew's phone call, I made sure there was a provision in the contract for a home warranty, and the Davenports are covering it."

"Oh, that's a relief. Thanks for being on top of that. We probably shouldn't tell anyone we took a leap like that without more due diligence, they wouldn't understand why we'd do something so irrational."

"Yeah, it wouldn't do any good—they couldn't possibly see this rabbit."

Felicity chuckled. "It always goes back to the rabbit, doesn't it? So many things we do just wouldn't make sense to others, but if they could see our rabbit, it would make all the sense in the world."

As they pulled up to the home, it felt just as inviting as it always had; but this time, their visions would be played out in the realm of physical reality. They pushed the heavy, beveled glass door open and wandered through the rooms with awe. As Richard turned a corner and opened a closet door, he discovered it wasn't a closet door at all. It revealed a stairway down to a basement level. "Felicity! It has a basement!"

"What?" Felicity declared with ecstasy.

Richard bounded down the stairs ahead of his wife, and from the tunnel echoed, *"no way..."*

"What? What is it?" Felicity ran down after him.

He didn't answer, but just stood, speechless at the bottom of the stairs. When Felicity arrived, standing on the last step and gazing over Richard's shoulder, she gasped.

There, spread in front of the stunned couple was a vast and empty room with a hand-painted garden mural on the far wall, and on the side, a ballet barre mounted under a wall-to-wall full-length mirror. Richard spoke reverently, "God's just sent us a tender mercy."

Felicity fell back and sat on the stairs weeping like a child.

That night, Felicity knew there was no hope of capturing her emotions in mere mortal language, so all she attempted to explain was this:

> *I know God lives. He knows I'm here. And you know what? He really does care. I always kind of thought (or hoped) he did, but until today, I had no idea how much. I'm sure I still don't realize how much. My poor little brain has a hard time comprehending all this. Is he really this merciful? I'm just so grateful.*

33

PRIORITIES

Two years later

After doing fairly well on his own, Victor relapsed and was grateful for the guest room at the Goodman home. Discouraged that his grief could have such a relentless grip, the spark of hope nevertheless flickered a little brighter, and he chose to view his setback as temporary.

"I'm sorry, guys—thanks for having me. I don't think it will take me so long to get back on track; I just needed a little time away from the house to reorient my thoughts again." His free time was spent reading and journaling. Saddened by his broken life, he still found a way to view it with frail optimism.

He wrote:

> *I've decided that success isn't a measure of the life I have, but a measure of how I live the life I've been given. I choose to live. I think Michelle would expect me to.*

On the other side of the house, toys were strewn across the family room floor as Sadie and Chloe tried to stay atop their bucking-bronco older brother Matthew. "Shhh! Guys—I'm on the phone!" Felicity whispered with intensity as she stood behind the kitchen counter with her hand over the receiver.

She spoke into the phone. "Yes, the program materials and costumes are on their way. You should receive them by Friday; if they don't reach you by then, let me know."

Felicity listened, nodding as though the director on the other end could see her gesture of understanding. The nodding switched to brief shaking, "No, you're all set to go—the graduation form has been processed and approved, and we'll expect to see you at the training. Oh, you're welcome. Yes, you'll get all the info then. Certainly. Yes, we're thrilled to have you on board! Thank you. Talk soon! Bye, now!"

Felicity hung up the phone and Richard appeared from his office down the hall to raid the fridge. "Who was that?"

"Oh, that was Laura Johnson from New Jersey—our newest director."

"Great!" Richard set out a pile of supplies to create an overstuffed sub sandwich.

Felicity continued, "She's a stay-at-home mom with an underutilized passion for dance, and heard about my Talent Team program from Lisa Vargas in Florida—they used to be college roommates, can you believe that?"

"Wow—thin threads! So, you're in New Jersey now, huh?"

"Yeah," Felicity beamed. "I can't believe how quickly it's spreading. Yet, at the same time I'm not surprised in the least. There's been such a crying need for a resource like this to give parents an alternative. They see how Talent Team has a unique way of empowering the youth, while promoting wholesome family values and uniting communities. They see that we train the competitive performer to compete, without excluding the non-competitive. It really meets the child at their level and inspires them to attain the next." Felicity bubbled with enthusiasm, "I love what I do!"

Richard smiled and nodded in agreement with his mouth full of hoagie bread.

She added, "Did you know that as of last week, we've got thirty-four directors now? And the participant lists are already in the thousands. I'm astounded that God could do something this big with such a simple idea."

After chasing his bite down with a swig of milk, Richard reminded her, "It was genius. You tapped into something genius."

Felicity mused, "I didn't *set out* to do anything *genius*, I just started honoring the idea that wouldn't leave me alone. One small step at a time."

"I'm convinced that genius ideas are just that: simple thoughts that someone stopped to notice and chose to honor." Richard was quiet for a moment then added, "What *I* love about Talent Team is that you haven't just created something to help kids; you've *created* an *opportunity* for *other* moms to earn some *seriously* good money doing what they love, on their own schedule." Richard concluded, moving in from behind and wrapping his arms around her. Eventually it was the kiss behind her ear that made her turn around to embrace him back.

Leaning her head on his chest and gazing out the back window she confessed, "Yeah, but something's bugging me."

"What's that?"

"Maria called me yesterday."

"Your friend from high school?"

"Yeah. I'm confused, because, she and I used to be so close, but now—oh, I don't know." Felicity eyes reddened and she forced composure so Richard wouldn't notice.

Richard stood quietly and kissed her head tenderly as he stared in the direction of the kids playing on the other side of the great room. Patiently he just listened.

Felicity continued, "I was confiding in her, about how overwhelmed I was feeling last week. It's like everything had come down at once and I just needed to vent. The accountant needed my reports, we couldn't find Matthew's homework folder, Chloe used permanent marker in the hallway, and I wasn't keeping up on the orders. I was just at a breaking point, you know? And I just needed to vent—I needed someone to lean on. Maria has always been good for that sort of thing before, but this time, her response really shook me up."

"Oh? What did she say?"

"She said, 'If you're having it so rough, maybe you should quit working.'" Felicity swallowed to hold back the emotion. "Then she said, 'Maybe if you weren't working so much all the time, Chloe wouldn't need to act out like that—to get your attention.' Oh, and then she even said, 'Sometimes I think that women who work have *no business* having kids.'"

"Are you *serious*? She said that?" Richard was incredulous. "Well, Felicity, that's what *she* thinks. But what *I* want to know is: what do *you* think?"

"I don't know, maybe she's right. She made it sound like I should have chosen between work and having the twins or something." Looking at her kids playing on the carpet, the thought that someone could criticize her for bringing such jewels into her family cut like a knife.

After a moment she admitted, "Sure, things get hard sometimes trying to be a good mom and build the Talent Team program at the same time, but deep down, I know I'm doing exactly what I'm supposed to be doing! It's like God carries me along, lets me struggle now and then, and shows me just one piece at a time what I'm supposed to do. I know I'm on the right path—no matter what anyone says. It just hurts when someone I care about so much can't understand why I do what I do."

"Oh, so you mean she can't see your rabbit?" Richard smiled. "Since when has it ever mattered whether others could see the object of your pursuit and the reason for your madness? Life's too short to spend your time with friends like that."

Felicity sniffled and quickly wiped her face on his shirttail to reclaim control. "You're right. With friends like that, who needs enemies?" She whispered weakly. "She thinks that people who are so ambitious can't be spiritual, like they're just focused on money."

"Well, you and I know the truth; and the fact is, none of the money we receive is ours anyway. You know that. We're just stewards. Just temporary stewards. Perhaps she'll never understand that. Maybe she'll always judge you—is that going to change what you do?"

"Of course not."

Richard looked down as she buried her face again and wiped her runny nose on his shirt. "Oh, thanks for that," he muttered in disgust.

"No problem, Sugar." Felicity looked up at him sweetly and smiled.

After a moment of silence, Richard counseled, "Honey, don't let it get to you. Think of it like opposition trying to *keep* you from doing what you're supposed to do. You already know this: your work is improving the lives of thousands of kids now, and will even affect generations to come in a positive, empowering way. I'm convinced opposition will always accompany the most incredible, worthy accomplishments and come at us from the most unlikely, unexpected places. This thing with Maria could be evidence that you're more on track than you know."

Felicity nodded; she knew he was right.

He concluded, "Sometimes life sends us the greatest pain through those we love, and it becomes our opportunity to choose the right path anyway. It's a gift—because we can become stronger for overcoming it. The reward on the other side of the challenge will be at least equal to, if not better than, the pain we had to endure to get there."

"Yeah, you're right."

Both let the silence linger for a while, then Richard eventually followed up with, "You okay?"

"I'm okay."

"Okay enough for me to tell you something?"

Felicity hesitated, and then cautiously responded, "What *kind* of something?"

"Well, I wasn't going to tell you this, but—I can't keep it to myself any longer. We have a little problem."

Felicity remained silent, bracing for whatever news was to come. Richard hesitated so long that she finally broke the silence herself. "So, you have some bad news that you were going to keep from me, and *now* you want to share it?"

"Well, look what you did to my shirt. I guess I feel obliged to share something back."

While Richard's eyes feigned good humor, Felicity sensed she was about to hear something heavy.

"Honey," he continued, "it's a paradox. I spend all my time teaching other people the principles of success. I coach them to have faith in the face of fear. And we've seen the principles work for ourselves, too. But even though I'm grateful we've been able to repeatedly, creatively find the resources we need to keep going, our net worth and visible resources are shrinking faster than the revenue is flowing in. Honestly, Felicity—it's hard not to worry about that. I get exhausted trying to constantly apply the principles, just to maintain this life we've built."

Felicity admitted, "I've sort of worried about running out of money, too; but I've been working really hard to push those thoughts away. I keep thinking our big breakthrough will happen any day now, but if it doesn't, well, it's just got to turn around before we get to the end of our reserves. You know, we're not *nearly* done yet. You've only scratched the surface of what I think you'll do worldwide, and I'm not going to be able to rest until I have at least two directors in every state in the country. What I'd really like is to find someone who's been in this kind of a spot before who can help us move through it successfully. Surely we're students who are finally ready again for the next teacher to appear."

"I'd like to think so."

"The one thing I know for sure that helps me return to peace with each panic attack is that we're doing all we know how with what we have—doing our best to follow the inspiration we get along the way. But I wonder sometimes if we've fallen into the trap of trying to solve our problems at the same level of thinking we're already at. We need a business plan. Don't you think?"

"Yes, and no. I mean, we're in an urgent situation here. We could either spend our time formulating an intricately detailed business plan, or we can let the big picture remain a *little* vague and focus all our energy on things that bring the cash flow *now*. Put our energy into the short-term objectives that we *can* see clearly. Felicity, if we spend too much time trying to *force* the details of the goal, we may not be in business long enough to get there! We've got to get profitable ASAP, so that our minds are freer to develop the details of the ultimate goal."

Felicity sighed. "Makes sense, I guess. I hope you're right. I just want to make sure the short-term goal is going to get us to the big one."

"We may get a little off course, but so long as we stay in forward motion, I believe there'll be opportunity for course correction as needed."

34

VICTOR'S GUEST

"Hey Richard?" Victor knocked lightly on the frame of the home office door, and Richard looked up from his desk with a smile, welcoming his brother in to sit down.

"Thanks, man. Um—" he paused, "I have a confession to make." Victor's mouth was sheepishly scrunched to one side.

Putting his pen down and leaning back in his chair, Richard offered Victor his full attention. "Confession?"

"I eavesdropped. I overheard you and Felicity talking about things—and I've been doing a lot of thinking."

Richard suddenly felt uneasy, unsure of which of their many conversations had been overheard. Letting all he could remember race through his mind, he concluded that the only conversation that might have caused a problem occurred earlier in the week when Felicity made a remark about Victor's loneliness, and wondering if and when Victor was going to start dating again.

Bracing himself for an awkward exchange, Richard replied, "I hope we didn't offend you—"

"Offend? 'Offend' doesn't capture how I felt. It just made me worry a little. You guys were having some natural concerns, and I think anyone in your situation would worry about the same thing. But I have an idea and hope you'll roll with me on it."

"Okay, shoot."

"I have someone I'd like you to meet. Do you think Felicity would mind preparing a special dinner, so I can make an introduction?"

Richard was astonished that Victor would be this eager to bring a girl home with him, and whether Felicity would agree was irrelevant as far as Richard was concerned. Thrilled at the news that Victor had found someone interesting, he determined he'd cook it himself if he had to! "Of course—how about Tuesday night?"

"I'll check on that, but yes, that would be fantastic." After an awkward pause, Victor nervously added, "Great," smiled warmly and left the office.

"Are you serious? That's wonderful!" Felicity beamed with excitement. "I wasn't sure if he'd ever get to this point—oh, this is such good news! What's it been, three years since the accident?"

Richard's joy was hardly containable, too. "Yeah, about three. Let's make sure this dinner is extra special—I'll help you."

"Really? Cool!" Felicity stacked some papers carefully and moved them to the edge of the counter near the wall. "And how about we let the kids have dinner with Grandma that night? It could be a double-date!"

"Yeah—let's do that. I'll call my mom—I'm *sure* she'd support this."

"What kind of a girl do you think she is? Do you think he's found someone like Michelle, or maybe she's someone completely different? I can hardly wait!"

Tuesday night came fast, and Richard was impressed with the condition of the home—despite the fact it had only experienced a light tidying up instead of the deep clean Felicity had hoped for. There simply hadn't been time to make it any better.

After dropping the kids off at Grandma's, the couple spent the afternoon busy in the kitchen, pulling together all the elements of a magnificent three-course meal.

Victor emerged from his room wearing a suit and Felicity looked at the clock on the wall. "Wow, Vic, you look great! I guess I'd better get myself cleaned up—Richard, can you stir this until I get back?"

"Sure. Just leave me enough time to spruce up, too!" Turning to Vic he smiled, "Are you nervous?"

"Nervous? No, why should I be nervous?"

Regretting his question, Richard recovered, "Oh, you're right. No big deal, huh."

Victor looked at Richard perplexed, and Richard quickly changed the subject. "So, things at work going good?"

"They are—ever since I began studying those laws in your book, my partners have been responding differently. Things have never been better, and I've been thinking, you've got to get out there more. People need to hear what you have to say, man."

"I know, I know. One step at a time. I'm not sure how to break into a bigger game, but expect that will come together when the time is right."

Victor just grinned knowingly and nodded his head.

"What's that look for?"

"Oh, nothing."

Richard's brows furrowed and he wanted a better explanation but could tell Victor had no intentions of saying anything more.

Felicity returned and said, "Your turn—and hurry. She could be here any minute!"

Victor turned to Felicity and looked confused. Finally, he shook his head and didn't say anything.

"What?" Richard noticed Victor's odd reaction.

"Hmm? Oh, nothing."

Richard glanced at Felicity and her eyes widened as if to say, "I don't know what he's talking about either."

Just then the doorbell rang and Felicity jumped.

"I'll get it," Victor announced.

As he walked from the kitchen to the foyer, his shoes clicked on the polished tile and his figure reflected below his feet.

Felicity whispered, "I can't stand it! Do you think he's gone for 'tall' this time?"

"I don't know—but it'll be interesting to see if he's still attracted to the intellectual type."

The door opened, and there stood an overweight man in a business suit. Richard and Felicity looked at each other, speechless. In the distance, they could hear Victor say, "Hey, thanks for coming. Right this way."

35

UNCERTAIN ADVICE

Confused, Richard pasted a smile on his face and welcomed the guest with a hand outstretched. Felicity remained frozen, stunned.

The gentleman shook Richard's hand and said, "So, you're Richard, huh?"

"Yes, and you are?"

Victor piped in, "This is Lou. Ever since last week I've wanted to introduce you two."

Felicity pulled herself together and nervously said, "Let's sit down! Dinner's ready. Right this way."

The men filed in behind her and sat around the elegantly decorated dining room table. It finally sunk into Richard's mind that this was not the double date he thought it was going to be.

Victor broke the tension, "Lou is one of my business partners. We played on the same team together in high school. He's brilliant at what he does, and when I overheard you were having some cash flow challenges in your business, I thought you should meet."

"Oh!" Felicity released a relieved chuckle and glanced at Richard. Smiling, bright-eyed, she added, "Tremendous!"

Richard tried to convey his apology and embarrassment with a weak smile to Felicity. He wondered how this mix-up could have happened.

Lou interjected. "I've heard about what you do, Richard. I've seen the change in Victor over the last three years, and I'm intrigued. Maybe I can help."

"Lou has been instrumental in creatively marketing and reorganizing our systems to turn them around. He's a financial advisor by trade, but does so much more than that."

Felicity looked at Richard and raised her eyebrows. Turning her glance toward Lou she responded, "Great—we're all ears."

Apprehensively Victor interrupted, "I hope you don't mind I overheard your conversation in the kitchen that day—it's just that you've helped *me* so much, when I realized what you're dealing with, I thought about all my contacts and resources, and truly, I think with some of the people I know, we can steer you through this and help you get solid. We have connections and partners all over the country who could benefit from what you do, Richard."

Lou pulled back. "Yes, but first things first. We need to get your cash flow under control." Lou proceeded cautiously, allowing the couple to exercise their choice in the matter. "That is, if you're open to some discussion on that."

Richard's journey in just the previous ten minutes left him stripped of his guard and he began to recognize this was probably the answer to their prayers. Pride aside, he accepted. "Yes, I think that could be helpful. I have questions, and I haven't known *what* to do—we're dealing with some things we've never faced before."

"Well, first, what's your passion?"

"Helping people break through their financial difficulties."

"And you say you're having financial difficulties of your own?"

Richard reddened with embarrassment. "Just because the principles are true, it doesn't mean I'm perfect at living them. But I'm trying—and have committed to share what I learn as I figure it all out."

"Sounds like you've discovered a portal, or a gateway to providing genius solutions." Lou smiled.

"What do you mean?"

"You're so passionate about making a contribution; you're even looking at your *challenges* in terms of how you'll use them to serve others. That's genius. Don't you think you'll continue to tap into brilliant solutions as you need them, with a mindset like that?"

"Yeah, but it's been tough. We've been throwing all our time, money, and energy into the things we're passionate about. But, as often as we've invested, we've wondered: *how long will we have to sacrifice before we can relax and enjoy the revenue our businesses produce?* They're doing well, we have no complaints—but when the money comes in, it always goes to inventory, or marketing, or whatever—it seems endless. There's never enough left over to feel like we can really start *living*."

"Don't be too impatient, Richard. This is normal for start-ups. There *does* come a day when things don't have to feel quite so intense."

Felicity piped in, "I get to where I think we're almost there, and then something always pulls the rug out from under us. We can see where we're going, but I can't help but wonder if it's like the proverbial carrot dangling out in front of us, getting us to do things we wouldn't otherwise do with no *real* hope of ever being able to sit down and enjoy the reward."

Richard was finding relief getting this all off his chest. "We've seen the principles work, again and again, and yeah, we're still here. It's not like we're at the end of all we have yet, but it appears to be fast approaching. We just reject the fear every time it comes up, but it's getting harder to do."

Jumping in before anyone else had a chance to vent some more, Lou said, "I'm sure you're doing all you can to reject thoughts of potential failure," he paused, "but as honorable as that is, there is a piece of you—your subconscious mind as you know—that is designed to keep you *safe*. All this time you're going unflinchingly toward your goal, it's down there trying to make sure you don't meet with disaster. It's constantly asking you, 'what are you going to do if the money runs out'? or 'what are people going to think if you fail'?"

Richard found some comic relief that Lou could blatantly call attention to the thoughts he had been trying to ignore for so long.

The businessman leaned forward and raised his voice, "For crying out loud, answer the question! Give your subconscious mind an answer—without a whole lot of emotional energy on it—and put its worries to rest!" Sitting back in his seat, he concluded, "It'll more likely leave you alone after that."

"What do you mean, 'answer the question'?" Felicity wondered.

"I mean, ask yourself, '*so what if* the money runs out? What then?'"

Richard immediately felt a surge of adrenaline and he could feel the panic rise from wherever it had been stuffed for a long, long time.

"I mean really; what if the money was gone, what then?" Lou repeated.

"Uh—" Richard tried to speak directly to satisfy this new mentor, "we'd lose the house and our neighbors might talk about our failures."

"Okay, so?"

"Umm, so, then we'd have to find a cheaper place to live."

"And what if you lost your cars, too?"

"Then, I guess we'd be taking the city bus everywhere."

"And, so?"

The more they drilled down, the less terrifying the potential life changes seemed to be. Richard felt that it became ridiculous, in fact, to bottle up so much fear over scenarios that, in the larger scheme of things, were not that big of a deal.

Lou concluded, "If everything fell apart, would you quit teaching? Felicity, if you had to move, would you still build your dance programs?"

"Well, of course—that's what we do. Wouldn't you agree, Richard?"

"Yeah, even if we lost everything, we'd find a way to keep doing what we do—it's become our passion."

"Right, even if you lost it all, you would rebuild. In fact, many successful people have had to do just that. Now that you've answered the nagging question, you can let the issue rest and get back to work finding and creating solutions. I think your subconscious mind will give you a little less grief now."

"So, if our reserves run out before the cash flow is what it needs to be, then there's the question of whether to get a loan or use credit cards to keep afloat. That's my fear—I don't want to go into debt again after working so hard to get out of it."

"Well, if it comes to that, you'll have to decide whether to quit altogether, or draw upon *all* remaining sources and resolutely complete the projects that promise to make your situation solvent," Lou stated matter-of-factly.

"But we *have* no other resources."

"No credit? Nobody you could call on?"

Richard felt his jaw tighten at the idea of using other people's money. Felicity interjected, "I'm with Richard on this. We *refuse* to go into debt—there must be another way. It took us far too long to get out of it the first time—we're not going there ever again."

Lou gently explained, "Whether you *should,* ultimately depends on whether *you* feel that the utilization of credit is to *delay an inevitable bankruptcy,* or whether it will allow you to plant the final seeds and supply the necessary sustenance that will *bring the long-awaited harvest.*"

"But we decided long ago we would not go into debt again, aside from our mortgage, which we hope to eliminate as well."

"I agree; it's critical to stay out of debt. I would never advise you to go into debt. But let me explain how 'debt' is defined in the financial world. To be in a 'debt position' means you owe more than the value of your assets. If your assets are greater than your liabilities, you are not in 'debt,' but in an 'equity position,' even if you owe money to creditors. So, in that sense, I *always* counsel my clients to stay out of debt. But if your decision to borrow capital brings you to an end that eventually allows you to repay *everyone* in full—instead of declaring bankruptcy—it may be something to consider. Your creditors would ultimately thank you for it, don't you think?"

"I suppose; but to me, being in debt fundamentally means you *owe someone something.* It's bondage; period. I feel *that* kind of obligation should be avoided at all costs."

"So, nobody should owe anyone anything, ever, if we lived in a perfect world; is that what you're saying?"

"Right. In a perfect world, there would be no debt."

"So, nobody would owe *you* anything, either, right?"

"In a perfect world; that's right. I think it would be best that everyone be one hundred percent free from bondage of any kind. Not that it could ever realistically happen, but in a *perfect* world, yes."

"Did you know you're regularly putting people in that kind of bondage now? You *are a creditor*, to which a lot of people are in bondage. If you are as fundamentally anti-debt as you claim to be, then you probably shouldn't be a creditor either."

Richard was perplexed. "What are you talking about? I don't know *anyone* who is in debt to me," turning to his brother, he chided, "except maybe you, Victor."

Victor smirked and muttered, "Yeah, yeah."

Richard turned again to Lou, "But I don't *expect* anything from him, I don't *require* anything."

"You just make me *feel* that way!" Victor teased back.

Lou put the conversation back on track, "Do you have any money in the bank?"

Richard chuckled, "A little bit."

"Well, do you realize you've put the bank, and the people who borrow from the bank, into *your* debt? If you don't believe in the debt/creditor system at all, then you need to withdraw all of your money and release the bank of their obligation to you."

Richard reflected on Lou's words. He had never thought of the banking system in that light. He never judged what the bank did as anything less than honorable.

As Richard and Felicity both quietly digested this advisor's perspective, Lou added, "And for that matter, you should never go to a restaurant that lets you eat before you pay, because for that span of time, you're in debt to them. You'd have to always pay in advance; but then wait a minute, if you paid in advance, you'd be putting them in debt to you."

The more their advisor painted such pictures, the more absurd their expectations for a perfect world seemed to be.

The advisor reiterated, "Stay out of debt. Yes. In other words:

avoid owing more than you could repay if all was liquidated. But also, don't be afraid to engage in the economic system, either. Stay focused on production, over and above consumption, and wealth can be created, not just for you, but also for those who are in business to profit from helping you have the capital you need for a time. Make sure if you engage in the system, do it with gratitude—not guilt. How you feel about borrowing the money has a real effect on your ability to stay on track with the strategies you have for paying it back."

Richard raised his eyebrows and glanced at Felicity who furrowed her brows in thoughtful introspection.

Victor interjected, "There was a time when I worried about the same thing, and I concluded that it's sort of like trying to get from New York to Los Angeles under a deadline, with the one rule to *never go east*, because that's backward and takes me away from my goal. But if I'm sitting in New York, and the Airport is thirty miles east of me," he looked at Felicity and continued, "am I going to travel east to catch the plane, or am I going to doggedly go in no other direction *except* west, and have any hope of arriving on time?"

His question was rhetorical and caused Richard to reflect on the dilemma from a different perspective than he had ever entertained in the past.

Lou affirmed, "That's right. But I'll just say this because I don't want you coming back blaming me if it doesn't go the way you hope: don't borrow money if it puts you into a mindset of fear. When you're operating from a mindset of fear, you'll make different kinds of decisions than when you're at peace. A decision made from a place of fear is like driving a car under the influence of drugs, and you'll probably do something stupid.

Lou paused and picked up what Felicity guessed was probably

his third roll. She passed him the butter with a knowing smile and enjoyed a small spark of pride in being a contentious hostess as he smiled back. Generously buttering his roll, he continued, "But if borrowing money puts you into a mindset of advancement, and allows you to finish your projects quicker, consider it. If it gives you the continued ability to make progress and solve problems with a clear and sound plan for paying it back, then do it without beating yourself up. Then, don't look back and *get to work making it pay* as quickly as possible. Understand, Richard, this is a completely different issue from using other people's money for consumption. In, other words, don't take out a second mortgage to buy a boat, unless that is, you know how to turn the boat into production that increases your cash flow. Utilizing other people's money for production can in some cases be the wise thing to do, while using it for consumption is always foolish. You've got to determine your motive, mindset, plan for repayment, and tolerance for risk."

Despite their efforts to avoid it, in less than a year, Richard and Felicity's fears were realized. With their savings depleted, they faced the very scenario that had been discussed with Lou at dinner.

Richard reflected on that night. "Felicity, do you think we created this problem by talking about it with Lou?"

"Oh, I don't know. I doubt it. I mean really, if you think back over the last twelve months, don't you think we've done everything in our power to stay positive despite the setbacks? What more could we have done? We absolutely handled every challenge that came along in a levelheaded way. When we fell back into old thinking, it didn't take long to recognize it and fix it. For the most part, we didn't get upset over the setbacks."

"You're right," Richard agreed.

"We even managed to view that ridiculous lawsuit in a positive way—knowing that if we could get through it without destroying our vision for the future, the reward on the other side of it would be amazing," Felicity stated with certainty.

Richard scoffed, "Yeah, that one came completely out of left field; it amazes me how dishonest and ruthless people—opportunists— can be."

"I'm sure there will come a day when we look at that and understand what we needed to learn from it."

Richard shrugged, "Maybe it was just an opportunity to practice right thinking. It's not like you can really practice these principles without problems to practice *with*."

Felicity was thoughtful, and then said, "I'm glad you kept writing through it all—you've demonstrated the principles you teach in action, and one day, you'll see the fruits of your efforts, too."

"I'm counting on it. I wonder sometimes; but I'm so far down this path that I have no other choice but to push through."

"Now, honey, you always have a choice," Felicity reminded.

"Yeah, I know—and this *is* my choice. I can see no other path than the one we're on—the one that's laid out before us. I'm going to keep going until I have *no other choice* than to take a different path. So long as there is *something* I *can* do, I'll keep going."

"So, we're going to start using other people's money?"

"Do you see any other way?" Richard wondered.

"It can't be a long-term solution, Rich. Do you really see how this can turn around before it runs out like our savings did?"

"Honey, I can't believe God would bring us this far to fail now.

I don't know, maybe this is one of those final tests to see if we can continue in right-thinking."

"How can utilizing other people's money be a test? That sounds totally backward to me."

"No, it's not that—I mean, we've sacrificed a lot over the years, and we've always said we'd do what it took, except for *borrowing money*. I think no matter *what* our exception was, it may have been the final test we would have had to pass. Would we be borrowing the money to simply delay an unavoidable bankruptcy? Or would we be borrowing it to keep us in business while the law of gestation carries out its processes? Since I can't imagine that all we've been through was for nothing, maybe it's our test to see if we can draw upon that last and final resource *without allowing it to mess with our psyche*."

Felicity didn't respond right away. Finally, she expressed her thoughts aloud. "It kind of ticks me off to think we'd have to cross that line—but it wouldn't surprise me. No, I feel like we only need to float a little longer, and our businesses will begin to pay what we need them to pay. This would *not* be to delay an unavoidable bankruptcy; that's not how I see this. Sure, I *can* let myself feel grateful to participate in blessing someone else's life. You know, letting someone else profit from the interest we'll have to pay."

"Okay, but let's put our exit strategy in place, too. If we don't achieve a set benchmark in six months, then let's use the remaining funds to move somewhere more affordable. We don't want to be completely destitute before we drop everything and transition into a more affordable lifestyle," Richard proposed, being careful to talk about it without fear or emotional concern about the outcome.

Not thrilled at the prospect of uprooting the children, Felicity bravely replied, "Sounds reasonable."

Talking about the situation with Felicity always helped Richard believe his own hopeful words. However, in quieter moments alone, Richard wasn't always so at peace about their future. With less than one week before they'd reach the end of their savings, and knowing the anticipated cash flow would still be grossly inadequate, Richard reflected again on his discussion with Lou.

Richard had never thought of "debt" in contrast to "equity" before, and part of him felt like it was just a dangerous rationalization. Regardless, in the position he found himself now, he could see no other choice but to either, abandon his long-determined purpose to bring his life-changing message to the world, and instead go find employment working for someone else, or continue to build their businesses and keep their commitments on borrowed money.

Lamenting that he even needed to make such a decision, he counseled again with Felicity and they agreed they must proceed, even at the risk of all they had accomplished so far.

"Richard," Felicity reasoned, "We've done just what we knew we were supposed to do. In fact, although I honestly don't believe we'll have to, I'm willing to *lose everything* and start over if that's what it takes." Felicity stated with resolve.

Amazed at the remarkable evolved version of his wife who stood before him now, Richard could scarcely believe how far they had come. Gratitude and a sense of awe filled his heart that they both were determined to fearlessly pursue their objectives.

He finally spoke, "Felicity, money or no money, home or no home, I *know* what I need to be doing. Whenever I'm completely engaged in living my purpose and utilizing the talents I know I'm meant to utilize, I *feel* successful. No amount of money in the world could ever duplicate that feeling."

Felicity chuckled and then embraced him warmly. "I know what you mean." With a melancholy sigh she continued, "So, now what? Is it time to pull out the credit cards?"

Richard didn't respond right away. After furrowing his brow and staring off into space he eventually responded curiously, "Wait a minute. *Maybe not.*"

36

DÉJÀ VU

"Honey, I'll be back in a bit—I have an idea." Richard abruptly dismissed himself, leaving Felicity standing alone perplexed.

He ran to the home office and snatched up the phone, pressing the speed dial for Lou. After a moment, he relaxed. "Ah, Lou? This is Richard, Victor's brother—I hope you don't mind me calling."

"Of course not. What's going on?"

"The reason I'm calling is because, well, it happened: we ran out of money, and we were just getting ready to pull out the credit cards when I had a thought. Do you mind if I run it past you? I'd like your input on it—I want to make sure I'm thinking right.

"Go ahead; shoot."

"Oh, thank you." Richard breathed, and then continued, "Okay, so I just remembered I have this retirement account where I used to work. I have no idea how much it has in there right now, haven't really had time to pay attention to it. It was preferred stock in the company."

"You mean you haven't been taking the quarterly dividends?"

"No, I haven't, because I set it up to just reinvest them back into the company."

"Why?"

"Well, because we wanted to avoid the 10% penalties."

"But couldn't you have been using them to fund your business?"

"Yeah, well, it used to be my 401K, so it was always considered 'retirement,' and the rule has always been that we *just don't touch it.*"

"So, what made you take it out of the 401K in the first place?"

"I realized that I needed to invest in something I believed in, and at the time, it was clear my success depended on the company's success, and I believed in *them*, so I bought into Stillwater Technologies."

"But you're not with them anymore."

"Well, right, that's why I thought it might be time to transition that money out of the company and into my own."

"I was hoping you'd say that!"

"Really? Well, here's my issue: I'm sure the account has at *least* seventeen grand in it, because what I put in, and they've really taken off over the last few years with that InnoValve."

"So, you don't know how much you have in the account? Do you know what you *need,* to bridge the gap until your business starts producing like you expect?"

"No, I'm not sure how much we need. It's hard to say, but I figure this training system could be ready to release in four more months. I figure we need twenty to thirty grand, *minimum*, to carry us through until it can start producing."

"And how much do you have in hand right now?"

"Oh, um, we're down to just a few hundred dollars, actually."

"Well, you probably should have requested your retirement long before now, did you know it can take a month or two for them to get it to you?"

"Are you serious? It takes that long?" Richard groaned and rubbed the back of his neck.

"You'd better call them right away. Find out how much money you have, and at least get the process started."

"Okay, I'll give them a call. If it looks like there's enough in there, then maybe you could help me figure out how to hold everything together until it shows up in two months."

"I'd be happy to."

"Thanks, Lou. Talk soon."

Immediately after hanging up the phone, Richard picked it up again and called the Human Resources department at Stillwater Technologies, hoping to talk to someone familiar, but uncertain whether anyone he knew still worked there.

"This is Betty, can I help you?"

Richard smiled, "Betty! It's Richard, Richard Goodman!"

"Well, well, well! If it isn't the old company maharishi!"

"Very cute, Betty. Hey, can you look at my stock? I'm thinking about cashing out."

"Oh, *you don't want to do that.*"

"Why not?"

"Because you'll get hit with some *serious* penalties."

Richard didn't need another reminder of the downside of this decision. He was on a mission to simply discover the balance. Avoiding the dreary topic, he replied, "Anyway, can you look it up really quick?"

"Sure, just give me a moment." Betty placed Richard on hold and Richard sat on the edge of his desk crunching numbers while he waited.

Finally, she clicked back on. "Sir, your account has $42,563.51. Would you like me to get you the paperwork?"

Richard jumped to his feet, ecstatic that the figure had grown so much, and answered, "Yes, please—the sooner the better."

"I'll fax it over. What's your number there?"

After Richard's abrupt departure, Felicity had made herself some hot chocolate and sat, reading a magazine in the kitchen. Richard bounded in and announced, "I've got it!" Then, as if as an after-thought he added, "Sort of..."

Felicity set the magazine down, and smiling, asked, "Oh? What is it?"

"I just cashed in on our retirement."

Felicity scrunched her eyebrows. "I think I'm having déjà vu, but I'm going to try really hard not to freak out this time. Honey, the rule has always been that we *don't touch that money*! It's our retire-ment! Haven't we gone through this before?"

"I know, we have, and I've learned something here. When our money was in the 401K, we didn't have any clue what it was being used for. For all we knew, it could have been used to support a product or service against our values. The fees were automatically deducted, so we never paid attention to it. I added it up once—and if we had been required to write a check for every transaction they drafted, we would have been up in arms! I determined from that moment that the money would serve us best if it was invested in something that carried meaning for us, and something in which we had some control over the outcome. But that was then; I no longer work for Stillwater Technologies, and so I believe it's time we use it for our own company."

"Wow, I never thought of it like that before. But, Richard, what about the *penalty*? We're going to get hit pretty hard—wouldn't it be better to just let it grow until we can draw from it *without* the penalty?"

"Felicity, how much interest would we have to pay if we accumulate more debt?"

"Oh, depends on where we get it. Somewhere between eight and twenty-two percent per year."

"So, if we need thirty grand to hold things together until the business starts generating enough revenue, then we can either pay ten percent *once* on the retirement draw, and owe nobody anything, or we can pay between eight and twenty-two percent every year and be liable until the loans are paid back. What if it takes us five years? The retirement account will have cost ten percent, around $3000 just *once*, but the loan will have cost between *forty* and a *hundred and ten percent,* anywhere between $10,000 and $33,000! If we take longer, the numbers only get more ridiculous; but in any case, the so-called penalty is a *much better deal!*"

Felicity was amazed. Nodding in agreement, she added, "And, our own money would be utilized once again to invest in *ourselves.*"

"Right. But here's the problem. We're already out of money, and the retirement funds won't be in our hands for up to sixty more days."

"What? Wow." Felicity raised her eyebrows and then continued, "Well, that sounds like a reasonable purpose for credit cards, then; what do you think?"

"You mean, use them now and pay them off when the retirement money gets here?"

"Yeah—I mean, now that we have an exit strategy in place?"

Richard smiled. "I like the way you think. You're amazing, you know that?"

"Yeah, and don't you forget it," Felicity chided.

37

BUNNY SLIPPERS

Four months went by, and the cash flow *still* wasn't in place. But the Goodmans refused to give up and used nearly every penny of their retirement, as well as resorting to some borrowed funds.

However, their time in the refiner's fire over the recent years had, in a strange way, taught them to be calm in the face of adversity. So, when the cash was nearly gone, and their debt load was larger than it had ever been in their lives, and even though the projects still required additional work, something dawned on Richard. Sharing his epiphany with Felicity, he said, "When you think longer term, like ten years out, today's catastrophe is actually reduced to a mere irritant."

Felicity chuckled. "Yes, when put that way, it really is *merely irritating* that our money is pretty much gone, and we still have a house payment due in two weeks."

With their savings spent, and their credit extended to its maximum, the moment they had held fearfully in the back of their minds all those years was finally theirs to face.

And inexplicably, they had never been more at peace.

It was as though they were finally required to fight the monster under the bed, and to their surprise, they discovered it was only a pair of bunny slippers.

"So, this is it, I suppose. We have a few hundred dollars left, and I'm not even worried. I can't remember ever being this content. If we lose everything and have to start over," Felicity shrugged, "we'll start over. If we have to move into a trailer or live out of the car, we'll *still* find a way to expand your training programs and I'll stil continue to build Talent Team."

Richard wondered at the serenity enveloping them both, here at the end of their resources. "I know, it's hard to believe I could have this much peace with external evidence appearing so disastrous." Richard's eyes suddenly sparkled. "Honey, I'd like to take you to dinner for our anniversary."

"What? We haven't allowed ourselves to eat out all year! Of all times, how can you justify it now? With our deadlines, Richard, it's not like we have time to just enjoy a social engagement, shooting the breeze together when it won't help solve the money problem."

"Felicity, it's *because* of our deadlines that we don't have time to squander *in any other way*. We've got to get back into the right mindset where solutions can come. Forcing them to come in any other mindset will bring us nothing. Besides, I want to celebrate— *you*. It's been so long since we've just let ourselves have a good time; just for tonight, can we just pretend everything is okay for a couple hours, and enjoy each other at one of our favorite restaurants?"

Felicity smiled, "Why not."

Dinner that night was wonderful, and after years of practice managing their fears, they had no trouble setting them aside for just another short hour and a half.

Richard expressed his gratitude and amazement for the journey, and their relationship. He rejoiced in their happiness and the unbelievable peace of mind they felt, knowing the good they had yet to accomplish—and the mark they knew they'd leave on the world. They brainstormed on what they could do right away to create value for someone else, and made plans to stay in service, to keep their minds off of what they lacked.

When they were done, together they walked to the cashier and Richard playfully elbowed her in the side. "Felicity, we're going to be wealthy."

Teasingly she replied, "Oh yeah? How on earth is *that* supposed to happen?"

"I have no idea, but I know where to start," Richard winked and then signed the receipt.

Stepping squarely in front of him, reaching around his waist and clasping her hands behind her husband, she looked him in the eyes with admiration, and a smirk. "You know, Richard, *more than ever*, it'll take a miracle."

He responded with a grin and took her hand in his. Leading her to the car he stopped before opening her door. Tenderly brushing the hair from her eyes, he replied, "Yeah? Well, Felicity," bringing his lips close to her ear, his words quieted to a whisper: "*I happen to believe in miracles.*"

He kissed her head and opened the door. Within moments the waiter rushed out of the restaurant waving a piece of paper. "Sir, the manager wanted me to catch you—for your anniversary," he panted, "the meal's on the house!"

A glance passed between the couple exuding amazement and gratitude, and Felicity's eyes became misty while she watched Richard thank the waiter and retrieve the voided receipt. She couldn't remember a time when they had felt so entirely united in purpose, so guided, and *so supported by unseen, heavenly help* as they were feeling in that moment.

As they drove home, Felicity reflected aloud; "I'm amazed and grateful for the meal, but you know what? Even more than that, to me it's just *assurance* we'll continue to have all we need if we just continue in faith, feeling joy now as though the goals are already accomplished, and taking one step at a time toward fulfilling our purpose. After all, what greater security could anyone ask for?"

That night, Felicity logged the events of the day in her journal, and concluded with a reminder to herself and to whoever would read it in the future:

> *Go boldly toward your goal. Do what you can do today. Make progress. Fall forward. When you're truly at the end of all you can do, that's where you'll find what you need to keep going.*

> *If you don't have what you think you need in this moment, you don't really need it. Do your best with what you have, and you'll find that all you had in the moment was enough.*

On a quiet morning a few days later, Richard opened his e-mail to find a message from Lou. It read:

> *Richard, I know a businessman in Europe who is thinking about having you to train his employees. Have you ever been to Belgium? I've told him all about you, and he's read your book. He says he wants to talk*

*with you about a possible semi-long-term contract—
and after the way I pitched you, he's expecting to pay
you handsomely. (You can thank me later.) But you'll
need to get yourself to his office in Brussels on Tuesday.
I've tried to get more details out of him, but he wants
to meet you in person first. Feeling adventurous?*

Taken aback, Richard called to his sweetheart: "Felicity, come check this out!"

"What?" Felicity called from the other room.

Richard hurried to her side. "I'm going to Brussels!" Pulling Felicity away from her computer, he scooped her into his arms and spun her around.

"Honey!" she shrieked.

Spinning across the room and setting her down on the sofa, he turned her face to his and kissed her so long that she finally had to gasp for air. Pulling away and giggling she said, "What's this all about?"

Richard shook his head enthusiastically. "This is just the kind of opportunity we've been praying for!" He waited for his words to sink in, and when she didn't respond, he continued more quietly, solemnly. "God just sent another tender mercy; let's pray and thank Him. I think we should kneel this time."

Felicity smiled with deeper adoration for her man than ever before. She hugged him, took his hand and they knelt together while Richard offered a heart-felt expression of gratitude that they had been carried through a refiner's fire, and showered with more blessings than they could number.

Surely, there was no better way to start another perfect day.

38

HASENPFEFFER IN ODENTHAL

As soon as Richard finished his prayer, he and Felicity stood and embraced each other quietly. Remaining in her husband's arms with her head on his chest, Felicity cautiously revealed a concern. "Richard?"

"Hmm?"

"You're going to *Brussels*?"

Richard hesitated and pulled away to look her in the eyes. "I think I *should*, don't you?"

"*What's in Brussels*? You haven't told me anything about this!"

"What do you *think* this is about? Have you just been humoring me, or what?"

"All I know is that when you're on fire, it's contagious. But now, well, the emotion has subsided, so I'd like to know what's really going on here."

Richard chuckled. "I'm sorry, Honey. Lou's been talking to someone in his network who owns a company in Brussels. He's read my book, and because of Lou's recommendation, the guy wants me to train his people. It could be a semi-long-term contract that's supposed to pay pretty well."

"Okay, but what does that *mean*? What about the family?"

"I'm not sure, but what choice do I have? Nothing else has come along, and we need the money!"

"We *always* have a choice," Felicity reminded him.

"Yeah, I know; but I'd like to just talk to him and see where it goes." Richard's eyes begged consent.

Felicity looked worried. "Only *after* you and I get absolutely clear on what we *will* and *will not* give up to chase a dollar."

"That's fine. Felicity, I'm only exploring this because it may be very the thing I need to advance the purpose that burns in my soul, getting this message out and transforming people's lives."

"Right, but what about *your family*? What if it's in *complete alignment* with the service you're uniquely endowed to render, but it leaves your family behind?" Felicity was becoming increasingly concerned because Richard still hadn't said the words that would put her mind at ease.

"Then it *wouldn't* be aligned with my purpose, now, would it?" Richard paused, then sighed. "Felicity, I haven't signed anything. Nobody's offered me a position yet. It can't hurt to meet with him and find out how long this contract would last, and how much he's planning to pay."

"But to fly all the way to Europe, just to meet with him before you even have a contract? What about airfare? Hotel? We don't have that kind of money right now."

"If we determine this is something I should do, we'll *find* the money. Remember: *goal first, way second?*"

Felicity sat down and huffed, inflating her cheeks. "So, what would make this the ideal contract? Let's make a list of characteristics with the intention to find an opportunity that matches it. After that, if this Brussels thing still feels like a good idea to explore, then, I say go for it. If it doesn't feel like a fit, then making the list will probably set things in motion to bring about an ideal contract somewhere else."

"Ooh, I like how you think," Richard smiled proudly. "Grab a notepad; let's do this."

The couple brainstormed for the better part of an hour and ended up with the following characteristics:

> My Ideal Contract
>
> Less than 30 minutes from home
> At least $15,000/mo net
> Trainees who benefit from my unique abilities
> Leadership who I enjoy working with/for
> Helps further my career
> An environment with an inspiring atmosphere
> Becomes, or leads me to, continual work
> All this, or something better

After the list was complete, Richard and Felicity looked at it quietly.

Felicity was the first to speak. "Do you believe such a contract even *exists*?"

"In a world of six billion people? Of *course,* it *exists.*"

"In Brussels, though?"

Richard sighed. "I know it doesn't fit the list, but I can't let go of the thought that maybe I'm supposed to meet the guy anyway."

Felicity tossed the notepad to the table in disbelief. "I actually feel the same way. Creating this list, for some reason, has only *increased* the intrigue I feel about the opportunity, whatever it is. It just doesn't make sense."

"Then I guess I'd better follow this rabbit and see where it leads. But I'll need a plane ticket in a hurry; let's find some money."

Richard landed in Brussels wide-eyed and nervous. As he arrived at baggage claim, he was relieved to see a gentleman by the door holding a large card with his name printed in large black letters. The men greeted each other, and Richard was grateful the gentleman knew English.

"I will take you to your hotel, and after you have a good sleep, I'll pick you up again at 8:30 to meet the company president, Dietmar Hoffmann at the office. He looks forward to meeting you."

"Thank you—what was your name?"

"I'm Hans."

"Thank you, Hans."

During the forty-five-minute ride to the hotel, Richard enjoyed a lively conversation with the company driver, who was visibly thrilled to be at his service. They talked at length about their backgrounds and experiences, and the conversation took an exciting turn when Hans learned that Richard at one time worked for a company that built medical devices."

"Is that so?" Hans asked with curiosity.

"That's right, Stillwater Technologies is best known for creating something called the InnoValve several years ago. It was revolutionary."

Hans' excitement mounted and he nearly forgot to keep his eyes on the road, "I know! I was one of the first in my country to receive the InnoValve!"

Leaning forward in his seat Richard exclaimed, "*No kidding*! Here in Belgium?"

"No, I'm actually from Dusseldorf, Germany."

"Well, I'll have to give the president a call—the man who invented it—Morgan. He'll be thrilled to know I met you." Richard fell back again in his seat and then asked, "You doing well?"

"Never been better!"

At the end of the next day, after an interesting meeting with Dietmar Hoffman, Richard returned to his hotel room and collapsed on the bed. Expressionless, he looked thoughtfully toward the ceiling and took a deep, slow breath. Thinking about the outcome of his visit with the president, he shook his head and then sat up abruptly. Before he could call home, he felt urgency to see if Morgan was available for a conversation first.

He checked the clock and calculated the time change between Brussels and Kansas, and determined it was nearly lunchtime back home, so he had the best chance of reaching Morgan at the office.

After a few rings he heard, "Stillwater Technologies, Linda speaking. How may I help you?"

"Linda—it's Richard Goodman, how are you doing?"

"Wow, Richard! It's been a long time! I'm great, thank you. And you?"

"Good." Richard was polite but distracted. "Hey—I'm looking for Morgan, is he available?"

"Actually, he's out of the country right now. He and Ray are working on a deal in Amsterdam and won't be home until Saturday."

"Amsterdam? Can I reach him while he's there?"

"You can try; I'll give you his cell number."

Richard recorded the number, thanked Linda, and then dialed Morgan's phone.

The line connected quickly. The voice on the other end spoke, "Morgan here."

"Morgan, it's Richard Goodman, long time no talk to," Richard spoke nostalgically, smiling.

"Richard? *Is that you*? For Pete's sake, it's great to hear your voice! What are you up to?"

"Actually, I just spoke with Linda; she said you were in Europe. I just had to call you and thank you for everything you and Ray did for me all those years ago. It put me on an amazing path, and I just landed the most incredible contract—it's a dream come true and I'm humbled by the tremendous difference you've made in my life." Richard choked up.

"Well, that's wonderful to hear, Rich."

"I also needed to tell you that I met someone today, someone else who is grateful you followed your passion twenty years ago. His name is Hans. He was my driver today, and he was the first German to receive the InnoValve. You saved his life, man. He's got a beautiful young family, and the kids still have a father around because of you."

The line went silent, and Richard began to wonder if the connection had been lost.

"You still there?"

"Yes, Rich. Thanks for letting me know." Morgan took a deep breath and continued, "So, where *is* this dream contract?"

"Actually, I'm in Brussels right now."

Ray interrupted, "Brussels? How long you going to be in Brussels?"

"I'm supposed to leave tomorrow."

After a brief pause, Morgan said, "Just a second, Rich." The line went silent again and after a minute Morgan returned. "Rich, can you take an extra day before going home? Ray and I have decided that we have some unfinished business to take care of in Odenthal, not far from Dusseldorf. What would it take to have you meet us there, with Hans?"

"Um, I don't know—actually Hans is *from* Dusseldorf. But, why? What's this all about?" Richard was perplexed.

Morgan continued. "This is big Richard—it's a long story, and even if you can't pull it off, can you get us in touch with Hans?"

"I enjoy long stories, so now you've got me curious."

"Just meet us tomorrow night and we'll explain everything."

Richard scoffed, "What am I supposed to tell Felicity?"

"Just tell her you've spotted a rabbit and need to delay your return by just one more day."

Richard was confused. "Or, is it more accurate that I'm helping *you* catch one of *yours*?"

"Probably so. Whatever it takes, Rich!"

After hanging up the phone, Richard called his wife. "Hi Felicity, how're you and the kids?"

"Hi Sweetie! We're doing just fine. How was the meeting? What happened?"

"I got the contract!"

Felicity didn't respond immediately. When she finally did, she spoke slowly. "And, what does that mean? How long will you have to stay there?" Her voice revealed disappointment.

"Dietmar asked me to train his sales team and track results with them over the next six months. He offered me a company condo to stay in while I fulfilled the contract, but I told him it wouldn't work with our family objectives. After some brainstorming, he determined that the job could be handled remotely. I'll be training his people from our home office in Andover!"

"What?" Felicity was ecstatic.

"I'll tell you more when I get home—would it be okay if I stay an extra day? Ray and Morgan are in Amsterdam and they want to meet me somewhere near Dusseldorf tomorrow night. I checked the map and we're both less than a three-hour drive to something they want to show me, or tell me, I'm not sure."

Felicity was thrilled about his new position, and that he wouldn't have to live in Europe for six months was compensation enough to allow him to stay the extra day.

To Richard's relief, Hans was enthusiastic at the prospect of meeting the man whose inspired invention had saved his life with the InnoValve, and he looked forward to hearing the story behind its creation. "I'll show you my home town! We'll visit my family!" In his words, it was 'unquestionably worth the adventure', so they left in time to put them in Odenthal by 7:00 pm.

Upon arriving at Café-Restaurant Heuser in Odenthal, Richard was greeted outside the front door by Ray and Morgan who had arrived only a few minutes ahead of them.

"Richard! So great to see you again!"

As Ray attacked him with an aggressive bear hug, Richard felt a laugh rising in his chest and heard Hans laugh as well.

After releasing Richard, Ray extended his hand to Hans and said enthusiastically, "You must be Hans."

Hans ignored Ray's extended arm and threw his arms exuberantly around him. Ray's eyes widened while Hans jolted the wind out of his lungs. Then turning to Morgan, Hans did it again. "It's wonderful to meet you both." Hans beamed, "Thank you—for life!"

An embarrassed, humbled Morgan diverted the men's attention. "Let's go inside. I'm famished!"

The men were seated near a wall where they could visit quietly, and Hans again expressed gratitude that he finally was meeting the men whose efforts had changed his life forever. Soon the waitress arrived and with a thick German accent asked in English, "Vat voot my guests haf tonight?"

Morgan glanced at Ray, visibly moved by the significance of the moment. Doing his best to maintain his composure, he replied, "Hasenpfeffer. *For all of us.*"

Hearing this, Richard stopped browsing and closed his menu. He looked at Hans and shrugged, not knowing what hasenpfeffer was, but willing to give it a try.

While they waited for their meal, Richard shared all that had been transpiring in his life, including his most recent struggle regarding whether he should explore the Brussels opportunity, even when it didn't *appear* quite right.

Morgan stepped in and began to relate the whole story of *their* journey, describing his invention and the "portal to genius" that inspired it, the nachos at halftime, as well as hasenpfeffer in Odenthal, and explained, "Richard, if you had *not* come to Brussels, we wouldn't have known about Hans. We always dreamed of the day we'd come to Germany and enjoy hasenpfeffer with a valve recipient."

"It's what kept us going through the hard times," Ray chimed in.

Abruptly Richard interjected, "That would explain my strange impulse to go to Brussels, even when the opportunity did *not* match my list." Richard thought the details through and then said aloud, "*Wow*. And the opportunity ended up matching my list anyway."

The men were quiet and the waitress brought their stew. Hans smiled. "Hasenpfeffer." Then he turned to Richard, "You know what this is, don't you?"

"Not so sure..."

"Well as the author of *The Jackrabbit Factor*, you *should* know; it's peppered rabbit."

Richard turned abruptly toward Hans and asked, "*Really?*" Then dazed, he turned back to stare at the place setting in front of him. He mumbled to himself, "*Rabbit.*"

As the other men chattered on, Richard was transported through time and space to Felicity. *It always goes back to the rabbit,* he remembered her saying. His mind was flooded with memories of the last ten years since his dream in the woods, and he sat in awe, grateful for all they had been through. So much had been learned. So much richness had been gained. He held the key now: a knowing that *all* their experiences had been for their good, and those moments of glory, relief, and joy are always waiting to be discovered on the other side of the pain, heartache, and frustration. He didn't need life to deliver *only* pleasure, but he did *find* pleasure knowing that there was always joy and peace to be found. Joy could be had, not just in spite of anguish, but only *because* anguish came first.

The men noticed Richard's attention had slipped away. "Hey, Rich, where'd you go?" Morgan asked in good humor.

Contentment radiated from Richard's face. "Oh, I was just thinking."

"Well, that's a good thing to be doing," Ray winked, elbowing Morgan and swallowing a bite of stew. "You keep that up," Ray smiled, shaking his fork first at Hans and then pointing it squarely toward Richard, "and you just might discover *another portal to genius.*"

Richard's eyes beamed warmth, and a grin spread slowly across his face as he nodded his head resolutely and replied, *"I look forward to it."*

EPILOGUE

The morning bell rang through the hallways and two young men carried on their conversation amid the crowds of teenagers trying to get to their classes before the tardy bell sounded.

"So, did you get the English project done for Ms. Bear?"

"Are you kidding? She'd have had my head if I didn't. I've got it right here, ready to go. What about you?"

Moaning, the young man replied, "Oh, I wish! Still have a couple things to do but plan on throwing it together at lunchtime."

"Oh, Kyle! You can't miss lunch! Matt's sixteen! Don't you want to see what kind of wheels his rich daddy gave him? He'll probably take us off-campus to get something from Lumpy's Lunch! Come ON!"

The young man who didn't finish his project was disappointed to miss out. "Sorry." Sighing, he added, "No, I need an 'A' on this one."

"Your loss. I bet it's a BMW. No, I bet it's a Lamborghini. Can you imagine the heads that'll turn when we go cruisin' with Matt? I bet Jenna would give you a second glance, you sure you can't turn in the project tomorrow?"

"There's no way, Josh. No can do."

"Your loss."

Just then a vibration rattled the ground and the young men felt it come up through their feet. With wide eyes, they looked at each other and then turned around to see an old beater truck coming their direction and in obvious need of a muffler. In fact, as it jiggled side to side on its approach, the boys could see that the dilapidated, gray and rust truck had been in a wreck, and one fender was barely held on with a wire wrap.

Heads did turn, including Jenna's. She was walking between classes, headed toward the main building on the campus when she saw the jalopy rattle in to the parking lot and approach the boys who were leaning against an old Volkswagen. The truck pulled in right next to the VW and Matt kicked the door open from the inside and climbed out.

"Hi, guys."

The boys were speechless. Kyle caught a glimpse of Jenna with a look of disgust on her face as she quickly turned away, hoping to avoid eye contact with them.

Matt took a deep breath and exhaled slowly. "Gotta go. Class is about to start." Matt slammed the door shut and began to head for the main building.

The two other boys looked at each other questioningly and then jogged ahead to catch up with Matt.

"Matt—what's going on? What was THAT?"

Matt didn't look at his friend. "What's what, Kyle?"

"The truck! Where'd it come from? Why'd you come to school in that thing?"

"That's my new car, Kyle. I use it to get to school. Have you got a problem with that?"

Josh piped in with a chuckle, "That's no new car, Matt."

"Yeah, Matt, where's the *wheels*?"

"What are you saying, Josh?"

Glancing at Kyle, Josh paused and then cautiously replied, "Matt, you're sixteen. You're dad's loaded. Where's the car? We expected something more along the lines of a BMW, or…"

"Lamborghini," Kyle interjected.

Matt stopped abruptly and turned to face Kyle and Josh straight on. "Look, guys. My dad's rich. I'm not." With that he glanced up at the big round clock on the wall above the junior class bulletin board and said, "I've gotta go. Later, guys."

As Matt jogged ahead, disappearing into the crowds, the two boys shook their heads. "What's Jenna going to think now?" Kyle whined.

"Forget it, Kyle. You just need to get your own wheels if you want to turn her head. If Matt had brought a new car, she probably would've fallen for him instead of you, anyway."

"Dad, I don't think I can take it. Everyone just glared at me today. There're kids whose folks are out of work that have nicer cars than me."

"Are you trying to outdo them? Do you think you deserve better than them?"

"No, it's not that, Dad. It's just that—it just isn't fair."

"When you can afford a nice car, you can get yourself a nice car. What's so unfair about that?"

"You always make things so difficult! Seems like everyone else is just given a car when they're sixteen: a car with paint."

Rich chuckled empathetically. "Son, one day you'll thank me. To be honest with you, I feel sorry for the kids who have everything just given to them. Mark my words; you'll have more going for you in the long run."

Matt growled and rolled his eyes. "You just don't get it." Storming away, Matt slammed the door behind him causing his father to wince. Rich simply shook his head, grinning, and then turned his chair around to get back to his paperwork.

One Week Later

THUD! Matt slammed his books on the floor of the home office, causing his father to spin around, startled.

"Dad, I CAN'T take it anymore! Rachel turned me down for Saturday night, and I know it's because she's embarrassed about the truck!" Matthew slumped onto the padded bench positioned near the office doorway, shaking his head.

"Son, then that relationship is not worth your time. Anyone who is that caught up in appearances needs to grow in maturity, and I'm sure she will, one day. Look for a girl who likes you for you."

"I know, I know. You've ingrained that in me for as long as I've cared about girls. I know that, Dad. It's just hard when reality hits, and you find out there aren't any girls out there like that."

"Do you really believe that, son?"

Matt sighed. He knew what his dad was getting at and decided to save his father the trouble of pontificating "lecture number six." Tipping his head from side to side, he rehearsed it all: "No, dad. There's a girl who'll like me for who I am, and who has enough integrity to abide by universal principles of right living." It was a canned line that he had repeated over and over thanks to a stubborn father who wanted his son to find the most possible joy in life.

"Son, you really want a different car?"

Matt's body slumped and his eyes widened, "Isn't that obvious?"

"Matt, you don't want a different car. Deep down you're completely comfortable with the old truck."

"Dad! How can you say that?! I hate that truck!"

"On the surface you hate it, but it's in perfect harmony with your subconscious mind, Matt. If you want different wheels, you've got to change what's in your subconscious mind."

Matt sighed. Sometimes his dad's lectures were downright unbearable.

Rich could read his thoughts. "Son, it doesn't matter to me what you drive. But when it matters to you so much that you're ready to learn, just let me know. We all pay a price for knowledge, your price is to gut it out and put up with a few lessons from your old man." With that, Matt's father tipped his head down, raised his eyebrows, and then swiveled his chair back around to face his desk.

Matt closed his eyes and shook his head. "Dad, I know I shouldn't want a new car just to impress the girls. Is it okay, though, to want one that isn't an eyesore? Just, I don't know, so our community is a little nicer with one less junk heap on the road?" Matt tried to sound less like a teenager and more like a grownup. Deep down Matt didn't wish for a new car primarily to impress the girls; he just didn't want the car to repel them, either.

Without turning around, his father said, "So do you want a nicer car or not?"

"I want a nice car, Dad. But I don't have the money, and I know you aren't going to buy one *even though you can afford it.*" Matt couldn't resist dropping the last line under his breath.

Rich didn't reply at all.

Eventually the silence made Matthew feel awkward, and he wished he hadn't tried to guilt-trip his dad. He knew better. His father was extremely principled, which made it impossible to persuade him against his standards. Pushing his father only left Matt feeling uncomfortable.

Matt relaxed his posture and shook his head. "I'm sorry, Dad. Will you just tell me how you think I'm supposed to get myself a nice car when I can only work part-time at minimum wage?"

Turning in his chair, his father replied, "I have no idea. That's a question only you will be able to answer. I can't be the one to tell you where to jump, to catch your rabbit. Only you will know that, once you spot it. You're the only one who'll know which way the rabbit will lead you."

The rabbit analogy was not a new one to Matt. He'd heard it all his life, but until now he never really felt the need to understand it.

After spending the better part of an hour rehearsing the analogy, and reviewing certain sections in his father's book, Matt decided he'd better write his goal down.

"Once you get it on paper, bring it to me and I'll check to make sure you've worded it properly."

Matt disappeared to his room for five whole minutes. When he returned, he showed his father a statement, which read, "I will have a nice car next week."

Rich looked at it and tried to hide his dissatisfaction, "Do you believe this is true?"

"No, but you've said before to write it down, even if it is unbelievable."

Quietly Rich mumbled, "This isn't quite right." Louder, he said, "Let me ask you something: If you already had a way, how long do you think it'd take to get the car?"

"If I had a way? Oh, I don't know. That depends on how good of a way it was."

"How good of a way it is depends on how good of a way it needs to be. It all depends on the GOAL. Goal first, way second. Not the other way around. The way only shows up after you've set the goal. If you never set the goal, you have no need for the way."

"Then how do I decide on the when?"

"Well, when do you want the car?"

"Yesterday!" Matt said through clenched teeth.

"Matt, since this is the first big rabbit you've ever tried to catch, I suggest you pick a date far enough out that it is relatively believable, but close enough that it keeps you awake at night."

"Oh, I don't know. Maybe three months?"

"That could be good."

Matt paused, but finally moaned, "But I don't want to have to wait three months, Dad."

"Son, sometimes waiting can be excruciating. But once I've helped you set the goal properly, you'll be just as excited as the day it'll be yours, and nothing anyone can say will get to you. You'll be locked on the dream, and you'll enjoy the journey.

Matt shifted on the bench and looked up to meet his father's brown eyes. Laughter from some neighbor kids and the buzz of a jet plane drifted in through the open window, but the distractions floated away as his Dad stated the principles his son had heard a thousand times.

Richard's blue t-shirt stretched across his broad chest and shoulders and he sat tall. "When someone teases you about your truck, you'll have an inner confidence that won't be rattled, because you'll know it's only a matter of time before you'll have your dream car. Trust me, when you're chasing a rabbit, you don't have time to worry about what people are saying about you."

Matt's defiant attitude had completely melted away, and he meekly listened to his father's counsel. Deep down, he truly respect- ed his dad. His father was well thought of in the community and at church, and Matt was proud of that. Life at school among his peers was rough, though. It wasn't easy to disregard the taunting at school. Still, all he had to do was look at the kind of life enjoyed by his dad; then compare it with the lives of his friend's parents. By doing so, he was smart enough to know from whom he should receive counsel.

"Now," his father continued, "go write the goal again, this time with a specific date at the top. And while you're at it, add some detail to the description of the car you want."

Later, Matt returned with, "April 14, [year]: I will have a new, shiny black convertible."

His father looked it over and said, "Good, that's a little more than three months from now. Only there's a problem."

"What's that?"

"According to this goal, in three months you'll still be driving your truck."

"What do you mean? It says I'll have a convertible."

"It says you 'will' have a convertible. That word insinuates that the convertible is still in your future. So, in three months, you are no closer to having it than you are now."

"Oh, wow. I never thought of that."

"Write it in present tense, as though it's already yours, and express how it feels to have it. And, it could use a little more detail, too."

"Why?"

"Because a vacuum cleaner can be convertible. Exercise equipment can be convertible. If you don't want a vacuum cleaner, you'd better be specific." Richard stood, moved some papers from his desktop and leaned against it.

"Son, I knew a lady once who set a goal to have ten thousand dollars in her hand by a certain date. She had long since put the idea out of her mind, but when the day came, she found herself at the bank filling out a deposit slip for her father's bank account. The date triggered her memory of the goal she had written much earlier, and so she slowly turned the check over to find the amount was exactly ten thousand dollars. Richard picked up one of the pieces of paper from his desk, and miming the woman from the story, turned it over. "She got exactly what she had asked for: ten thousand dollars in her hand on that date. But the problem was that the money didn't belong to her; she was making a deposit for her *father*. She hadn't been specific enough when she committed her goal to paper."

"Is that a true story?"

"That story is absolutely true. The woman's name is Camille."

"Why do we have to be so specific? If what we want comes to us from the Universe somehow, isn't God smart enough to know what we want, and get it right without all the fuss of us writing it down perfectly?"

"Of course, he already knows what we want, but we're told to ask for it. I believe we often get what we ask for, even if it isn't what we meant, simply to teach us a lesson about how much control we really have over the kind of life we live. How specific we want to be is entirely up to us."

"What if I say it this way: 'April 14, [year]: I now have a shiny black convertible Mustang and it feels great.'"

"That's closer. But it needs more description, more feeling."

"You sound like Ms. Bear now, my English teacher."

"Come on, make it real."

"Um, how about, 'April 14, [year]: I am so excited now that I have a shiny black convertible Mustang that is less than five years old. It is so much fun to go cruising with my friends, and I don't have to be embarrassed about it looking hideous."

"Okay, that's better, but since our subconscious mind takes entire sentences and registers each word rather than complete phrases, that goal would program your subconscious mind to help you find a hideous and embarrassing shiny black convertible Mustang that is five years old."

Matt sighed. His dad was being just like Ms. Bear: so picky, and hard to please.

"Son, to help you understand this, let's talk about people who try to 'lose weight.' So long as they are focused on 'losing weight,' they are setting themselves up for failure. Why? Because when their subconscious mind hears that they've 'lost' something, it automatically kicks into gear to help them 'find' what they've lost. When it hears the word 'weight,' it might associate the term with synonyms such as 'heaviness' or 'paperweight,' or 'weights and measures'.'" Richard picked up a paperweight from his desk and tossed it to Matt. "So, to set a goal to 'lose weight,' a person is actually programming their subconscious mind to 'find heaviness'!"

"So, what should they do instead?" Matt tossed the paperweight back and Richard set it on his desk.

"They should write a date, and then express how grateful they are now that they enjoy a healthy, energetic, slender body."

"Hmmm. Nice!" Matt perched on the edge of his chair and craned his head when he heard the traction of tires on asphalt.

"Looks like Mom's home with the groceries. We'll hear about it if we don't head out to help."

Richard agreed, "Yeah, let's go."

As they hefted grocery bags from the trunk of the car, Matt teased his Dad, "I always thought you were fit from exercise and healthy eating."

Richard grinned and flexed his grocery-filled arms, nearly spilling a head of lettuce out of the top of the bag. "It's easier to make good choices if you're in the right mindset. It can help to spend more time looking at slim and fit pictures of themselves than at images of themselves in the mirror. Doing so can help their subconscious mind become more in harmony with the results they seek, and so the results can come more naturally, and more permanently. Looking in the mirror all the time and checking the scale every day can reinforce the heavy image they are trying to overcome. It wouldn't do any harm to manipulate the display on the scale to show the number they want, either. Doing so could help their subconscious mind believe it's true, and automatically help them desire the proper diet, or lead them to the right so-called 'weight loss' program."

"Makes sense, I guess."

After setting the last of the groceries down on the kitchen island, Richard added, "Same thing goes for getting out of debt. People need to be careful about setting goals for 'getting out of debt' because they can accidentally program their mind to focus on debt. Doing so can attract a constant supply of debt into their life. Not only that, but training their subconscious mind to constantly pay down debts can backfire. When their bills are finally paid off, their subconscious mind might panic: no debts to pay, but a well-established order to *pay off debts*. To solve this problem, it can subconsciously lead that person to get into more debt."

Matt's mind was drifting, since dealing with debts wasn't something with which he was personally familiar. His father nevertheless continued, as if lost in the memory of previous conversations he had with people who often sought his advice.

"Instead, a debt-ridden person would be wise to create a gratitude statement like, 'I'm so happy and grateful now that I keep my financial promises on time, and that I am independently wealthy. It feels absolutely empowering now that I hold the title to my car and the deed to my home! I feel so free to always have all I need to do all that needs to be done.'" Rich paused. He was obviously contemplative, as if attempting to fine-tune his philosophy on the matter.

Politely Matt humored his father and said, "Remind me about all that when it's news I can use, Dad."

Snapping back to the present, Rich obliged, "Matt, what I'm trying to say is that you're subconsciously in harmony with the old truck. If you want to own a nice car, you must switch the self-image you have deep inside your subconscious mind. You do that by writing your goal properly, and reading it often enough that you begin to feel how it'll be when it's yours. See, our subconscious mind accepts anything it receives as truth. Then it kicks things into gear to make sure that what it believes to be true becomes or remains the reality. Emotion reinforces subconscious ideas. Every day you feel emotionally upset about having an ugly truck, your subconscious mind is told you're your ugly truck is *important*. It solidifies the truth that you own an ugly truck."

"My *truth* is that I own an ugly truck? Because I let myself feel emotional about it?"

"That's right. If you want to *change* your truth, you must have a stronger emotion about a replacement idea such as, 'I feel ecstatic that I now own a nice, shiny Mustang,' and so forth. If you can genuinely feel how you expect to feel, you essentially hand your sub-conscious mind a *new* truth. On a conscious level, you might feel like you're lying to yourself, but do it enough and you'll drown out the old, undesirable programming. You'll put yourself in tune with the new circumstance you desire, and all you need to see it through will be drawn to you."

"So how do I write the goal properly, then?" Matt's eager voice showed fascination.

His father replied, "Let's say you wrote a goal like, 'April 14, [year]: I'm so happy and grateful now that I own a [model year] shiny black convertible Mustang with low miles. I am grateful it runs properly and gets me where I need to go. It's so much fun to cruise around with the blue sky overhead." Richard smiled at the idea, and stopped to ponder his son's desires. "I'm grateful it's a de-pendable way to get me to school and my other responsibilities. I'm amazed at the worthy money-making opportunities that presented themselves to help me get this car. The Mustang was affordable and leaves me free financially to pursue other goals such as college. I'm grateful that I had plenty of time for the money-making idea which presented itself and allowed me time to pay sufficient attention to my studies to keep my grades up." Richard paused, his eyes turned upward in thought and his pen tapping, "The kids at school are inspired by the example I've set, and are curious to know what Dad has taught me. I selflessly share what I've learned and encourage oth-ers to set worthwhile goals. I attract the kind of friends who respect me for my integrity; after all, I only wanted the car for respectable reasons.'"

"Wow, Dad. That was a mouthful. Are you serious?"

Rich just smiled. "Son, it's all up to you. You set a goal like that, and read it often, and eventually you will begin to believe it's all true.

Once you're already living the dream in your mind, it's only a matter of time before it's really yours. You'll be in tune to opportunities that come your way, which will assist you in attaining your goal."

Matt was intrigued. He believed what his father was saying, because his father had obviously practiced his theory successfully for years, and soon Matthew's mind was racing with anticipation. Abruptly he declared, "I'll be in my room Dad. Thanks!"

He ran upstairs and pulled out a page from his notebook. Carefully and thoughtfully he composed a statement that described how he felt about his car, and life in general, or how he expected it to be, three months in the future. After about two hours, he returned to his father's office, but his dad wasn't there. "Dad? Where are you?"

"I'm in the kitchen with your mother!" His father called from the other room.

Matthew ran to the kitchen and slid to a stop on the polished floor, nearly falling over but catching himself by grasping onto the granite countertop. "Dad, I think I've got it! Look at this!"

Rich read the statement. It was nearly a whole page long, and it was obvious that Matt had scrutinized each word. "You know how I can tell you've discovered a portal to genius, Son?"

Felicity had just poured three tall glasses of iced lemonade and beamed with pleasure.

"How, Dad?"

"Because you're genuinely excited about your new car. Look at him, Honey. He can hardly stand still."

Matthew *was* jittery. He couldn't wait to do something about finding a way now. "Dad, that's my car! I'm getting a new car."

"I know, Son. How are you going to do it?"

"I don't know yet, but somewhere that car sits, just waiting for me to find it. And somewhere, there are people who need me to do something for them, and they'll give me the money I need. I just know it, Dad. I'm going for a ride. We'll see where it leads me."

"Take your phone in case we need to find you." Felicity reminded.

"Son, don't be discouraged if you don't find something right away."

"Oh, Dad. I already know that. This trip today might only lead me to think of something else I should do instead tomorrow. It's all good. That's what you've always taught me."

"And Son, if you feel fear or anxiety before you act on a hunch, just know it's simply your subconscious mind wrestling with two contradictory truths. It is trying to believe, 'my car is an ugly truck,' and, 'my car is a shiny black Mustang' all at the same time. The anxiety is only a sign that your new image has found its way solidly into your subconscious mind. It's simply a positive sign that you've *done it*. You've successfully planted the new idea in your subconscious, so take action anyway!"

Matt stopped just before disappearing out the door and said, "Huh?" He couldn't seem to concentrate on what his father just said; his mind was already miles down the road.

"Oh, never mind. We'll have that conversation soon enough, I'm sure."

"Okay, Dad!" With that, he was gone. His parents smiled and gave each other a squeeze. This experience alone was worth all the agony of refusing to give him the world on a silver platter. Felicity confessed, "I was wrong, Rich. I shouldn't have given you so much grief over what to do for his birthday."

"I can't blame you. It's hard to do the right thing. Sometimes you're the one who sets me straight. I'm just grateful we've endured the hard times together and can now help each other remember how to live by principles."

"Isn't it interesting? We've been trying to teach him this for ten years, but until he wanted something badly enough, he wasn't ready or willing to listen and apply. Apparently, you can't force kids or anyone else to get it until they want something to change bad enough."

"Hey, guys, let's go off campus for lunch today. I'd like to swing by the used car lot down on the corner," Matt said as he approached his buddies near the lockers.

"What, and take your truck? Thanks, but no thanks. Besides, I heard Jenna's sticking around at lunchtime to work on some posters for student council," Kyle glanced over his shoulder in case he could spot her across the way.

Josh jumped in, "Matt, I can't believe you'd want to drive your truck at lunchtime when all the other cars from school are out on the road. Save it for the 'to and from,' my friend."

"Look, who cares what I'm driving?" Matt's demeanor was solid. "I'm going to take my truck at lunch, and I am going to the used car lot. I saw a black convertible Mustang there on my way to school, and I've gotta see if it's mine. I have to check the year, and the mileage, and if it's the one, find out how much money I need to make in order to get it. I'm gonna sit in it if they'll let me, and I'm gonna see how it feels."

"You're a goofball, Matt," Kyle chuckled.

"See you after lunch, guys." Matt turned, threw his backpack over his shoulder, and was gone.

"Hey, Matt! You think you'll get a Mustang? In your dreams!" Josh hollered and laughed out loud.

Matt didn't turn around. He just grinned and thought, *That's precisely* why *it's gonna happen: because it IS in my dreams.*

Walking to his truck, he heard Kyle say, "Oh, he's just excited, Josh. Give him a week."

Matt glanced back at the guys making their way to the cafeteria. He wondered why they had to try to pull him down. *I guess I need to add something to my goal about the kind of friends I spend my time with.*

His trip to the lot occupied his entire lunch period. He even forgot about and never missed the lunch he brought from home: a peanut butter sandwich in a brown paper sack. After all, *he was simply too busy chasing his rabbit.*

The End

ABOUT THE AUTHORS

Leslie Householder is the award-winning, internationally published bestselling author of *The Jackrabbit Factor: Why You Can*, and *Hidden Treasures: Heaven's Astonishing Help with Your Money Matters*. As wife to her best friend, Trevan, and mother of seven children, Leslie is also a contributing author to multiple *Chicken Soup for the Soul* publications.

She and her husband are the founders of an organization dedicated to helping families prosper against the odds. She is also the creator of *Genius Bootcamp*, the *Rare Faith Podcast* and the life-changing *Mindset Mastery Course*.

As popular speakers and educators, Trevan and Leslie both creatively use humor and story to connect with their audiences, helping people overcome obstacles that keep them from achieving their highest potential, in all the areas of life.

To learn more about Trevan and Leslie, visit RareFaith.org.

Garrett B. Gunderson is an entrepreneur who started his first company at the age of fifteen and became a multi-millionaire by the age of twenty-six. As the winner of Utah's Young Entrepreneur of the Year award, Garrett has founded several prosperous companies, including an Inc 500 company that was named by The Utah Fast 50 program as one of the top companies in the state for entrepreneurial spirit, innovative business tactics and skyrocketing revenue growth.

Garrett co-authored the highly-acclaimed Curriculum for Wealth series, and is the author of the New York Times bestselling financial book *Killing Sacred Cows*. Garrett coaches large groups of business owners and financial service professionals nationwide, and is a sought-after speaker and personal finance coach.

To learn more about Garrett, visit www.WealthFactory.com.

FOR THE READER

Just like the characters in *Portal to Genius*, you have also been endowed with unique abilities to enrich the world and bring success. To help you discover, identify, and cultivate *your* portal to genius, the authors have a gift for you:

The FREE '*Portal to Genius* Principles Guide'
This was already provided if you requested the Character's Guide at the beginning of the book. But if you did not obtain it, get the complete, condensed list of success principles from this story in one convenient document for quick reference and easier implementation. Did you find the hidden ones? Download your free copy at www.PortaltoGenius.com/guide

Tell a friend
If you loved this book, did you know? It can be downloaded FREE at PortaltoGenius.com!

Take the free assessment
How well do you think according to the laws? Take the FREE Mindset Quotient Test at RareFaith.org to find out.

Stay on course

Subscribe to the Rare Faith newsletter or stay connected on social media via RareFaith.org to let Leslie help you stay on course.

Internalize the concepts

Listen to the *Rare Faith Podcast*, or enjoy Leslie's other book: *Hidden Treasures: Heaven's Astonishing Help with Your Money Matters* (available in paperback, audio, or as a FREE download). Enjoy it all at RareFaith.org!

Be inspired

Watch the FREE full-length video, "The Visual Aid that Changed Everything" at RareFaith.org.

Get help

From home:

If you need help making a change, Leslie's *Mindset Mastery* course will take you step-by-step through twenty-four empowering lessons and assignments that help you understand and apply that Rare kind of Faith that causes things to happen. Learn more at ProsperTheFamily.com.

At a workshop:

Ready to be immersed in a *Portal to Genius* experience of your own? Register for our next Genius Bootcamp and enjoy the environment, training and support for getting your own inspired solutions to your most pressing dilemmas. Learn more at GeniusBootcamp.com.

For bulk order requests, or to share your comments
and success stories, send a message through RareFaith.org.